AN ILLUSTRATED GUIDE TO
WINE

Dedication
To my guide, philosopher and friend, the late
André Simon (1877-1970)

AN ILLUSTRATED GUIDE TO
WINE

George Rainbird

PEERAGE BOOKS

Contents

First published in Great Britain in 1983 by Octopus Books Limited

This edition published in 1990 by Peerage Books, Michelin House, 81 Fulham Road, London SW3 6RB

© Octopus Books Limited 1983

ISBN 1 85052 1778

Printed in Hong Kong

Introduction

Above: The wine of the domaine de Montmélas, a Beaujolais property, in bottle and glass.

'Wine maketh glad the heart of man' chanted the psalmists and this is what this book is about. But we must first define what we mean by wine: wine is the fermented juice of *freshly gathered grapes*. It is not a concoction made from parsnips, potatoes, dandelions, elderberries, and so on, and no further reference will be made to such beverages in these pages. Neither is it the kind of concentrate that you buy in packets and bottles from pharmacists, take home and make into something called wine in your bath or sink or basin, which is, I believe, known as DIY. It is true that what is contained in these packets and bottles was once incorporated in the grape but that was a long time ago. Neither is wine, in my definition, any of the liquids marketed in this country under the pseudonym 'British wines', which again are made from dried fruit. I *will* include brandy, although a spirit, because brandy is distilled from wine that has been properly made in the first place.

Wine may mean many things to many people, from the connoisseur delving in his cellar for his last bottle of Château Mouton-Rothschild '45, to the French farmer reaching for his litre bottle of local red wine from the nearest *alimentation*. To the connoisseur the Mouton '45 will mean a great moment in time when the true magic may be revealed and he and his privileged friends (for great wine is never drunk alone) will discuss and compare the bouquet and colour, the after-taste and manifold merits of this incomparable wine. They will shake their heads slowly after the last drops in their glasses have been drunk and will give thanks to God for having been privileged to be present, and hope devoutly that they will be spared to share such another miracle. To the farmer, wine is life itself, just as important as his daily bread and more important than almost anything else. The wine he drinks, as like as not, will come from the Midi, a large area under the Pyrenees stretching roughly between Carcassonne and Avignon, where an enormous quantity of ordinary wine of no great distinction is made. He will take it for what it is, one of the more agreeable necessities of life, providing both food and drink and making the world a rather better place to live in. On high days and holidays he may indulge in a bottle of sound red, fruity Bordeaux or Burgundy according to whether he likes his wine dry or rich, and he will be well satisfied thereby. He will probably die without ever drinking the wine of one

Right: A vineyard in autumn colours; the leaves turn yellow and then red before falling with the coming of winter.

of the great châteaux of Bordeaux or famous domaines of Burgundy.

Somewhere between the connoisseurs and the peasant there lies an enormous group of human beings who like wine. People who, having tasted wine and having found it good, want to know rather more about it, though not necessarily wanting to join the ranks of those connoisseurs who compare only the greatest and rarest wines, which, in any case, are beyond the purses of most of us. Let us assume that we *like* wine, and as long as we have this in common we can use our intelligence and at least four of the five senses to discriminate and to select wines that for us will be the best wines within a certain price category or class. One doesn't have to be a wine snob to appreciate good or great wine, but it is a great mistake not to be able to know and appreciate one when you find it. The important thing is to like wine for what it is; to drink only honest wines whether they be cheap or not, and then to enjoy

them for what they are and not what they might be. I hope that you will find in this book a useful guide to moderately priced wine.

This book, then, is intended as a guide to what constitutes an honest wine. This is harder to come by than you might think. Some blending goes on, mainly from French and Italian wines; but it is now totally illegal to blend European Community with non-EEC wines. The average drinker will not worry very much about it.

There is a good deal of truth in the saying that Paris alone consumes twice the annual output of Beaujolais, largely, possibly, because of the unscrupulous barman's habit of refilling bottles carrying *appellation contrôlée* labels from the bulk 'plonk' tank. If we add together the demands for Beaujolais from all over the world and subtract the known supply, it will be seen that the genuine Beaujolais is quite difficult to come by. This is an example of a potentially dishonest wine, for in order

Above: The hilly vineyards of Torgiano in Umbria in the morning mist.

Opposite: View of the Napa Valley, California.

to meet the world demand for Beaujolais (even if we leave out Paris) the custom is to blend (or 'stretch' as they say in the trade) the true Beaujolais with cheap, sound, red wine from any EEC country. The result is not as bad as it sounds, because the shippers know their job and also know perfectly well that if they do not produce a palatable wine, which is sold at a rather higher price than ordinary 'plonk', the demand for so-called Beaujolais will decline, and they will be out of business. Nevertheless, there is some real Beaujolais in most of the Beaujolais sold outside of France today. Probably a lot of it comes from the Beaujolais, but is just poor *négociants'* wine. I suppose it would not be far from the truth to say that comparatively few drinkers of this excellent wine have ever tasted a really genuine one. But you have one sure way of protecting yourself. You can buy only Beaujolais that is shipped by a reliable firm and from a wine supplier of strict reputation. You have at least then obtained wine from Beaujolais with a good pedigree. It can mean no more than that, for as in every other wine, there are good, bad and indifferent Beaujolais of good, bad and indifferent years. There is not much difference in the price, although there is bound to be some between that of a reputable and genuine Beaujolais and most of the fake wines bearing that name. The object of this book is to help discerning and intelligent readers to distinguish and discriminate.

One last word – in order to know wine you must drink wine. When you drink wine, use those taste buds with which you are endowed and, above all, develop a curiosity about wine in all its legitimate forms. Make your own classifications and your own rules. Learn to know what you like. If, for some reason or other, you prefer to drink a white wine with your steak, drink it. If you travel a lot you will know there are a good many places in this world where you can buy only the local wine to drink with whatever you are eating. When in a red wine country, as in some parts of Spain, for instance, you would drink red wine with your fish and like it, and the meal would be none the worse for it.

Since this is a book about wine and the enjoyment thereof for plain people, I have avoided wine jargon and too much technical description; only the most important grapes used in wine making are named. If you are tempted to know more, there is an important wine glossary by Michael Broadbent MW on page 214 and there are plenty of large books about each chapter subject for you to read, which I hope you will, glass in hand and bottle at side.

Which cheers the sad, revives the old, inspires
The young, makes weariness forget his toil,
And fear her danger; opens a new world
When this, the present, palls.
Byron: *Sardanapalus*

Understanding Wine

The soil, the sun, the grape and its vinification

Wine, as I have said, is the fermented juice of the freshly gathered grape and wine has been made since before the beginning of records. The vine thrives in all kinds of climate and on all types of soil, except in the frozen north or south and in equatorial regions. The vine will grow where little else will thrive. This is true also of the olive, and between them the vine and the olive tree can provide most of what is necessary to keep man healthy and wealthy and wise.

Wine has been found and is also depicted in wall paintings in the early Egyptian tombs. The most reliable proof of the length of the reign of Pharaoh Tutankhamen is the wine jars found in his tomb. He died about 1350 BC, long before the Israelites left Egypt under Moses.

In AD 92 the Emperor Domitian ordered that a large part of the wine-growing areas in Gaul should be denuded of their vines in order to plant wheat to fill the granaries of Rome. But in Champagne, where the soil is thin on the chalk hills of the valley of the Marne, wheat would not flourish, and he lost his labour and the Gauls lost their wine – a very poor bargain for both parties.

Italy at that time (or at any time since) had no need of wine from abroad. It grew the vine prosperously everywhere, and the making of wine had reached far greater refinement and development centuries before the French made full use of their natural resources in the making of fine wine. Even before Rome, in the days of classical Greece, wine was made and venerated according to its district and the vintner, and the symbols of the vine, its grapes and leaves, and its protecting deity, Dionysus, all decorate profusely the famous and beautiful attic *kraters* (wine-mixing jars) and pottery cups of the period.

Four things go into the making of wine, whether it be good, bad or indifferent. First of all, the soil from which the vine grows; second, the climate, particularly the sun or the amount of sunshine which shines upon the vine in any given year; third, the type of grape used in the making of the wine; and last, but by no means least, the hand of the *vigneron* who makes the wine. The first is immovable and permanent, the second variable, the third important, and the last human. When these four come into alignment, the result can be a near miracle, and by the grace of God this sometimes happens.

The soil

Obviously, the first element, the soil upon which the vines are grown, does not alter from year to year, but like any soil it can become exhausted if it is not constantly fed with the right kind of nutriment, although its mineral-bearing qualities will be unimpaired, whatever happens. It is the soil which harbours those mysterious saccharomyces, or yeasts, which form the bloom of the grape and which, in conjunction with the various acids and the fermenting elements in the sugar of the grape itself, form the special flavour and character of the grape.

It is unquestionably true that the grapes from which the finest wines are made grow on the thinnest of soils, and consequently are those with the smallest of yields, and from which it must follow that the wine made therefrom is in the smallest quantity. In France the quality of the soil can vary from field to field, and one only has to travel through the countryside by car or train in the early spring when the fields are fresh-harrowed to see the change in the soil, especially in chalky country. One-half of the field may be quite white and then suddenly the whole

Below: Viticulture goes back to ancient Egypt: detail of a tomb painting from the fourteenth century BC – treading the grapes and storing the wine in amphorae.

Right: Vines growing in the hard slaty soil of the Moselle.

Below: The chais of Château Mouton-Rothschild. The quartz pebbles of the Médoc contrast with the slate of the Moselle.

colour value changes and the other half is brown. So it is with many vineyards, and it is quite true that only a narrow path will separate the vineyard making the wine of the very first order from another producing grapes which are of the third or fourth growth.

The sun

The second factor is the sun itself, which is responsible for most of the worries of the vineyard. By sun, I also mean the lack of it for, generally speaking, it can be assumed that if the grapes ripen, you will get good wine, and if they do not ripen properly, you won't. But there are varying degrees of ripeness, and it is this factor which makes all the difference to a good, bad or indifferent year. The function of the sun is to promote the sugar in the grape which becomes alcohol in fermentation.

If the sun shines when the buds are burgeoning on the vine, it is a very good thing; and if the sun shines when the flowers are blooming, that is also a good thing; but most of all the sun is wanted when the grapes have formed and are beginning to swell. Then a little rain will not hurt, and if a fine month is experienced before the vintage, you are likely to get some extraordinarily good wine; 1982 was a good example of this. If the weather is wet and damp, all the very horrible diseases that the vine grower has to contend with will start to raise their ugly heads. All take their toll to reduce the crop, and thereby spoil the wine.

Too much sun, on the other hand, will also do damage, although not by any means on the same scale. The grapes become *brûlé*, or burnt, and the wine is hot and rather harsh. This is the reason that some of the ordinary Greek and Mediterranean wines are harsh.

By and large, it can be taken as a fairly competent guide to assume that there can be little good wine in a year with below-average levels of sunshine, although it is quite possible to have a bad wine of a good year. Some wine suppliers will not subscribe to this for fairly obvious reasons, but I defy anybody to give me a good honest claret of 1951 or 1956 or, to be nearer, 1963, 1965 or 1968. There may be good wines in these years, but I have never seen one. This does not, however, mean that the wine is necessarily undrinkable, because here the *vigneron* will sometimes bring art to the aid of nature, and by the judicious and extremely skilful addition of a little sugar can put into the wine what the sun and weather have failed to provide for it. The result is not a true wine, or even by any manner of means a fine or great wine, but it is certainly palatable. A good example of this is 1951, when the weather was so bad in the Bordeaux district that a special regulation was introduced to allow the growers to *chaptalize*, or sugar, the wine, a method which used to be proscribed by law in the Bordeaux area under normal circumstances. The resulting wine is not by any means unpalatable but it is distinctly odd and, as a friend of mine remarked on being given a bottle of first-growth 1951, 'As Bordeaux, this is extraordinarily like a poor Burgundy.' The great years, however, have been uniformly sunny with just enough rain to put heart into the berries. Such a year was 1929, and some of the finest wines that I have ever drunk have been 1929s. The great Cheval Blanc is a perfect example of 1947, another great year, and 1953 wines were rather similar. But even great vintages do not last forever. The 1953s are lightening and fading, and have been replaced by the 1961s as the pinnacle of claret quality. If you have some '53s, drink them soon.

We have now dealt with the soil, which is permanent, and the sun, which is extremely variable; and assuming that we have the soil and we get some sun, we can agree that we shall have some very good wine provided that it is well made.

The grape
It is the grape which produces the wine and it is the grape that gives the wine its basic flavour and character. It is most important that the grapes are

Left above: Traditional training in Tuscany; a tall vine with two branches.

Left below: In contrast, the much lower pruning of Chablis, so that the grapes can absorb heat from the ground.

Below: Spraying against rot in the vineyard of Bougros on the slopes of the Chablis grands crus. Note the limestone soil.

Above left: Pinot Noir, the grape of fine red Burgundy; the bunches are said to be shaped like a pine cone, hence its name.

Above right: Chardonnay that makes the best dry white wines in Burgundy and elsewhere; there is a village of the same name in the Mâconnais.

Below left: Merlot, one of the grapes that contributes to the quality of fine claret, and especially St-Emilion and Pomerol.

Below right: Sauvignon Blanc, found at its best in Sancerre and Pouilly-sur-Loire.

suited to the soil in which they grow and the climate in which they are expected to ripen. Some varieties do particularly well on chalk, some are more suitable for gravelly soils and so on. Thus we have Chardonnay in Champagne and Cabernet Sauvignon in Bordeaux. If the soil is too rich and the climate too kind, the vines will overcrop and the grapes will be larger and more luscious, but with none of the concentration necessary to produce fine wine. In Germany, where the climate is cold and the summers relatively short, recent emphasis has been on planting the newly developed early-ripening grapes, such as Optima or Ortega, in order to harvest an early crop with a high sugar content and still produce their famous sweet wines even in the mediocre years. Much research has also been done in California, where the wine-growing area has been divided into climatic regions and the most suitable vine varieties allocated accordingly.

Vines are grown to suit the soil, the climate and the grower and, eventually, the wine-buying public. Hundreds of varieties are grown around the world, all of which contribute to the essential quality and flavour of the final product, the wine.

Vinification

The principles used in the making of wine from the grapes are permanent and unalterable. The techniques of vinification, however, are many and even in the last decade have undergone great changes for the better. Thus, there is very little badly made wine, and what there is can only be due to human failure to take advantage of the more sophisticated kinds of machinery available. As an example, when I researched my book on the wines of Spain in the very early 1960s, there were many wines which, although universally honest and good, were earthy to taste, although I will not say unpleasant. But they did not have that clear, clean flavour and could not be drunk as fine wines or with great pleasure. They were also absurdly cheap. Today, I very much doubt if you will find a wine from Spain that is not clearer and cleaner, from whatever part of the Iberian Peninsula it comes. Alas, they are considerably more expensive. There was nothing wrong with the great wines of Rioja and other famous wine-growing districts in Spain, but the fault lay mainly in the large areas, such as Valdepeñas, producing common wines.

The method of wine making is simple: for red wines the grapes are gathered, brought to the winery and fed into a crusher and stemmer, which

Left: Finishing the vintage at Château d'Yquem.

Below: Pinot Noir grapes arriving at the press-house.

removes all the stems and superfluous detritus that has been gathered from the vine. Then they go into the fermentation vat. After fermentation the young wine is pressed to separate it from the skins. There may be a second or third pressing of the grapes, which will naturally produce an inferior and coarser wine, but this is not done everywhere – usually only when the grapes are very expensive. The main difference for white wines is that the grapes are pressed immediately and the juice fermented. In this way, even if black grapes are used, the wine does not become discoloured.

In the vats the juice soon begins to ferment and it is at this stage, if *chaptalization* is permitted, that sugar is added to correct a lack of sun or for any other reason that has caused the grapes to be

An old wine press, no longer in use, at Château des Capitans, a domaine at Juliénas in the Beaujolais.

gathered in less than perfect condition for wine making. I am bound to add that it is sometimes added even unnecessarily when the grapes are gathered in perfect condition, but not by responsible growers.

The object of *chaptalization* is to assist fermentation. The sugar in the grape is turned into alcohol by the process of fermentation and the addition of more sugar merely promotes alcoholic strength. While it cannot on its own make the wine sweeter, because it is turned into alcohol (which is not sweet), it gives more body to the wine. If it is not overdone *chaptalization* does not destroy the flavour. If properly carried out, it does in fact improve the wine and it is the job of the *vigneron* or grower to know how far to go. In Bordeaux it is only

in recent years that general permission for *chaptalization* has been given. There was a time when sugar could only be added in very small quantities, possibly only one or one and a half per cent, and only in bad years when the vines were producing rather sour grapes. Now it is far more general and even in good years a small, possibly minute, quantity of sugar is added at fermentation by all growers, from a *grand cru classé* château down to the smaller grower, but probably more in the last class than in the first.

In Burgundy things seem to have gone rather haywire, at least according to Mr Anthony Hanson's book *Burgundy* (Faber and Faber, 1982). Mr Hanson's contention is that far too much sugar is added in every class of Burgundy and there is little or none of the true, delicate wine to be had. He explains at great length the reasons for his findings and, having lived in Burgundy for some years and since he is a Master of Wine and a wine merchant, one must pay respect to his opinion. On the other hand, perhaps he overstates his case. However, I myself have drunk too much lovely Burgundy not to know when the sugar bag has been overused and I do not think there is any doubt that there is far more of it than there was in the past.

I remember, many years ago, André Simon – then about eighty-seven years of age – took a group of members of the Wine and Food Society, of which he was the Founder and President, to Beaune to the Hospices de Beaune. He said it would be his last visit, and it was. At that time the fermenting vats in the Hospices' cellars were all full and bubbling with

fermenting wine. The year, I think it was 1964, had been perfect for the grapes. The sun had shone and everything had happened at the right time. As he was showing the group round a workman came with a sack of sugar, climbed to the top of the vat, and threw it in.

'My dear man,' said André, 'why do you add that? The sun has shone, the grapes have been beautiful, they are full of sugar. Surely you don't need any more?'

'Ah, monsieur,' replied the workman, 'we always do it.'

So, having said all this, I am going to come into the open and say that I myself am not against *chaptalization*. I think that any way of *improving* wine is a good thing and that, after all, is what it is all about.

Above: Bottles maturing in the cellars of Château Grand Pontet, a grand cru in St-Emilion.

Left: The maître de chais at Château Pétrus takes a sample of wine from a cask.

Excesses have been the ruin of many good things and nowhere more than in the case of wine, both in its making and, alas, in its consumption. Because a wine tastes sweeter than you think it ought, the reason may not be due to *chaptalization*. It could be due to adulteration or it may be that you did not know enough about the nature of the wine. Adulteration is quite another thing and so is 'stretching', which simply means using a wine of a provenance and quality and adding to it a more common, inferior wine and selling it under the label of the better one. This practice is far more common than you would think and that is why you should always avail yourself of the services of a very reputable wine supplier, learn to read a label and respect certain shippers and disrespect others.

But all this is not so easy. Let us take the great wine scandal in Italy only a few years ago when vast quantities of 'wine' were being shipped abroad that had nothing to do with the fermented juice of a freshly gathered grape. Or the scandal in Ipswich, England, not so long ago, when it was proved that quantities of labels, very pretty ones too, had been printed in batches saying, for instance, 'Clos de Vougeot' or possibly 'Nuit-St-Georges' or again 'Côte de Beaune-Villages'. When orders came in the bottles were simply labelled with whatever was ordered, although it was all the same wine.

This may all sound rather discouraging, and indeed it is, but dishonest people are to be found in every trade, profession or calling, and the wine trade is no exception. It behoves you and me, therefore, to put ourselves into a state of knowledge so that, if we are being deceived, at least we stand a chance of knowing it.

During fermentation, the black grape skins are left in for red wine, for it is the pigment in the grape skins, dissolved in fermentation, which gives red wine its colour. White wine is often made from black grapes, such as in Champagne, but the skins are removed by pressing before fermentation starts. This initial fermentation is boisterous; that is, it bubbles away rather like a muddy volcano. At just the right time, the *vigneron* will draw off the wine into barrels or, in the case of bulk wines, into storage vats.

If it is in barrels, and this will be true of all great wines (the storage vats being more or less used for the ordinary wines), these will go into what is called the *chais*, which is above the ground, where the wine is stored for the first year of its life. The red and white wines will be racked three times in the first year, that is to say, the wine from one barrel will be run into another, leaving the lees (sediment) in the first barrel to be emptied away. Before the third racking a further operation called fining takes place by mixing white of egg into the wine. This then spreads and sinks to the bottom, taking with it any

Above: Madame Emmanuel Cruse, the owner of Château d'Issan, judging her wine in her own cellars.

Left: Nosing the wine at Château Léoville-Las-Cases.

Opposite above: The oenologist at Château Pétrus, Monsieur Berroulet, measuring the specific gravity of his new wine.

Opposite below: A cool damp cellar in the Côte d'Or; the ceiling is covered with fungus that thrives on the wine fumes.

remaining impurities. Only the best, old-fashioned growers use white of egg now. There are substitutes which I am sure are no less efficient, but I like the sound of white of egg.

The barrels are then taken to the cellars, where the wine is racked for the third time. There it rests for a year or such period as the grower considers right for the bottling of his wine at its very best. In Bordeaux the period in wood is eighteen months to two years for a light wine or three years for a good vintage of especially good wine. In the case of minor wines and more common wines (perhaps 'little wines' is a better expression), the secondary fermentation is accelerated by technical processes as it is intended for quick consumption. It is not expected to adorn your cellar or mine for ten or twenty years before it is drunk.

The wine is then ready to be sold to the *négociant* or to the wine merchant, but it is not necessarily fit to drink. I remember a friend of mine being given a case of Lafite '45 round about 1949 and within a year it was drunk. Of course it was drinkable, but oh! what a waste. Four decades later, the '45s are still beautiful, but in 1949 they were hard, full of tannin and not at all great or even fine.

On the subject of when to bottle wine I will add a story that was told me by the venerable Pierre Dubos, the owner of Château Cantemerle, which is

The fully automatic bottling machine at Pommery in Rheims.

Awe inspiring bottles of Brunello di Montalcino in the cellars of Biondi Santi – these are wines with a fabulous reputation and a price to match.

at the bottom of the fifth-growth Bordeaux but *should* be well into the second. I share David Peppercorn's experience of regard for this grand old man and, as in David's case, his was the first château in the Médoc I ever visited in 1948 on my first visit to Bordeaux and I have held him and his wine in affection ever since.

Old Pierre Dubos liked to reminisce, and since he and his family have been making wine for I know not how many years – several generations – he knew quite a bit about it and could express himself well. The story he told when he was describing the essential mystery of wine was that there are three times in the year when the wine in the *chais* must not be touched: at the time of the budding of the vine; at the time of the flowering; and at the time of the vintage. He said that at these times the wine in the cask is 'troubled' and nobody knows why. However, he said that it was well known that, even in casks of wine in places as far away as Tokyo or South America, the wine became troubled during these seasons *in Bordeaux* and the good wine merchant never attempted to bottle it at these times. I know not whether this is legend or truth. Frankly, I don't care. I like it.

In all these conditions of wine, there is a very human factor – that of timing. In the moment of time when God ordains that a wine should be at its most perfect, the vintner must first transfer the wine from the fermentation vat into barrels. Then he must choose the exact time (and by exact time I don't mean to the minute, but certainly within a very limited period of days) at which the wine in its first year should be racked, and again in the second year, and above all, the moment in time when the wine in the barrel should be bottled.

Bottling

When it comes to bottling there has been a great revolution in method. Whereas until recent years the vast majority of wines were exported in bulk, this no longer happens because wine merchants realised that it is much easier to import wine bottled at source and in the special cartons used today, than to go through the adventures of bottling their own wine. There is a school of thought, and I subscribe to it, that certain wines are not greatly improved by this and I personally have usually bought wine bottled in the United Kingdom. Wine merchants may do a better job than some of the bottling that takes place in the country of origin. Not so long ago, there was, in the UK, a firm named Lovibond, who ran a chain of wine shops very far removed from the multiple wine shops or supermarkets of today. They retained the flavour of the old-fashioned wine merchant and put as much care into each branch and the wines therein as if they only had one shop. In due course, they were taken over by a conglomerate, which promptly sold all the wines off and stocked the shops with gin, whisky, etc., and no doubt some good wine too, but the whole thing lost its flavour. It is an ill wind that blows nobody any good and I was able to buy at simply ridiculous prices a very large quantity of 1961 London-bottled clarets, and I still have quite a lot I am very pleased to say. They are quite delicious but are the products of minor châteaux and will not stand up to the great château-bottled wines. It is now illegal for a *grand cru classé* château not to sell in the bottle, although one or two continued to do so until quite recently.

The wine is now in the bottles and we must assume that whether it is done in the château or whether it is done in the cellars of a local and trusted wine merchant, or in a bonded store, that the expert has done his job properly and the wine has been given its best chance on the day of bottling.

Corking the bottles

Now there is the little matter of the cork, and it is upon the cork that the whole reputation of the wine will rest from the time of bottling forward, for wine is rendered bad only because air is allowed to contaminate it. Air obviously cannot reach the wine through the bottle and therefore must come through the cork. It should be remembered that if the wine is bad before it goes into the bottle, the best corks in the world will not make much difference. If you buy your wine château bottled or if you buy it through a first-class wine merchant, you will find they are using what is called the long cork (which is 6 cm/2¼ inches long) even on moderate qualities of wine. Wine merchants who wish to save money (and indeed if the wine is to be drunk very quickly after bottling there can be nothing wrong in this) use a short and, therefore, cheaper cork. The better the cork the longer it will protect the wine.

Nowadays one sees all kinds of corks for cheap wine – plastic or even crown corks for *ordinaires* in France – and I do not doubt they do their job for wine intended for consumption within a few days.

The bottle by your side

These are the many natural and human factors that militate against the production of the truly great bottle of wine, and so it must be; but you and I are not wine snobs. If we come across a really great bottle of wine we shall drink it on bended knees (metaphorically at least), but we will also take our pleasure when we can and be satisfied with a good deal less, and by satisfied I mean extremely happy, too. As I write these words, I have at my elbow an excellent glass of a commercial *blanc de blancs* dry white wine. It cost but very little. It is clean, it is honest and I am very happy with it.

Above: Champagne bottles in an old-fashioned wicker basket.

Great bottles and vintages; 1945 is one of the finest post-war vintages in both Bordeaux and Burgundy.

How and where to buy wine

Above: Advertising the Riesling wines of the Moselle in a wine shop in Koblenz.

To say that the buying of wine is important is a very considerable understatement. We *may* have rich relations who died too young and left us the wine in their cellars, but that we must discount as being improbable. Consequently, our whole interest in wine will only develop, and to the extent that we shall sooner or later become connoisseurs, if we buy it, and this quite honestly is not so easy to do. For the purposes of this chapter I will define wine under what I will call The Three Estates:

1 The great and the fine
2 The good and the moderate
3 *Les vins ordinaires* ('plonk')

The great and the fine

For the enthusiastic amateur to gain any first-hand tasting experience of the great Bordeaux châteaux wine, that is to say, wines of first or second growth, or the domaine-bottled *grands* or *premiers crus* of Burgundy will be difficult if not impossible. The growers simply cannot afford to open bottles of Lafite or whatever when the price today in Bordeaux, if you want to buy it ex-cellars, is no less than £20 per bottle for last year's vintage. Much the same applies in Germany for the great *Trockenbeerenauslese* wines. So how do we get this experience?

One way would be to join the International Wine and Food Society and attend some expensive tastings of these wines, and I think you should if you can afford them. If you are a sufficient buyer of important and expensive wine, it is not improbable that your wine supplier will be able to introduce you to the agents of the shippers, and when they hold their periodic wine tastings for the trade you may get an invitation.

When I was first in Bordeaux in 1948 I carried introductions from André Simon to the principal wine houses. These were the great houses of Cruse, Eschenauer, Calvet and others, and since I was one of the first amateurs to visit Bordeaux after the war, I was received with great honour and pleasure and was shown the best of everything. I remember that at Mouton and Lafite where the proprietors were bottling the famous 1945 vintage, my wife and I were given a bottle of that vintage from both the châteaux as a memento and indeed it was a memorable visit. But one cannot expect these things any more. Bordeaux and Burgundy are now full of tourists who come without introduction or anything else and expect to be fêted, but they are not well received – especially at vintage time. It is in this respect that you will find the services of your wine supplier to be invaluable. But do not expect a red carpet down at a *grand cru classé* château. Take your chances as they come along and go to very considerable trouble to find friends who will share a bottle with you. Buy it if you can – save up if necessary. Where there's a will, there's a way, but drink it you must.

The good and the moderate

This is very much easier because there are still plenty, possibly thousands, of excellent wines that cannot boast a famous name but, nonetheless, have the whole tradition of good wine making behind them. In Bordeaux alone there are more than 2,000 minor châteaux, many whose names are virtually unknown but who make excellent wine. Some of them are château bottled and most are bottled in France and exported in bottles. It is now illegal in France for *crus classés* of the Médoc, whether they be first, second, third, fourth or fifth growths, to be bottled elsewhere than at the châteaux. That should be a sufficient birth certificate. It can be no more. It simply means that the wine is bottled at the moment in time chosen by the proprietor as doing most justice to his wine, it is not a guarantee that the wine was really worth it in the first place. This is a chance you will have to take and you can only judge it when you know how to taste wine, and this can only be achieved by experience.

Three *bourgeois* clarets from Bordeaux are in my memory at the moment, having just 'looked at' them. Château d'Angludet (which is owned by Peter Sichel) in Margaux, and Château Sénéjac and Château Cissac both in the Haut-Médoc. But they are only three among more than 2,000. There are others equally good, perhaps some even better, but you and I would do very well if we never drank anything worse. The recommended wine lists in this book will give you some guidance.

Les vins ordinaires

Of these *vins ordinaires* there is a great deal to be said, for and against. At the lower end of the 'plonk' division, I would put the wine that is dispensed in the crush bars of theatres, and in pubs where the

Opposite: The vineyards and village of Montmélas, one of the several villages entitled to the appellation Beaujolais Villages.

Château Olivier produces red and white wine in the Graves. One of Bordeaux's most beautiful châteaux, it dates back to the eleventh century and was once a hunting lodge of the Black Prince.

proprietor has no interest in wine and it is usually served in quite small glasses at relatively high prices. It is not worth drinking. At the top end of the scale there are the wines sold by the great conglomerates, people in the supermarket business or people specialising in wine at low prices, but who do know their jobs and have enough knowledge to take some pride in what they dispense (such as Marks and Spencer and Sainsburys in the UK). In between these two classes there are hundreds and hundreds of table wines that are not worth the money and give no pleasure, or do not instil any desire to have more. The conglomerates I have mentioned do go to a great deal of trouble to find wine worthy of their name, but there is no question of an identification in the blends that go into the making of it, which is not to say that you cannot buy quality wines from these supermarkets. You can get lots of *Appellation Contrôlée* (AC) wines, Italian *Denominazione di Origine Controllata* (DOC) wines and *Qualitätswein bestimmter Anbaugebiete* (QbA) wines from Germany at comparatively low prices, but most of the cheap wine, and it can be very cheap today, is not to be recommended.

Under this heading should come the 'bag in the box' or 'square' wines, which I am told are becoming very popular all over the world. These are wines contained in polythene bags and housed in cardboard boxes. They contain between 2 and 8.5 litres (3½ to 15 pints) although you can get bigger ones in France. They have a tap and you merely keep them on a shelf in your cellar, cupboard or refrigerator and tap off the wine when you wish to drink it. The wine does last because, unlike opening bottles, no air is allowed into the bag once you start tapping off the wine. These wines are not expensive, but they are not all that cheap. I suppose they are convenient, but I cannot find it in my heart to recommend them. However, I did once buy a French 'bag in the box' holding 20 litres (35 pints) at a cooperative in the Midi for a ridiculously low price and brought it home in the back of the car. Very good it was too, right to the very end. That excellent wine magazine *Decanter* made a special investigation of 'bag in the box' wines some time ago, and did not think a great deal of them. The magazine reported that most of the wines so packed were those that come, alas, not from France but from Australia and South Africa for red wine, and Austria, Germany or Hungary for white wine.

The wine supplier

All of this brings us naturally to where we buy our wine, and I must say that for people who have a natural curiosity about wine and wish to drink well, the reputable local wine supplier is the best bet and today he need not be all that local.

The main point about it is that specialist wine suppliers are trained in the job. They have a natural instinct for it. I never knew one who did not love his wine and was not prepared to discuss it with me. A specialist will be interested enough to suggest wines from time to time when he knows your particular tastes, to help you to improve them, and to suggest interesting wines within your financial compass, and I doubt whether he will ever sell you a bad wine. A specialist will hold periodic tastings for his customers and keep a very comprehensive stock. Furthermore, he has a reputation he does not want to lose. The strength of the specialist wine supplier compared to conglomerates can be summarised as follows:

1 A small merchant can deal in small quantities with individual vineyards and producers. These quantities would be insufficient for supermarket and national distribution.
2 He has no national advertising appropriation or distribution costs.
3 The duty for wine is the same, irrespective of what it costs, so that if you spend a bit more on your wine you are paying the extra money for the quality of the wine, whereas with the cheapest conglomerate wine, you pay for the duty, packaging and distribution and very little over for the wine itself.

Having said all this, I must add that your reputable wine supplier is unlikely to be the cheapest on the market, although he will be competitive. His expenses are quite high, but he will not impose upon you, or at least I can only say that I have never had anything but satisfaction from any of the wine merchants I have dealt with over the years.

If you are in the right hands, the name of your wine supplier should be a sufficient guarantee of the integrity of the wine in the bottle, but it sometimes happens that you will want to buy elsewhere from a strange source. When buying wine in its country of origin, especially in France, there are one or two things to remember. All the information you want should be recorded on the label. You will find details of many of the local requirements in the chapters in this book, or in the glossary.

In Bordeaux the name of the château, especially if it be a *cru classé*, will be sufficient to tell you where it came from. You can look it up in your books without any trouble if you have not heard of it before. But if the wine is not château bottled then it is as well to know the names of a few first-class shippers in Bordeaux who have a reputation to lose and who are unlikely to risk it. The firms I would suggest are as follows, but I must make it absolutely clear that there are many many others in the same class but for which space does not permit an inclusion. There are Schröder & de Constans, Cordier, Moueix, Eschenauer, Nathaniel Johnston, Mähler-Besse and Peter Sichel (now Gallaire & Fils), and Shroder & Schyler & Cie. I have had much help,

friendliness, and not a little excellent wine from the houses of Calvet and of Cruse, and although they have not come out too well from the Bordeaux wine scandals I still believe in them and will continue to buy from them, but that is my affair.

In Burgundy, apart again from the domaine-bottled wine, it is important to know the shippers upon whom one can rely absolutely, especially as the vineyards are so small (in many cases only two or three acres). So it behoves one to know from whom one is buying, even directly through your wine supplier. The labels of Louis Latour, Louis Jadot, Bouchard Père ct Fils, Joseph Drouhin, Drouhin-Laroze, Clair-Daü and Chanson, Père et Fils have formidable reputations, as has Mommessin, although their wines are considered to be a little on the sweet side for Burgundy. In southern Burgundy Georges Duboeuf is highly thought of, as is also the house of Paul Jaboulet Aîné on the Rhône. Among the German wines, after the jaw-breaking estate names, look for the names of Dr Bürklin-Wolf or von Simmern on the Rhine; and on the Moselle, Saar and Ruwer, if you buy anything with the names of von Schorlemer, J. J. Prüm or the Bischöfliches Priesterseminar on the label, you certainly will not go far wrong, and will probably do very well indeed.

Above: Bottles of Jordan Cabernet Sauvignon, one of the most prestigious new wines to come out of California.

Below: Château Léoville-Las-Cases, a second growth and finest of the wines of St-Julien.

The service of wine

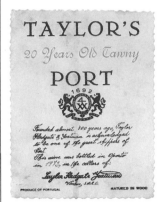

People who do not trouble to serve wine properly in their own homes hardly deserve to drink it, because there is all the difference in the world between wine which is brought to the table at its best and wine which is merely poured out of a bottle without thought to its condition. Let us begin with the wine in your cellar if you have one, or in the cupboard where you keep your wines if you have not.

Storing wine

Wine is best kept at a temperature of 13°C (55°F) but will not come to much harm if your cellar (or cupboard) goes down a few degrees in winter or goes up to 15.6°C (60°F) in summer. Temperatures must, however, be kept reasonably constant and if you freeze your wine in winter and boil it in summer, you can hardly expect to get much more than an intoxicating liquid out of the bottle, or perhaps only vinegar. If you can control your cellar, there should be ventilation of some sort, but no great harm will come to the wine if there is not. This has been proved by the well-authenticated stories of fathers who traditionally wall-up a specially stocked cellar of wine on the birth of their first-born son, to be opened after he comes of age, or later. In some places, like Limberg in southern Holland, this kind of thing has been going on for some hundreds of years, so we may take it that if ventilation had much to do with the keeping quality of wine, the practice would have stopped a long while ago.

The next point to remember is that wine must always lie on its side and the reason for this is twofold. In the first place, the wine should cover the cork and keep it moist. This stops it shrinking and thus helps to stop air entering the bottle. If there were a space between the cork and the wine, this would certainly be a breeding ground for the kind of microbe that would start trouble in the wine. Second, this allows any sediment or crust to settle in the bottom of the bottle while it is resting. There have been many tragic tales on this subject.

The best way to store your wine is in bins, if you have a cellar, or in simple wire racks. They can be made in any size to fit whatever space you have available, and if you like they can go up in steps to fit in a cupboard under stairs.

With your wine in reasonable condition, it can be served, and this is the moment which the wine lover has long awaited.

Opposite: A cellar scene: bottles in racks, an opened box of Château Léoville Barton and a bottle in readiness for decanting, candle and corkscrew at hand.

Above: The cellars of Robert Ampeau in Meursault, with traditional oak barrels, or Pièces, for ageing his wine.

Opposite: Red wine and port decanted in preparation for dinner.

The right temperature

White wines can be taken direct to the table, and, according to the temperature of your cellar, may be served at any time, provided they are cold. I keep the light beverage wines like Chablis, Bordeaux, the dry white *blanc de blancs* or white wines from Spain in the refrigerator, so that they can be taken out at any time and are always very cold, as indeed they should be. On the other hand, it is a very great mistake to serve really fine white wine like white Burgundy from Meursault or Montrachet, or the fine German Hocks and Moselles quite so cold as this. They need to be chilled and not frozen, and are quite all right if served straight from the cellar provided the temperature is not more than 10°C – 13°C (50°F – 55°F), plus a little extra cold which can be provided by no more than, say, a quarter or half an hour in the refrigerator. Champagne is at its very best when really cold, but not frozen.

Rosé wines, which are uniformly light beverage wines (there are one or two exceptions), should be served really cold and indeed, to my taste, are not really palatable otherwise. Even important rosé wines, like those from Tavel near Avignon in the Rhône Valley, are best served very cold.

There are very few red wines, however, which derive any benefit from being chilled (the red wine of Provence is an exception) and, in general, the best way to serve them is at room temperature. Another possible exception to this rule is Beaujolais. There is an informed school of thought which thinks that Beaujolais should be drunk very cold. Certainly it tastes delicious either way. It must be remembered, however, that good red wine can be spoiled by being too warm and I have far too many recollections of being honoured by my host with a superb bottle of claret served, it seemed to me, just off the boil and completely ruined. It is much better to serve red wine too cold rather than too hot, but there is really no reason for either, especially in your own home. My general practice, and I can recommend it to you, is to decant red wine for luncheon after breakfast, and red wine for dinner any time after five or six o'clock. Leave the decanter or the bottle open in your dining-room, or, better still, put it with the saucepans on the rack in the kitchen for a couple of hours, and it should be about right. NEVER plunge the bottle or the decanter into hot water – it merely warms the outside of the wine and causes all sorts of circulations to be set

up, and does the wine no good at all. I prefer to decant all my red wine, whether it be cheap, medium or dear. I personally think wine looks better in a decanter, and it will certainly give the wine a chance to breathe before drinking. On this matter of decanting, it is necessary to use intelligence and sometimes care, but it is always simple.

Serving fortified wines and brandy

The rule for Madeira and Marsala is that they should be served at room temperature, but sherry, apart from the old *amontillados* and *olorosos*, should be served chilled, especially the *finos*, which are their very best when slightly iced – but not with ice *inside* the glass!

Brandy is another thing again. In some restaurants, it is considered the thing to heat the brandy glasses on a little spirit stove before pouring the brandy in and handing it to the customer. This is a very great sin and should not be tolerated. Nearly always, the brandy is at room temperature anyway, but it should be served in small glasses and held in the palm of the hand and warmed, if warming be needed, naturally. Nothing really good is to be said of the huge *ballon* glasses, which again are sheer ostentatious affectation and leave most of the liquid round the glass anyway.

Decanting

For your beverage wines – that is to say, those wines which you will probably drink as a matter of course with some or all of your meals – it is not necessary to go through the ritual of decanting over a candle. Use a decanter that is perfectly clear and white, i.e. colourless, and pour your wine in just as though you were pouring it into a glass. That is all you need do. With the better clarets, some Burgundies and port, especially vintage port, you have to be more careful but, again, it is always a simple and rather pleasant ritual.

If you have a few days' notice of serving, merely stand the bottles at room temperature, then decant straight from the bottle in front of a candle or an electric torch. The light helps you see when the sediment is beginning to come with the wine from the bottle into the decanter. You must stop pouring at this point. If you are drinking your wine on the same day, use this method. You will need a cradle, just the usual wicker cradle that can be bought from almost any store, and which you see commonly and quite unnecessarily used in restaurants. Take the cradle to the bin or wine rack, take out your bottle from the bin and place it in the cradle in the same position in which it is lying in the bin, that is, with the sediment still in the bottom of the bottle. Take your

Opposite above: Removing the cork without disturbing the wine.

Opposite below: Decanting over a candle flame so that the sediment is immediately visible.

Below: A selection of the many different designs of corkscrew.

cradle to the table and remove the cork carefully. Wipe the neck and shoulders of the bottle and wipe the top, both before and after the removal of the cork. Grasp the bottom of the bottle and remove it from the cradle. Hold it in front of a lighted candle or electric torch so that you can see the light through the wine at the point where the neck joins the shoulder of the bottle. Decant the wine steadily in one pour, not letting the wine regurgitate back into the bottle by altering its position. Watch the light through the red wine, and as the bottle empties you will see the crust at the bottom of the bottle starting to come through the neck. It does not matter about an odd wisp or two, but when the main body of the crust starts to move through the neck stop pouring immediately and either use the rest of the wine for cooking or throw it away. Even though there may be a quarter of a bottle left, it is of no earthly use and you will only spoil what you have already decanted by continuing to pour. When this operation is finished, you should have a candle-bright, crimson wine in your decanter, which should be a delight to see and a greater delight to drink.

Vintage port is, however, a special subject, especially if it is one of considerable age. You may have trouble in getting your cork out in one piece, because this type of wine tends to rot the cork and that is why many of the older ports have been recorked. If the cork breaks, then I advise you to use an ordinary glass jug and a very fine tea or coffee strainer. Put the strainer on top of the glass jug and pour as though you were pouring into the decanter. Then fish out the pieces of broken cork as best you can. You will also find in the port a substance known as 'beeswing', which is not in itself as harmful to the wine as the very much heavier crust at the bottom of the bottle. If you are using a strainer, the beeswing will be caught in it, but if you are not and are decanting straight from bottle to decanter, it will do no great harm if a few pieces of beeswing get in. Both beeswing and crust are formed from living organisms in the port and seem to play an essential part in the development of this superb and now rather out-dated wine.

In my opinion, port is about the most difficult wine to decant properly and most worth the trouble. I keep in my cellar a pair of bottle tongs for really special bottles (or I did when I had special bottles; alas, they have long since gone). For my last bottle of Sandeman's Jubilee 1887, for instance, I nipped off the top of the bottle complete using the tongs – it is quite a simple operation. The tongs, which are of the right size for the neck of a port bottle, are heated until they are nearly white-hot, put round the neck of the bottle for a few seconds and then a wet rag is wrapped round the top and the neck snaps off quite cleanly without disturbing the cork, which would almost certainly have been bad.

From my experience, the only wines that need to be dealt with by the kind of careful decanting which I have described are clarets over five years old, and these include all the red wines of Bordeaux, such as St-Emilion, Pomerol, the red districts of Graves and, most importantly, the Médoc. Some old Burgundies need the same treatment, and almost all the classic Burgundies from the Côte d'Or (but only if they are a few years old). Crusted or vintage ports certainly need decanting, but I cannot really think of any other red wines that need special treatment. Most of the little red wines of France, including the famous Beaujolais, and all the wines of the Loire and the Rhône, throw hardly any sediment and need not be fussed with. If in doubt, wipe the bottle and hold it over a candle and you can see for yourself.

The affectation of most restaurants in bringing wine to the table carefully nursed in the cradle is, in most cases, pure undiluted nonsense. The first-class *restaurateur* will decant the wine if it needs it and bring it to the table, or put the bottle on the table just as it is, standing upright, which is all that is necessary. There is a very good piece on this in George Orwell's *Down and Out in London and Paris* (Secker and Warburg, 1933), where he describes how, while working in a Paris restaurant, the wines would be taken from the bin, thrown from hand to hand until they finally reached the bar and would then be brought to the table in a cradle with a napkin round the neck with all the pomp and ceremony imaginable. This, I think, is what usually happens, judging from the condition of some wine when it reaches the table. Of course, most of them are quite clear because there never was any sediment to be disturbed anyway.

Madeira and Marsala, although having many affinities with port for they are made and matured in much the same way, do not normally need very special treatment, as they form little or no crust. I have myself drunk eighteenth-century Madeira

that certainly showed no sign of crust, and although Madeiras may be of considerable age, even when they are vintage wines made in a particular year, they do not seem to throw much crust, possibly because they have been matured so long in wood.

Sherry is usually entirely free from crust, but I have drunk some very old *amontillado* (1770!), which proves (for I still have a bottle) almost impossible to decant because its loose sediment has the consistency of mist, and the mere taking of the bottle from the bin, even though the greatest care is used, is sufficient to cloud the wine.

The resting time
It goes without saying that wine requiring ritual decanting must be rested before the bottle is opened and the time will vary enormously. Cool white wines and most of the minor wines can come straight from your wine cellar and they won't hurt, but fine claret, Burgundy and port can require to rest in the bin for at least three or four weeks from its coming into your cellar. Vintage port needs three months, and must of course be binned very carefully with the white stripe or the label facing up. It does not like to be moved at all, and it was not for nothing that a wine-loving vicar refused a bishopric because he could not again contemplate moving his port!

Finally, use a sense of proportion in this matter of the service of wine. All good things, great or small, are worth a little trouble, but to take too much trouble, that is to take everything to the fraction of a degree with younger and cheaper wines, is not necessary. You will have nothing to complain about if you serve your white and rosé wines quite cold, and your red wines at room temperature. Great wines deserve respect and your special attention and, indeed, if they do not get it, you will only have yourself to blame if the wine is cloudy and dull, for the greater the wine, the more delicate it is and the more easily ruined by bad serving.

Above: Flutes for Champagne, tall-stemmed Hock glasses and classic red and white wine glasses.

Left: A traditional sherry copita (far left) and a small brandy glass (far right), with other glasses for red, white and rosé wines.

arms, or the name of a château, or in the case of port, the initials of a private person or college or club lucky enough to be able to buy bottles in sufficient quantity. Some châteaux will celebrate a very special vintage by putting up their château bottles with a shoulder seal of this kind. Lafite did in 1945, for instance. The enterprising people who devised the bottle for the alleged Napoleon Brandy (whoever they may be) emphasized that it was in fact Napoleon Brandy by putting a shoulder seal on the bottles with a very beautiful 'N' moulded on it. Could any further proof be necessary that it came from the cellars of the Emperor himself? Nonsense, of course!

It is perfectly true that the bigger the bottle the better the wine. The main reason for this is that the wine in large bottles develops more slowly and lasts longer, and also, possibly, that since all impurities must get into the wine through the cork there is chance of fewer impurities entering through one

cork than through, say, six in the case of a jeroboam. Certainly I have drunk some very splendid wines from big bottles. On the other hand, it can be pretty disastrous to find a corked jeroboam of Champagne that must be consigned to the sink.

Just as the first bottle was a jar, so the first glass was a cup, and it was not until clear glass became available that the pleasure of drinking a lovely wine could be enjoyed to the full. It has been well said that in enjoying our wine we indulge four out of five senses – taste and smell, hearing (for is not the popping of the cork a nice thing to hear?) and, not least of these, sight. The contemplation of a glass of red wine in a clear glass against a lit candle is an extremely pleasant experience, and if the glass be beautiful and rounded and nicely made, we can perhaps indulge the sense of touch too. A sixth sense may also come into action, that of anticipation, but this is nothing to do with glasses.

For hundreds of years, glasses have been made in

many shapes and sizes. They have been beautifully engraved and sometimes they are made of coloured glass. Those glasses which have been designed by modern designers for wine lovers are nealy all tulip shaped, large or small, wide or slim, according to the type of wine they are intended for, and made of clear crystal with little or no cutting, so that the sight of the wine is unimpaired.

Champagne can be enjoyed out of flute glasses – that is to say, tall, thin glasses from whence the bubbles rise interminably for the whole time the wine is in the glass, which is not usually all that long. The use of the Victorian, wedding-reception, flat-bowled type of Champagne glass is to be deplored – the wine explodes in it, effervesces and goes flat very quickly and does the wine no justice. You will not find these glasses in general use outside England or America. Brandy glasses should be *ballon* or thistle shaped, but small enough to hold in the palm of the hand so that the wine may be warmed.

Good clear wine glasses are not necessarily expensive, and indeed they should be cheap because they should be in general use and breakages are, unfortunately, all too frequent. I suppose the general principle is to pay as much as one can afford. Even the plainest glasses by Baccarat, the famous French glass manufacturers, are extremely expensive by any standard, but they are lovely things and, if I were a rich man, I should certainly use them all the time. As it is, I use a perfectly simple, plain (Czechoslovakian I suspect) goblet, which I can buy in all sizes, which does full credit to the wine inside it. The use of large glasses, *grandes pièces* they are sometimes called, in fashionable restaurants is harmless enough and, of course, tends to use up a bottle very much more quickly (which I suppose is the general idea). It is, I confess, rather a pleasant conceit and one restaurant that I have in mind only uses it for the very best Burgundies at very high prices, which enables the host to show his guests and the other people in the restaurant that he is buying the most expensive wine. If you would like a demonstration, this habit is very common in Beaune and in Burgundy generally.

Cellars and cellarage

Above: A warming sight: a glass of wine awaiting tasting.

A cellar can be defined in two ways: physically as an underground chamber in which is stored wine, or coal, or perishables, or any other kind of material best kept underground; and as a collective noun for bottles of wine. Consequently, you may not have a cellar in your home, but you can have a cellar of wine in almost any part of it, provided that the temperature is fairly even and it does not get terribly cold in winter or terribly hot in summer. I happen to be blessed with a particularly good cellar under both definitions. It behoves every lover of wine to have a cellar of some sort, not only for convenience because you can get at your wine easily and quickly, but because you may need supplies suddenly when all the shops are shut. Apart from that consideration, you will, as a wine lover, from time to time come across parcels of wine (that is, if you are curious enough to look around for it) that you will want to treasure and keep until some suitable occasion when you can share it with your friends.

It is perfectly true that a fine wine cannot be drunk by oneself. It is made to be shared with your friends, and particularly those friends who will appreciate what they are drinking. The late André Simon said, 'A man dies too young if he leaves any wine in his cellar.' This is, of course, a very nice calculation but it is in the nature of things that we shall all leave wine in our cellars, because we are too mean to give it away or, when it comes to our precious bottles, quite unable to drink it alone. You always have to keep a few in reserve – even André Simon left two magnums of Lafite '53 when he died in 1970. I hope it will never happen to me, as it did to the late George Saintsbury, that my doctors should forbid me ever to touch wine again. George Saintsbury, on receiving this advice, sold his cellar entirely and lived to a ripe old age, cherishing the memories of the great wines he had drunk, hence his famous *Notes on a Cellar Book* which is the great classic of its kind. More of this famous cellar book anon.

As a collective noun for bottles of wine, a cellar can be started with two bottles up, but that could hardly be termed a substantial reserve. I started mine with eight dozen, well-selected bottles of which I still possess perhaps a couple, and that goes back thirty-eight years. As wine is drunk, so it must be replaced and one tends more and more to take care for the future and put a few reserve bottles by. This is the principle which I have firmly adhered to. I

Right: The cellar book, an invaluable record of past and future drinking.

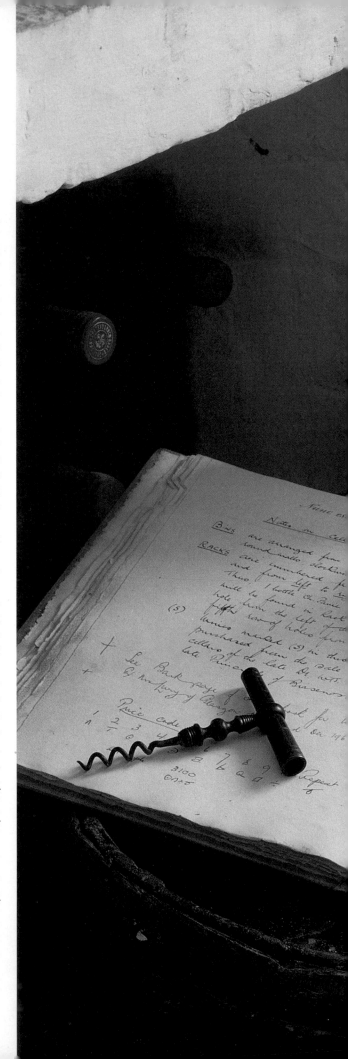

Bottles ageing in the cool cellars of Château Lafite; this is an essential part in the development of all fine claret.

Opposite: The author decanting in his own cellar, surrounded by some of his favourite wines.

bottles at a time as your purse or your capacity dictates. The second principle is to cellar what wines you wish to reserve for high days and holidays and for special friends. In other words, those that you wish to share with other people. These wines should be selected with careful interest and bought from the indispensable, reputable wine supplier. The actual cellarage may pose some small problems, but there is usually a cool room or cupboard somewhere in the house which is large enough to take care of a reasonable number of good bottles. If it can be kept at a temperature of 13°C (55°F), this is ideal, but five or six degrees up or down will not hurt the wine a little bit, providing the temperature remains fairly steady. In the case of a small cellar the simple racks with holes for up to one dozen bottles are purveyed by most stores. They can be made and fitted to any size. They are not terribly expensive, and are by far the best way of using the space to its fullest advantage.

In the case of the cellar in its true physical sense, the best way is to fit bins, each containing quantities of a dozen or two dozen bottles, with some larger bins of up to ten dozen bottles. These can be built on three sides of the cellar for wines bought by the dozen, with some racks on one wall. The racks are for small quantities of up to a dozen bottles, for which you do not want to use your bin spaces. The bins should be numbered consecutively, and the racks numbered in rows from top to bottom and from left to right. Then with your cellar book in hand you know exactly what is in each bin and in each hole in the rack. There should be a table in the centre of the cellar containing the essential implements for opening the wine: corkscrews; a candle stuck in a bottle for decanting; hammer and chisel for opening wooden cases; and, if you are lucky enough to have really old port, perhaps bottle tongs for nipping off the neck.

If you are very rich you can also have a sink fitted and a collection of glasses ready to hand for tasting the wine after you decant it, and if you are a millionaire or very very rich there is a firm in New York making some beautiful temperature-controlled wine cabinets to take up to 700 bottles. The advertisement says that: 'they cost no more than a case of Lafite '61'. Enough said!

To finish the complete equipment of the cellar you will need a cellar book and there are one or two simply laid out cellar books on the market. Again, one good one that I know can be bought from the IEC Wine Society, and there are others. These printed books are by no means necessary. One of my most treasured possessions is the original cellar book of George Saintsbury which served him so well for thirty years. It is simply a sixpenny exercise book which he used indiscriminately from both ends at once, sketching in a map of the cellar at

can honestly say I have had more pleasure out of my cellar than I have out of most things in this life. I recall those pleasant moments, possibly running into a quarter of an hour each, when I have looked round the cellar, cellar book in hand, to choose the wine for some luncheon or dinner party. I consider one, discard it, take up another, and finally choose a third, at the same time thinking of the food with which the wine is to be drunk and the company that is going to be privileged to partake thereof. Each bin or rack has particular associations, according to how, when and where it was bought, and what it tasted like when a bottle was last drunk.

Having thus dealt briefly with the philosophy of keeping a cellar, I will proceed to more practical details. First, it is by no means necessary to build a cellar for every kind of wine. Your beverage wines – that is to say those wines which I hope you will drink with your lunch and your dinner, with or without company, and which you will probably buy quite cheaply – can be kept in the cellar for convenience and bought in two or three, or two or three dozen,

one end, roughly dividing it up into bins, and noting the wine that he laid down in those bins. When a bin was finished (and he never recorded the wine as it was drunk) he would make one of his salty and appropriate remarks against the wine, so that after about thirty years he was able to compose his book *Notes on a Cellar Book* (Macmillan) from this sixpenny exercise book. I myself use a simply ruled book divided up into Bordeaux, Burgundy, Rhenish, Ports and Sherries, Champagne and other wines, and this has served me very well. But each to his choice. Keeping a cellar book is not only an essential operation if you take an interest in the wine and have a great number of different sorts of it, as I hope you will, but in turning the pages, when you mark off your wine as it is drunk, it will provoke some very pleasant memories.

From the foregoing the reader will see that there is no great problem about starting a cellar. To sum up, it can be started almost anywhere, at any time, and any number of bottles can play.

Advice to the beginner

Now I will proceed to give some advice to the beginner who wants to start a cellar and has, we shall assume, a limited amount of money to spend and wants to know what to put into his cellar. This is very largely a matter of personal taste. If you like claret better than Burgundy, you will have more claret than Burgundy in your cellar; this is natural. But if you are a true wine lover, as you almost certainly will be if you are starting a cellar, you will be curious about it and will want to have a wine for most occasions and to suit the food you serve.

Starting at the bottom end, and if you have space available, you can buy your beverage wines more cheaply by buying a few dozen at a time. Some specialist wine suppliers will sell mixed cases of better wines. They can be put down and brought up as you wish to drink them. This will at least save the trouble of popping round to the wine shop too often, but it may deprive you of variety.

It is mainly, however, the good wines with which we are concerned and it seems to me that if I were starting all over again, I should go (and remember again this must to some extent be personal) for some *grand cru classé* claret, if I could afford it, of the years 1970 or 1971 for ready drinking, 1961 and 1966 for keeping. I should be lucky if I could get any 1945s, 1949s, 1953s or anything earlier, which are now only available at auction. I have them now for the simple reason that I had a cellar and bought them when they were young and, by present-day standards, very cheap. But mostly for my clarets I would go for the second, third, fourth and fifth growths with some good *crus bourgeois* in Médocs, and some good first-growth St-Emilions, and perhaps some red Graves. One can still get wines at

a reasonable price, like Pontet-Canet or Cantemerle, which, although fairly expensive, are much better than their fifth-growth status would suggest. In fact, they should be, in my opinion, second growths. The Léovilles – Poyferré, Barton or Las-Cases – are all good wines and not too highly priced. Château Lascombes is a second growth and is a sound wine. But search among the *bourgeois* growths and you will find some comparative bargains if such there be in this year of grace.

Remember as an axiom that there is rarely good wine of a really bad year, whatever the name on the label. Conversely, there is not much bad wine of a good year, provided the wine be honest, and on this you must rely to a great extent upon your personal taste backed up with the reputation of your supplier. Burgundies are considerably more difficult to choose because, despite the *appellations contrôlées*,

A cosmopolitan mixture for inclusion in the complete cellar, from Spain, Italy, California and Germany.

there is a great deal more fake Burgundy than there is fake claret. In the first place, all Burgundies have a fair amount of sugar added when the wine is made. Many clarets are also *chaptalized*, but not to anywhere near the same extent. In the second place, the vineyards in Burgundy are very much smaller and there are a great many smallholders providing their wines to be 'packaged' by *négociants* in Beaune and Dijon and Nuits-St-Georges. The bottles bear geographical details on the labels which do not always even approximate to the vineyard from whence the wine came. Again, and I cannot say this too often, you must rely on your wine supplier. But in choosing Burgundies for your cellar, you should, if your taste is for big, even great, suave wines, I suppose, have a few bottles of the Romanée-Conti wines, but you are fortunate indeed if you can afford them. Meanwhile, commune wines from

Chambolle-Musigny, or vineyard wines like Bonnes-Mares and Les Amoureuses (which is in Chambolle-Musigny) are quite delicious and good keepers. You should, of course, choose a wine of a good year.

Going from Burgundy to Mâcon and Beaujolais, one must be very careful in one's choice. There is more poor Beaujolais on the market than anything else, but there are excellent estate-bottled examples from Moulin-à-Vent, like for instance Clos de Rochegrès or Clos de Grand Carquelin, which are universally good. Among Beaujolais wines of the *grand cru* districts, Fleurie is excellent, and Morgon and Moulin-à-Vent produce very good wine. Once you have found a good, honest Beaujolais, you have an excellent wine that can be drunk very young indeed. It is fashionable to drink *vin de l'année*, which is the Beaujolais of the current year, but I

personally prefer those made for drinking at two or three years old, and they will keep a lot longer.

Do not by any means despise some of the best Spanish wines. The good wines of the Rioja will last for donkey's years, and so, rather unexpectedly, do the best Italian wines. Italian wine has the merit of being rather cheaper than French wine. It is very good and, in my view, no well-contrived cellar should be without a few bottles. Like Spanish wines, the date on the label of Italian wine is not terribly important, neither is it always very truthful, but the wine itself can be good. I have drunk, and still drink, wines like Gattinara and some of the best Chiantis of some age that are very good quality.

If you have a large cellar and want to have a few interesting wines, try some of the very best Australian, South African or American wines. Certainly, a few fine bottles of these wines will be rewarding and worth the trouble of getting. They have a quality of their own which does not always suffer by comparison with European wine and, in some cases, they are even better.

White wines, which are not by their nature terribly long lived, can be taken according to taste. My preference has always been for white Burgundy and the few bottles of the great Montrachet, Bâtard-Montrachet or a Meursault Genevrières are essential to any good cellar, but they are, like all great wine, very expensive. There are many lower-priced and excellent white Burgundies and Chablis available with which you can achieve variety with excellence.

The best German wines can be even more expensive than the French; the *Trockenbeerenauslesen*

Some of the best that France has to offer, from Champagne and Chablis to red Burgundy and claret, all deserving a place in a well-stocked cellar. Magnums mature more slowly than the ordinary bottle.

Nantes, Sancerre and Pouilly Fumé (not to be confused with Pouilly-Fuissé of Burgundy). They are excellent value and well worth keeping in your cellar.

As to sherries, you have no need to put them down unless you want some very fine vintage or very old *solera* sherries. These must be kept in a cellar because they throw a fine but heavy crust. They are difficult to decant, but incomparable in their nature. Bottles can be bought from your specialist suppliers as and when required and should be kept in adequate supplies of such quantities as you consume.

Port again must be cellared, especially vintage port. Tawny ports do not throw a crust, neither do the commercial rubies, and here again you may buy as and when you wish.

Champagne is certainly a wine which must be represented in your cellar and the famous *marques* can be obtained in small quantities when you wish. Non-vintage Champagne is sold ready to drink, though it can improve with a year or so's cellaring. Vintage Champagnes are at their best at seven years old. A good vintage will last up to twenty years, but may be unreliable after that. Most non-vintage wines are best for being kept in the cellar a few months before drinking to achieve bottle age. The consumption of Champagne is now so great that although it arrives in good condition from the shipper and will be three years old or more, it comes straight from Rheims or Epernay and is all the better for being stored for a while before it is drunk. Do not neglect the sparkling wines of South Africa, Australia and America.

To sum up, the composition of your cellar must be essentially a matter of your personal taste, coupled, if you are inexperienced, with the advice of a really reputable supplier. It would be comparatively easy for me to give you a list of wine to start a cellar with, say, ten dozen bottles, but what you would get would only be my personal choice, and it might not be at all what you would want yourself. Remember also that to know wine you must drink it and it is the experience which drinking wine brings that will enable you to build up your cellar in the best way possible.

One final word: keep in mind that wine has steadily increased in value for as long as I can remember now, and the wines which I bought fifteen to twenty years ago are now not only unprocurable, except at auction, but I could not afford them if they were. Consequently, it is probably true to say that starting and developing a cellar today will not only be a gracious and absorbing hobby but will also be a sound and worthwhile investment.

My personal policy has always been that: *when things are good I buy a little wine, and when things are bad – I buy a little wine!*

of the Rhine and Moselle are in a class by themselves. But sound wines from the Moselle, Bernkasteler, or Wehlener Sonnenuhr, can be bought at reasonable prices and are quite delicious, as are also the Niersteiners and Rüdesheimers from the Rhine. These wines should be represented in every cellar.

White Bordeaux wines have never been great favourites with me and indeed I keep very little of them, except for Sauternes headed by the great Château d'Yquem. Then, perhaps Climens, Coutet and Lafaurie-Peyraguey, which are available at reasonable prices. The Graves and Entre-Deux-Mers and other white wines of Bordeaux are sweetish, sound and not impressive. The wines of the Loire in recent years have developed a character of their own, for example Muscadet, from near

Wines of the World

FRANCE

Vendangeuse *at Château d'Yquem, warmly dressed against the autumn chill.*

To say that the whole of France is one great vineyard is not quite true, but only seven of the eighty-nine *départements* are free of vines. All the rest grow grapes and make wine. No longer is France the largest wine-producing nation in the world; Italy now has pride of place and produces something like 80,000,000 hectolitres per annum compared to the 69,000,000 hectolitres made in France. However, French wine has long been rated the best in the world, and even if some wines produced elsewhere are now as good, there is still none better. Nowadays there is little chance of a really bad French wine being sold as more sophisticated vinification techniques have been introduced, and the general upsurge in wine consumption has resulted in a corresponding appreciation of and interest in quality. The same concern for standards may well exist in nearly all wine-making countries.

The French have the greatest and longest tradition of wine making and they have, in their time, overcome, for the sake of quality and excellence, some really appalling problems of vinous pests and diseases that beset the vineyards in the last century and part of this. Notwithstanding these difficulties, the performance is simply amazing. First of all, in 1854, oidium reduced the quantity of wine to a little more than one-eighth of the average production. After oidium came phylloxera, a tiny spider-like insect which attacked the roots of the vines and devastated all the vineyards in France except for one or two tiny enclaves. These enclaves continued to produce wine from pre-phylloxera vines until recently. In 1910, after phylloxera, came mildew, which again wrecked French production for a year or two. But the Frenchman has always managed to find the antidote to these plagues, and while he has undoubtedly suffered, most of the vineyards today are healthier than they have ever been. It is fashionable among my older friends to say that wines have never been the same since phylloxera hit the vineyards of France, but like most of my contemporaries, I have had very little opportunity of tasting pre-phylloxera wines – that is, wines made before about 1880. I have indeed tasted some excellent wine that was certainly pre-phylloxera, but I have also tasted some that, while being post-phylloxera, seemed to me to have such pure magic that I cannot conceive that any wine could be better. Phylloxera was accidentally imported into France from North

Wine label terms

Name of property
District
Classification
Appellation Contrôlée
Vintage
Name and address of proprietors
Content by volume
Bottled at the château

Name of property
Country of production
Name of the region followed by its quality category, *vin délimité de qualité supérieure* (VDQS).
Official stamp showing that the wine has been tested and approved as a VDQS wine.
Content by volume. 'e' denotes that the wine has been bottled in accordance with EEC regulations, but it does not have to appear on the label.
Name and address of bottler
The merchant for whom the wine was bottled.

French wine law

There are basically four categories of wine:
Appellation Contrôlée (AC). The highest appellation for quality wines, covering all the fine wines of France. Every aspect of viticulture and vinification is strictly controlled, i.e. area of production, grape varieties, quantity produced, wine-making procedure and alcohol level. Most wines are now tasted before the appellation is granted.
Vins Délimités de Qualité Supérieure (VDQS). Wines good enough for quality control but not yet up to AC standards. Similarly controlled are: area of production, grape varieties, minimum alcohol. In addition, all wines have to be tasted.
Vin de Pays. Little wines with an indication of geographical origin only. Origin, grapes, alcohol and acidity are controlled. Tasting is obligatory.
Vin de Table. Basic wines, subject to a government intervention system to keep the market stable.

vines. The vineyards of France today, therefore, grow grapes on American stock.

Such is the importance of wine to the general economy in France, and to the whole well-being of the nation, that the strongest controls are exercised by the Government and by the wine-growers' associations to maintain these pure standards upon which the French reputation has been built but which, by reason of the great demand, have been in the past subjected to all sorts of adulteration and misdescription. The fine wine-growing districts and sub-districts of France now have what is called *appellation contrôlée* (AC). This means that the wine with the AC tag has been made subject to strict standards and specifications, it is up to certain degrees of alcoholic strength, made from approved grape varieties, and comes from within the very clearly set out geographical limits of the district. This ensures that wine sent out with this certificate has come from the district from which it purports to start, and is composed of the wine of that district and from none other. At least, it starts that way. It is not a guarantee of high quality.

The wine-growing districts

The main wine-growing districts of France are Bordeaux, Burgundy, the Loire, the Rhône Valley, the Midi, Alsace, and, last but not least, Champagne. They all have their special characteristics and their special virtues. Good wine is made in all, fine wine in some and great wine in three only. They can be bought, these wines, for a reasonable price for the young wines of less importance, to quite a lot of money for a first-growth Bordeaux of a good year. Over the last few years there have been many auction sales of bottles of old wines for tens of thousands of pounds. To pay prices like this merely shows complete lack of all sense of proportion. It is possible, however, to drink well by choosing carefully the lesser growths of the right years and for them, it is not necessary to pay any more than you can afford.

America in the roots of some experimental hardy stocks, which were immune. Once these stocks were planted in France the insect quickly transferred its attentions to the native stocks, which were not immune, and it spread like the proverbial wildfire. Finally, the ravages were stopped by the wholesale importation of immune American stocks into France on to which were grafted the old French

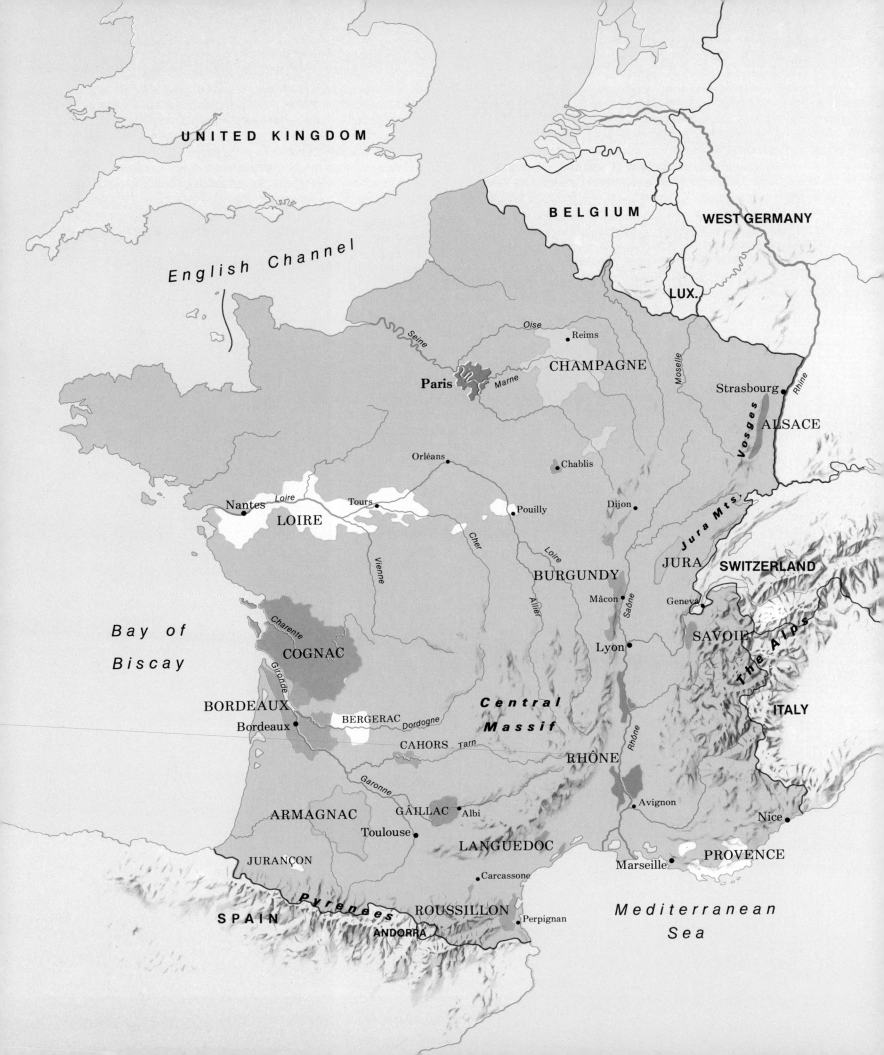

Bordeaux

Opposite: Château d'Yquem, most famous of all the Sauternes châteaux.

The red wine of the Bordeaux district is in general called claret, whereas the white wines can be Graves, Barsac, Sauternes, Entre-Deux-Mers, and so on. Bordeaux was, from the twelfth to the fifteenth centuries, part of the English Crown and it is generally accepted that claret derives its name from one of the Earls of Clare, who held fief under Henry II of England and his successors. There are many English names still active in the Bordeaux district, for instance Talbot, whose name still lives in the wine of Château Talbot, one of the best wines of the Médoc. (The original Talbot was killed at the battle of Castillon in 1453, when Bordeaux and Aquitaine were lost to the English Crown.) Before it was known as claret the wine was known in England as Gascon wine. It was very popular during

Above: Old vines, identifiable by their thick gnarled trunks, in the vineyard of Château Margaux.

Below: Château Ausone, since its revival at the beginning of the 1970s, now makes one of the best wines of St-Emilion.

the Middle Ages, if for no other reason than that it was a royal monopoly, which the King had given to the city of Bordeaux; consequently, there was hardly any competition.

There are three main types of wine made in the Bordeaux area and this applies, to some extent, to both red and white wines, but principally red. First of all, we have the very finest wine, which is made from the grapes grown on the low hills above the Gironde in the Médoc to the north of Bordeaux and in the Graves to the south, and in the Dordogne above the villages of St-Emilion and Pomerol. The hills of the Médoc are but gentle slopes not rising much above the river level. They were once upon a time under water and the effect of this is a soil composed of gritty sand and pebbles which, although it can grow hardly anything but vines, has within it those salts and mineral substances which give the wine delicacy and tremendous staying power. The second type is made in vast vine-growing areas around Bordeaux like Bourg and Blaye and Entre-Deux-Mers. This is very good vine-growing land with slightly richer soil and higher yield, but the wine is not great. Third, there are the wines made from the low-lying river areas (at one time called the *palus*), but they can never be great, although some, like the wines of Château de Terrefort in Cubzaguais, can be very drinkable.

The best dry white wine is made in Graves and the finest sweet white wine is made at the world-famous Château d'Yquem in Sauternes. The clean and cheap white wines of Entre-Deux-Mers (which literally means 'between two seas' but is, in fact, between the Garonne and the Dordogne rivers) and Premières Côtes de Bordeaux are made in great quantities and are refreshing and only slightly sweet.

The good red wines of the Côtes de Blaye and Côtes de Bourg are thoroughly satisfactory, inexpensive, full-bodied and have that 'kiss' which signifies the true Bordeaux: a faint touch of sharpness that one finds in all wines of the district, more or less pronounced according to the quality of the wine and the amount of sun in that particular year. The wines of Pomerol and St-Emilion are rather richer and fruitier than Médocs, and here are made some very important wines indeed.

The red and white wines of Graves have the reputation, and deservedly so, of being by nature fine, well-bred wines. They are not as generous as St-Emilion wines and they have not the suave dignity of the great Médocs. One of their number, Château Haut-Brion, is named as one of the five *premiers crus classés* of Bordeaux, and most of the wines are fully up to Médoc standard, but have perhaps greater finesse. They have the reputation

Principal wine-producing districts of Bordeaux

Médoc	Barsac
Graves	Sauternes
St-Emilion and Pomerol	Cérons
Fronsac	Ste-Croix-du-Mont
Côtes de Blaye	Entre-Deux-Mers
Côtes de Bourg	Premières Côtes de Bordeaux

Bordeaux appellations contrôlées

Bordeaux, Bordeaux Rouge, etc. Generic appellations for the whole areas of the Gironde. The least expensive of all Bordeaux
Basic district appellations: Haut-Médoc, Graves, St-Emilion, etc. A higher standard is required. Should be marginally less expensive than château labels. Reds from the Médoc, St-Emilion, etc., and plenty of whites from Graves and Premières Côtes de Bordeaux. Rich sweet whites from Sauternes and Barsac.
Pauillac, St-Estèphe, St-Julien, Margaux, Moulis and Listrac. The six Médoc communes with their own appellations. Almost entirely red wines. With increased demand for minor châteaux wines, generic wines under these labels are found less and less.

Classifications

• The famous classification of 1855 covered the wines of the Médoc (but included Haut-Brion from the Graves) and Sauternes. Sixty Médoc châteaux were listed: four *premiers crus classés*, fourteen *deuxièmes crus*, fourteen *troisièmes crus*, ten *quatrièmes crus* and eighteen *cinquièmes crus*. (See list on page 60.) The classification of Sauternes included eleven *premiers crus* and twelve *deuxièmes crus*, with Château d'Yquem the only *premier grand cru*. (See list on page 61.)
• The *crus bourgeois* of the Médoc were first officially classified in 1932 and most recently in 1978.
• The classification of the Graves (for both red and white wines) took place in 1953 and was most recently revised in 1959. (See list on page 61.)
• The district of St-Emilion was classified in 1954 and reclassified in 1985. At present there are 11 Premier Grands Crus Classés, with Châteaux Ausone and Cheval Blanc in a special category at the top, and 63 Grands Crus Classés.
• Pomerol has never been officially classified but Château Pétrus is acknowledged as the outstanding wine.

Bordeaux prices

The price range for Bordeaux wines covers the whole spectrum from the very expensive first growths right down to basic Bordeaux *rouge* or *blanc*. As a guide, the lists of recommended wines on the following pages are divided into four categories (★—★★★★) although the price range within each is fairly wide.

Pascale Delbeck, the régisseur of Château Ausone, tasting in the cellars. His shirt provides the essential white background with which to judge the wine's colour.

of being very good keepers and of outliving the wines of the Médoc, but this I would very much doubt. The soil is poor and stony, hence the name Graves, or gravel, and the output is singularly small, and that is why, with the rising cost of production, many vineyards in Graves have gone out of cultivation or have ceased to cultivate the whole of their acreage.

Château bottling

It is necessary to say something at this point on château bottling, which is so much a feature of the best Bordeaux vineyards. Château bottling simply means that the wine is actually bottled at the château where the grapes are grown and where the wine is made and matured, and it should therefore represent the wine of that château at its very best, always provided the *vigneron* knows his job. Usually it is safe to assume that he does, but château bottling can never be more than a birth certificate in that you know that it has come from a certain place and is the wine of a certain year bottled at the time the *maître de chai* judged it to be at its best. The corks of château-bottled wines are stamped with the name of the château, sometimes with the owner's name and always the date.

There have been in the past several châteaux that have not practised château bottling – but have kept what they wanted for their own consumption, and sold the remainder in bulk to reputable shippers and wine merchants who bottled the wine. Château Pontet-Canet and Château Langoa-Barton are two of these, but both are now of course château bottled as, since 1972, it has been illegal for any of the sixty Médoc *cru classé* wines to be bottled outside the château. In the case of minor wines being sold through a Bordeaux *négociant* with a monopoly, corks will sometimes be branded with the name of the château and date, although the wine is in fact bottled by the *négociant* in Bordeaux. This is in some measure an added security to the buyer. The procedure is called *étampé* and the wine may be, and quite probably is, just as good as that which is

The wines of the Médoc and Graves are briefly described below, followed by a selection of recommended wines. The first growths (★★★★) are very expensive; other classified growths (★★★) are moderately expensive and the bourgeois growths (★★) are reasonably priced. The symbol ✩ indicates a wine expensive in its class; ✩✩ indicates a wine very expensive in its class.

Médoc

Pauillac. Deep concentrated colour; firm and powerful full wines; long lasting. The commune boasts three out of five of the first growths and produces arguably the best red wines in the world.
First growths ★★★★ Lafite ✩, Latour, Mouton-Rothschild ✩.
Other classed growths ★★★ Batailley, Grand-Puy-Lacoste, Haut-Batailley, Lynch-Bages ✩, Mouton-Baronne Philippe, Pichon-Longueville Baron, Pichon-Longueville Lalande, Pontet-Canet.
Bourgeois growths ★★ Colombier-Monpelou, La Couronne.

Margaux. Less heavy and quicker-developing than Pauillac with tremendous delicacy and charm. The appellation includes wines from four neighbouring villages: Cantenac, Labarde, Arsac and Soussans, which all produce wines of a similar style.
First growth ★★★★ Margaux.
Other classed growths ★★★ Giscours, Lascombes, Malescot-St-Exupéry, Palmer ✩✩.
Bourgeois growths ★★ d'Angludet, Bel-Air Marquis d'Aligre, Labégorce, La Tour-de-Mons.
St-Julien. Classic claret. Very characteristic on the nose. The wines seem to have the breed and finesse of Margaux and the richness and weight of Pauillac. No first growths but five seconds.
Classed growths ★★★ Beychevelle ✩, Ducru-Beaucaillou ✩, Gruaud-Larose, Langoa-Barton, Léoville-Barton, Léoville-Las-Cases ✩, Léoville-Poyferré, Talbot.
Bourgeois growths ★★ du Glana, Gloria ✩.
St-Estèphe. The most northerly of the four great Médoc communes, producing big, tough, long-lasting wines. No first growths but a large number of excellent *crus bourgeois*.
Classed growths ★★★ Calon-Ségur, Cos d'Estournel, Montrose.
Bourgeois growths ★★ Beau-Site, Haut-Marbuzet, Pomys.

Moulis and Listrac. Two lesser known communes lying inland from the Gironde, west of Margaux. The wines have a heavier style but can be fruity, firm and attractive. No classified growths.
Bourgeois growths ★★ Chasse-Spleen, Gressier-Grand-Poujeaux, Moulis.
Haut-Médoc. The southernmost part of the Médoc (including the above six communes) and the highest appellation to which wines from other communes are entitled.
Classed growths ★★★ Cantemerle (not to be confused with Château Cantemerle of the Côtes de Bourg), La Lagune.
Bourgeois growths ★★ Bel-Orme-Tronquoy-Lalande, Caronne-Ste-Gemme, Cissac, Citran, Coufran, Lanessan, Liversan, Sénéjac, La Tour du Mirail, Villegeorge.
Bas Médoc. Usually simply called the Médoc and extending north from the Haut-Médoc to the mouth of the Gironde. Wines slightly lighter in style and generally less distinguished. No classed growths.

Graves

A large area stretching south from Bordeaux. Red and white wines from the most ordinary to very fine. Reds are particularly dry with great finesse. Whites vary from the old-fashioned slightly honeyed dry style (e.g. Laville-Haut-Brion) through medium-dry to the sweet wines of the south.
Red wines ★★★★ Haut-Brion; ★★★ Domaine de Chevalier, Haut-Bailly, Larrivet-Haut-Brion, Latour-Haut-Brion, Malartic-Lagravière, La Mission-Haut-Brion ✩✩, Pape-Clément, Smith-Haut-Lafitte; ★★ Bouscaut, La Louvière, La Tour-Martillac, de Portets, La Tour-Bicheau, La Vieille-France.
White wines ★★★★ Haut-Brion; ★★★ Domaine de Chevalier, Laville-Haut-Brion, Olivier, Pape-Clément; ★★ Baret, Bouscaut, Carbonnieux, de Portets.

château bottled. Apart from the château-bottled and monopoly wine, wines bottled in France need be no better than those bottled by a first-class supplier elsewhere, but bottled wines are more expensive because of heavier carriage charges. However, it is only fair to say that wine transported in bulk does not always reach its destination in the best possible condition.

The Médoc

Our tour of the Bordeaux wine country starts with the Médoc, which is itself divided into two districts, Médoc and Haut-Médoc. In the latter, the southern area, are found all the greatest wines, although fine wines are made in the Médoc or northern part. The Médoc must be dealt with in some detail because of its tremendous importance to wine lovers all over the world and its influence on wine making everywhere.

Along the west bank of the Gironde right down to the Bay of Biscay there is a stretch of land some 64 kilometres (40 miles) long. It is not very picturesque, though it rises in parts to low hills, and there are swamps and arid wasteland between the wine-growing areas. Along this strip are grown the grapes that make the finest wine in the world.

The actual vine-bearing strip varies in width from a few hundred yards to a mile or so and it is not continuous. There are pockets of vine-growing land that start as suddenly as they cease and a mere footpath may divide worthless land from land that will grow the grapes capable of making the very finest wine. Within these pockets, too, there are grades of soil. All of it is poor, sandy, gritty, stony and hardly seems capable of growing a single blade of grass. But there are minerals in the soil which, in their turn, feed into the grape that quality which in fermentation develops and flavours the wine. One château is not exactly like another, either physically or in the wine it produces. There are hundreds of châteaux, or estates, in the Médoc and Haut-Médoc all producing good wine.

The 1855 classification of Médoc wines

Bordeaux wine, because of its 2,000 years of recorded history, its English court monopoly in the Middle Ages and its lasting properties giving it export potential, has always made the region prosperous, but never more so than in the first half of the nineteenth century.

It was about 1850 that the Chamber of Commerce in Bordeaux was invited to sanction the Bordeaux brokers' classification of the great wines of Médoc and in 1855 the official classification was made. This was based on the general principle that the best wine gets the best price and by and large this is perfectly true. The pundits therefore classified the leading wines of the Médoc according to the aver-

Above: A quartz-pebbled vineyard, the typical soil composition of the Médoc.

Left: Vines resplendent in autumn colours, overlooked by the eccentric chinoiserie *towers of Château Cos d'Estournel.*

age prices obtained for the wines by the different estates over a period of years. No fewer than sixty estates were divided into five categories. In the first category or class there were but three – Lafite, Latour and Margaux, and then in honesty and decency the Chamber of Commerce had to let in an outsider – Château Haut-Brion from Graves, whose wine was undoubtedly equal to the best of the Médoc, though it has not always remained so. A few years ago, because of the excellence of its wine, the top of the second growths, Château Mouton-Rothschild, was granted first-growth status. There are now five *premiers cru classés*: Lafite, Latour, Margaux, Mouton-Rothschild and (in Graves) Haut-Brion.

Of the fourteen second growths, there are many names which are well known, including the three famous Léoville wines, Léoville-Las-Cases, Léoville-Poyferré and Léoville-Barton; Lascombes makes excellent wine, as do the Pichons – Pichon-Longueville, Baron and Pichon-Longueville, Comtesse de Lalande; Cos d'Estournel of St-Estèphe is a wine that is reputed to be scented with pines (but I must admit that my imagination has never taken me so far); and Montrose is of great and historic interest. There are fourteen third growths, ten fourth growths and eighteen fifth growths, and it is among the fifth growths that one can expect to see some fairly rapid promotion when the long-talked-of reclassification comes into being.

It is now more than one hundred and thirty years since the great classification was made, and there have been many changes. Most of the great estates have remained in good hands, although there have been ups and downs. Haut-Brion had a long period of over twenty years of poor or unhappy management, but it is now back on the right road. Château Margaux had a bad patch from 1929 until 1947, but has recovered. Other châteaux fell out of cultivation altogether, although I think most of them have been brought back now, but when a château goes out of cultivation a good deal of the expertise goes out too: new vines have to be planted, and time is not always on the side of the *vigneron* when he wants to resuscitate a good estate. On the other hand, there are some very notable improvements. I have already mentioned Mouton-Rothschild, but within the fifth growths there are several names like

The beautiful moated Château d'Issan, one of the oldest châteaux of the Médoc, dating back to 1600.

Médoc: 1855 classification

Château	Commune
Premiers crus (1st growths)	
Lafite	Pauillac
Latour	Pauillac
Margaux	Margaux
Mouton-Rothschild	Pauillac
Haut-Brion	Pessac, Graves
Deuxièmes crus (2nd growths)	
Rausan-Ségla	Margaux
Rauzan-Gassies	Margaux
Léoville-Las-Cases	St-Julien
Léoville-Poyferré	St-Julien
Léoville-Barton	St-Julien
Durfort-Vivens	Margaux
Lascombes	Margaux
Gruaud-Larose	St-Julien
Brane-Cantenac	Cantenac
Pichon-Longueville Baron	Pauillac
Pichon-Longueville Lalande	Pauillac
Ducru-Beaucaillou	St-Julien
Cos d'Estournel	St-Estèphe
Montrose	St-Estèphe
Troisièmes crus (3rd growths)	
Kirwan	Cantenac
d'Issan	Cantenac
Lagrange	St-Julien
Langoa-Barton	St-Julien
Giscours	Labarde
Malescot-St-Exupéry	Margaux
Cantenac-Brown	Cantenac
Palmer	Cantenac
La Lagune	Ludon
Desmirail	Margaux
Calon-Ségur	St-Estèphe
Ferrière	Margaux
Marquis d'Alesme-Becker	Margaux
Boyd-Cantenac	Cantenac
Quatrièmes crus (4th growths)	
St-Pierre-Sevaistre	St-Julien
Branaire	St-Julien
Talbot	St-Julien
Duhart-Milon-Rothschild	Pauillac
Pouget	Cantenac
La Tour-Carnet	St-Laurent
Lafon-Rochet	St-Estèphe
Beychevelle	St-Julien
Prieuré-Lichine	Cantenac
Marquis-de-Terme	Margaux
Cinquièmes crus (5th growths)	
Pontet-Canet	Pauillac
Batailley	Pauillac
Haut-Batailley	Pauillac
Grand-Puy-Lascoste	Pauillac
Grand-Puy-Ducasse	Pauillac
Lynch-Bages	Pauillac
Lynch-Moussas	Pauillac
Dauzac	Labarde
Mouton-Baronne Philippe	Pauillac
du Tertre	Arsac
Haut-Bages-Libéral	Pauillac
Pédesclaux	Pauillac
Belgrave	St-Laurent
Camensac, de	St-Laurent
Cos-Labory	St-Estèphe
Clerc-Milon	Pauillac
Croizet-Bages	Pauillac
Cantemerle	Macau

Opposite: The famous tower of Latour, originally intended as part of a line of defence against ocean-going pirates. Roses are also a traditional feature of the Médoc vineyards.

Graves: 1959 classification

Château	Commune
Red wines	
Haut-Brion	Pessac
Bouscaut	Cadaujac
Carbonnieux	Léognan
Domaine de Chevalier	Léognan
de Fieuzal	Léognan
Haut-Bailly	Léognan
La Mission-Haut-Brion	Pessac
La Tour-Haut-Brion	Talence
La Tour-Martillac	Martillac
Malartic-Lagravière	Léognan
Olivier	Léognan
Pape-Clément	Pessac
Smith-Haut-Lafitte	Martillac
White wines	
Bouscaut	Cadaujac
Carbonnieux	Léognan
Domaine de Chevalier	Léognan
Couhins	Villenave d'Ornon
La Tour-Martillac	Martillac
Laville-Haut-Brion	Talence
Malartic-Lagravière	Léognan
Olivier	Léognan
Haut-Brion	Pessac
(added to the list in 1960)	

Sauternes: 1855 classification

Château	Commune
Premier grand cru	
d'Yquem	Sauternes
Premiers crus (1st growths)	
Guiraud	Sauternes
La Tour-Blanche	Bommes
Lafaurie-Peyraguey	Bommes
de Rayne-Vigneau	Bommes
Sigalas-Rabaud	Bommes
Rabaud-Promis	Bommes
Clos Haut-Peyraguey	Bommes
Coutet	Barsac
Climens	Barsac
Suduiraut	Preignac
Rieussec	Fargues
Deuxièmes crus (2nd growths)	
d'Arche	Sauternes
Filhot	Sauternes
Lamothe	Sauternes
Myrat	Barsac
Doisy-Védrines	Barsac
Doisy-Daëne	Barsac
Suau	Barsac
Broustet	Barsac
Caillou	Barsac
Nairac	Barsac
de Malle	Preignac
Romer	Fargues

Cantemerle, Pontet-Canet (which, incidentally, is only across the path from Mouton-Rothschild) and Lynch-Bages. These wines will almost certainly be up-graded, perhaps even to second-growth status.

Other Médoc wines

So much for the classified wines, but what of the *crus bourgeois* and the *petits châteaux*? The latter are the wines that you will be drinking when you buy a simple bottle of Médoc, St-Julien, St-Estèphe and

so on. They are all good wines if bought from a reputable wine supplier. They are clean, rich in colour and with all the character of a Bordeaux. They cost more, by and large, than other French beverage wines, but they are worth it. Nowadays, they are increasingly marketed under their own names. The *crus bourgeois* are the less well known châteaux, which rank below the *crus classés* (they were first classified in 1932), and account for some of the best value wine in Bordeaux today.

Just to give one last statistic, sixty great châteaux of the *grand cru* class only produce one-sixth of the total wine in the Médoc. Médoc is in demand wherever good wine is drunk and there is never enough of it. You must expect to pay well for this wine, especially if it is château bottled.

Graves

The district of Graves stretches from Langon in the south 20 kilometres (12½ miles) along the west bank of the Garonne through Bordeaux itself, until it reaches the Blanquefort stream, where starts the Médoc. It is even more stony and gravelly (hence its name) than the Médoc and its production is much smaller. It produces some of the finest red wine in France, and some excellent, sometimes great, white wine, too. *Vin de Graves* is synonymous with white wine, yet most people would be surprised to read that Graves produces as much red wine of excellent quality as white wine of good and moderate quality. Take, for instance, the great first-growth Château Haut-Brion just outside Bordeaux, in the *commune*, or parish, of Pessac. Its wines have

Below: Brand new oak barriques *arriving at Château Mouton-Rothschild in preparation for the vintage.*

Evocative and mouth-watering names on the tourist circuit of the Graves.

been famous for hundreds of years and it is mentioned in Pepys's Diary as Ho Bryen. Until the château fell upon evil days (which in wine making means that the owner thought he knew better than the experts) thirty or forty years ago, it always made a fine wine of superb quality. A change of ownership put the matter right but, alas, a generation or more was lost.

The principal characteristic of red Graves, and it is about red Graves that I sing, is what is called in wine jargon *finesse*. It is an extremely well-bred wine, slightly thin by comparison with the more full-blooded, dignified Médocs, but bright in colour, good to the palate, and with tremendous lasting properties.

I know something about Graves and its red wines because a few years back I took one of the more famous of the red wine châteaux, Château Smith-Haut-Lafitte in Martillac, for a month and lived there with my family, when I saw a good deal of the country. Graves is just a little too arid and Château Smith-Haut-Lafitte is like many others. The prosperous châteaux are those being worked by proprietors who live on the premises, and who, in many cases, work themselves. In nearby Château Bouscaut, where wines both red and white of the very first quality are made, the proprietor could be seen on his tractor, cultivating his vines, bare to the waist in the burning sun, while his family enjoyed themselves at the seaside. I talked to him a good deal during my sojourn at Château Smith-Haut-Lafitte, and I got to know and like his wine, most of which goes to Belgium and Holland. His wine is a classified growth and indeed it deserves to be, but as he says: 'One cannot let up in Graves; the production is too small and a bad year may spell

near ruin. Nevertheless, the prices of wine have risen, and a living is made.'

Among the great red wines of Graves, we have the Haut-Brion itself at Pessac, and, literally across the road, La Mission-Haut-Brion, making a wine hardly less good. The Domaine de Chevalier, Châteaux Pape-Clément, La Tour-Martillac (its 1955 is fragrantly superb), Haut-Bailly, and many other famous châteaux all produce very worthy wines.

I find it much harder to write about the white wines of Graves than the red. Although there are some very good ones, I have never tasted a great one. Apart from the few château-bottled white wines, it should be noted that white Graves should never be highly priced, because the wine just is not worth it. This is the root of the whole problem in Graves: the production is too small and the price is not enough. One might well ask why the *vignerons* do not grub up their white grape vines and plant red and indeed some have, but the problem lies in the fact that Graves is traditionally noted for its white wines and therefore cannot give them up easily.

Of the principal white wine châteaux, apart from Bouscaut which I have just mentioned, Château Baret makes an excellent wine, Château Carbonnieux an extremely good one, as does the Domaine de Chevalier. Château Olivier also has a well-deserved reputation. Château La Tour-Martillac makes excellent wines, both red and white, and a little wine is also made at the very lovely Château de La Brède at La Brède, which is a perfect example of a small medieval castle. It is still preserved as it was when the residence of Montesquieu, the philosopher. Graves in itself is not particularly beautiful, but La Brède is an exception and well worth a visit. According to André Simon, the optimum output of La Brède used to be something like 15,275 litres (3,360 gallons), but I have never seen it on the market, still less tasted any, outside of France.

St-Emilion and Pomerol

A few miles above Bordeaux and just past the Blanquefort stream, which marks one boundary of the Médoc, the Dordogne and Garonne rivers join, and from thence to the Bay of Biscay become the River Gironde. If we follow the Dordogne from its confluence with the Garonne back towards its source, about 32 kilometres (20 miles) from Bordeaux almost due north, we go through the prosperous town of Libourne, which is the commercial centre for St-Emilion, Pomerol, Lalande-de-Pomerol and Fronsac. The St-Emilion district lies in the hills above Libourne and the Dordogne in broken, rolling countryside, with vine-clad hills spreading here and there. The heart of the district is the ancient town of St-Emilion itself with streets winding uphill and downhill. It has a monolithic

Above: Vendangeur stopping for a break in the vineyards of Château Carbonnieux in the Graves.

Left: Château Bouscaut in the Graves, in autumnal mists. It makes mainly red and some white wine.

The hilltop town of St-Emilion, with its fine church and ruined castle, seen from vineyards across the valley.

Red Bordeaux vintages

1961 Arguably the best wines of the century so far. A small crop of exceptionally high quality wines, concentrated in colour and flavour. The better wines will last another ten years.

1962 A good vintage of attractive wines but overshadowed by 1961. Drink up.

1963 Poor. Should have been consumed years ago.

1964 Basically a good vintage, but inconsistent.

1965 A bad year because of the weather.

1966 An excellent vintage of delicious wines. Most wines lovely now but some will last another ten years.

1967 A large but patchy vintage. Drink up.

1968 Another bad year with the worst weather in August for twenty years. Better weather later but no really good wines.

1969 Moderate. Most wines should have been drunk.

1970 An excellent vintage with both quality and quantity. Lovely wines, deep in colour and packed with fruit.

1971 A good to very good vintage. A fairly small crop but some very good wines, particularly from St-Emilion and Pomerol. Drink soon.

1972 Poor. Miserable weather and a very late harvest.

1973 A moderately good vintage with light, pleasant, easy-to-drink wines. Most wines need drinking.

1974 Another moderate and uneven vintage spoilt by heavy rain in September. Hard, ungracious wines unlikely to improve much. Most should be drunk now.

1975 An excellent vintage that has repaid keeping. A small, fine quality crop, vintaged early. The best wines have further to go yet.

1976 Another good vintage, but variable. Attractive fruity wines. Drink before the 1975s.

1977 A very moderate year of dull wines, unlikely to improve.

1978 A very good vintage. Attractive and interesting wines turning out well. Ready to drink now, and the best will last about fifteen years.

1979 A good vintage. An abundant crop of sound wines, generally to be drunk before the 1978s.

1980 A very moderate vintage, the result of a miserable summer.

1981 A good vintage, but variable. Time will tell.

1982 An excellent vintage. Wines with magnificent colour and heaps of fruit, a vintage to lay down for the years to come.

1983 A very good, well-balanced vintage with attractive wines in all ranges.

1984 A problem year, wines overpriced.

1985 An abundant harvest promises to produce some classic wines. Some wines lack concentration.

1986 Another large harvest of high-quality grapes. Promises well: good petit châteaux for early drinking, and top wines will last.

1987 Patchy, not as good as 1985 or 1986. Careful selection needed.

cathedral and spire, a château and a monastery and, above all, vines. Here on this plateau is to be found a similar soil, although not quite so bleak, to that in Graves and the Médoc, and some of the greatest wines are made from grapes grown on the so-called *Graves de St-Emilion*. Here again there is that fascinating difference from one vineyard to another which we have already seen in the Médoc.

St-Emilion

Wines have been made in St-Emilion for the last 2,000 years. The records are exact, for the Roman poet Ausonius in the fourth century AD lived at his villa on the hills overlooking the Dordogne. There he grew his vines and made wine and sang their praises. Near the site of his ancient villa stands the present Château Ausone. The fact that the vineyards round St-Emilion and especially those of the Château Ausone have been cultivated for 2,000 years means that the sum of knowledge of viticulture to be found in the people who now own the vineyards, cultivate the vines and make the wines is very great indeed. At Château Ausone, for instance, the *maître de chai*, or wine maker, who retired some years ago was in direct succession from the eighteenth century – that is to say, father and son had been *maître de chai* for over two hundred years. This, in the cultivation of vines and the making of wines, means quite a lot.

The wines themselves have most of the virtues of Médoc and red Graves, but they are slightly more fruity; their colour is deeper, more purple; they are big, good, hearty wines, and if they lack what we might call breeding, they certainly make up for it in other directions. They have a kind of honest voluptuous beauty which mightily appeals to me. Taken collectively – that is to say, St-Emilion and Pomerol – they are the nearest Bordeaux will ever get to Burgundy, and I suppose that is as far as one ever wants to go.

The classification of St-Emilion, which was last reviewed in 1985, is comparatively simple. There are two first great growths in a category of their own: the historic Château Ausone and Château Cheval Blanc; the first from the vineyards on the slopes known as the *Côtes* and the second from the more gravelly vineyards on the plateau or *Graves* district. There are nine other first great growths: Châteaux Beauséjour (proprietor Duffau), Belair, Figeac, La Gaffelière, Magdelaine, Canon, Trottevieille, Pavie and Clos Fourtet. Below the *premiers crus classés* come the *crus classés*, or great growths, a long list of lesser known wines, such as Châteaux L'Angélus, Fonroque and Clos St-Martin. All of these wines are uniformly excellent and if the prices are not as high as their opposite numbers in Médoc, this ought not to be counted against them, rather to the contrary.

Châteaux Ausone and Cheval Blanc cost nearly as much as first-growth Médoc or Graves and quite rightly so.

Like some of the other châteaux, the cellars of Château Ausone and Clos Fourtet are cut into the living rock and it is an experience to be much recommended to travellers, who can arrange an introduction through their wine supplier, to visit either or both of these cellars and there taste the wines of the two or three vintages preceding their visit. There are many other well-known châteaux in St-Emilion and the *mis en bouteilles au château*, the certificate of château bottling, will prove a good reference for the wine inside the bottle.

Below: Château Cheval Blanc, the property that produces the finest of all St-Emilion.

Bottom: The vineyards of Château Trottevieille, a small but highly reputed property.

The wines of St-Emilion, Pomerol, Sauternes and the minor red and white wines of Bordeaux are briefly described below, followed by a selection of recommended wines. The first growths (★★★★) are very expensive; other classified growths (★★★) are moderately expensive; the petits châteaux (★★) are reasonably priced and minor wines (★) are inexpensive. The symbol ☆ indicates a wine expensive in its class; ☆☆ indicates a wine very expensive in its class.

St-Emilion

Rich, supple red wines, slightly higher in alcohol than the Médocs. *Classed growths* ★★★★ Ausone, Cheval Blanc; ★★★ Angélus, Bel-Air, Canon, Figeac, Clos Fourtet, La Gaffelière, Magdelaine, Trottevieille; ★★ Clos St-Martin, Grand-Barrail-Lamarzelle-Figeac.
Wines from the St-Emilion satellites. The surrounding villages entitled to tack the name St-Emilion on to their own, such as Lussac- and Puisseguin-St-Emilion. Château Lyonnat is good.

Pomerol

Closer in style to St-Emilion than the Médoc. Wines tend to develop earlier than Médocs. No classification.
★★★★ Pétrus ☆☆; ★★★ La Conseillante, La Fleur-Pétrus, Gazin, Nenin, de Sales, Trotanoy ☆, Vieux Château Certan; ★★ Le Gay, Taillefer.
The wines of Lalande-de-Pomerol (which appellation includes the wines of Néac). Similar in style to Pomerol but less well known. ★★★ Châteaux Bel-Air and ★★ Siaurac among the best.

Minor red wines ★–★★

Fronsac, Côtes de Canon-Fronsac. Honest and straightforward clarets, e.g. Châteaux Canon-de-Brem, Haut-Mazeris, Bourdieu-La-Valade, La Dauphine, Rouet, Tasta.
Bourg and Blaye. Good ordinary claret.
Bourg: Châteaux de Barbe, du Bousquet, Guionne, Plaisance, La Croix de Milorit; *Blaye:* Châteaux Bordieu, Le Menaudat and Videau.
Premières Côtes de Bordeaux. Very light early-drinking wines, e.g. Château Nenine.
Côtes de Castillon. Mostly sold as Bordeaux Supérieur. More akin to St-Emilion than to Médoc. Good wines.
Entre-deux-Mers. Ordinary wines generally sold as Bordeaux Supérieur.
Cubzaguais. Two large estates: Châteaux Timberlay and Terrefort-Quancard.
Bordeaux Rouge, Bordeaux Supérieur, etc. Basic appellations, mostly used for minor châteaux or merchants' brands and blends. Look for one of the more important shippers' labels, e.g. Schröder & Schÿler, Sichel, Calvet, Nat. Johnson, etc.

Sauternes

A small area within the southern part of Graves. Wines should have a honeyed bouquet of ripe fruit; a deliciously sweet taste in the mouth. Styles vary from Château d'Yquem, the heaviest, to the lighter more delicate wines. The classification covers the villages of Sauternes itself, Barsac, Bommes, Fargues and Preignac. Barsac wines may also call themselves AC Barsac.
Classed growths ★★★★ d'Yquem ☆; ★★★ Coutet, Climens; ★★ Doisy-Daëne, Filhot, Sigalas-Rabaud.

Minor white wines ★–★★

Ste-Croix-du-Mont and Loupiac. More minor areas around Sauternes, producing attractive, light sweet white wines, e.g. Clos du Pavillon, Château de Tastes.
Cérons, Illats and Potensac. Agreeable sweet white wines under the Cérons appellation and dry white wines under Graves. More often sold as generics than with château labels.
Entre-deux-Mers. A large quantity of minor whites, slightly sweet or dry.
Premières Côtes de Bordeaux. Some good medium-dry whites.
Bordeaux. The basic appellation for white wine. Sometimes very good, e.g. Château Reynon, and mostly from the Entre-deux-Mers.

Pomerol

Pomerol adjoins St-Emilion to the north and runs down to the town of Libourne on the Dordogne. If one had to make a distinction between the wines of the two districts, one would say that those of Pomerol are, if anything, more generous than those from St-Emilion. But again there is the splendid ruby colour and again the charming bouquet. The vineyards are contiguous to those of St-Emilion and any difference between the wines is slight.

The Pomerol châteaux were near enough to share, with a few others on the other side of the St-Emilion border, the devastation caused by the great frost of 1956. This catastrophe occurred after a warm February when the sap had started to rise in the vines. Then came a cold snap of unprecedented hardness combined with snow, lasting for some weeks, which froze the rising sap in the vines and killed everything above the graft. I well remember visiting vineyards later in that year when I was living at Château Smith-Haut-Lafitte in Graves and being shown by the late Madame Loubat, then in her eighty-fifth year, for sixty years proprietress of Château Pétrus, the tragedy of the vines shooting from below the graft – that is to say, on the American stocks so that the fruit which came from them eventually was the American vine and not the traditional French, and useless for making the fine wine of Pomerol. Up to that year, Château Pétrus had retained a corner of the vineyard planted with pre-phylloxera vines which, for some reason or other, had not been wiped out during the infestation. These have now gone, the last of the very, very few.

Madame Loubat was not to be depressed by this. 'Well,' she said, 'in my long life I have seen a few devastations and troubles: I saw oidium, mildew and phylloxera. We have come through them all. I don't doubt we shall come through this, but I doubt if I shall see it.' She was, of course, quite right in both respects, for the vineyards have been replanted and she, alas, is gone. But never let it be doubted that Château Pétrus has retained its traditional title of first great growth of Pomerol. Madame Loubat was an indomitable character and because her vineyard was small and the quality consistently superb, she would never sell her wine at any lower price than that of Mouton-Rothschild, which is among the highest priced of the Médoc wines. Her view was that her wine was as good and the price should be the same, and while there may be two opinions about this, certainly it was good enough for the shippers and merchants of Bordeaux to pay up and look big.

The tragedy of the great frost of 1956 was that it wiped out most of the oldest vines and the making of fine or great wines depends to some extent on the use of grapes from old vines. Generally speaking,

a vine takes five years to come into fruit; from the fifth to the tenth year it yields well, and from the tenth year onwards yields well and produces the best fruit. Probably the best of all grapes are produced on vines fifteen to twenty-five years old, and, in the making of fine wine, a proportion of grapes from the old vines is not only desirable but necessary. The damage of the great frost has been made good and the young vines have come into full fruit. The wine is as good as ever except, of course, for that which was made from the pre-phylloxera vines at Pétrus.

After Château Pétrus, indisputably the leaders are other important châteaux like Vieux-Château-Certan, Château La Conseillante, Château Certan, Château Petit-Village, Château L'Evangile, Château Trotanoy, Château Plince, Château La Fleur-Pétrus, Château Beauregard, Clos L'Eglise, Château de Sales, Château de Bourgneuf, Château Gazin and many others. The neighbouring areas, Néac and Lalande-de-Pomerol, make excellent wine of similar character, from vines grown in a clayish soil, producing soft, fruity wine with an agreeable bouquet. Lalande-de-Pomerol, which is rather larger than Néac, produces a wine that may be compared with the leading growths of Pomerol. One of the best of the Lalande-de-Pomerol wines is certainly Château de Bel-Air, a lasting wine. Château La Commanderie, Château de Loge Couzelles, Château de Musset and the Clos des Nouaves all produce good wines and should be mentioned.

Vintage years of St-Emilion and Pomerol

The good vintage years are much the same as for Médoc (see Bordeaux vintages on page 64). Generally, it can be said that St-Emilion produces very evenly with the Médoc, for the sunshine is much the same everywhere in the Bordeaux area. Great

Top: Red hydraulic presses at Château d'Yquem. The plates come down very slowly and gently on the grapes.

Above: An old wine press in the wine museum at St-Emilion.

Above left: Oak fermentation vats at Château Léoville-Barton. This fine château maintains traditional methods.

Gnarled old vine in the vineyards of Château de Sales in Pomerol.

years are uniformly great and bad years uniformly bad. I must refer, however, to the excellent wine produced in the great St-Emilion and Pomerol character in 1947 and 1971. This is some of the best claret ever made, while many of the Médocs of those years, including some of the first growths, were of good but not extraordinary quality.

The little red wines of Bordeaux

After leaving Lalande-de-Pomerol and descending to Libourne, face north from the eastern or right bank of the Dordogne and you will be looking at the vineyards of Fronsac, and beyond them, through Bourg, where the Garonne joins the Dordogne to form the Gironde, and so north through Blaye. The countryside is beautiful with its rolling hills, and here are made most of the little red wines which you will buy from your supplier as AC Bordeaux Rouge or Bordeaux Supérieur if not under the legitimate *appellation* of Fronsac, Bourgeais or Blayais, as the case may be. These are all good sound wines and there are many prosperous châteaux producing wines under their own labels, and sometimes château-bottled wines. You and I will do very well to buy these for our ordinary consumption. They cost very little compared to the giants of the Médoc and they have the character of a good Bordeaux: rich colour with that infinitesimal touch of sharpness to the palate which gives a 'kiss' to a claret.

There are no good or bad years for these wines as such, because blending is carried on to a considerable degree – that is to say, the wines of different years are mixed in order to produce a first-class average bottle of non-vintage claret.

The fine white wines of Bordeaux

Graves may be said to produce the driest white wine of Bordeaux. The sweet wines, ranging from what we should call the medium up to the luscious sweetness of Château d'Yquem, are produced on both banks of the Garonne, starting with Cérons in the north, passing through Barsac, through Sauternes with its four *communes* of Preignac, Bommes, Sauternes and Fargues, crossing the river above Langon to Sainte-Croix-du-Mont and turning through Loupiac. All the vineyards in these districts, which are extensive, make good sweet wines of considerable reputation. Sauternes was the only white wine district to be classified in 1855 (see list on page 61).

The principle of making sweet wine is first to use the right kind of grape and these are almost exclusively the Sémillon or Sauvignon. The grapes are left on the vines until much later than in other districts. Under the action of the sun they become wrinkled, even, to outward appearance, rotten. The grapes are not picked until the last possible moment, and when they are brown they are

Above: A bunch of Semillon grapes affected by noble rot; shrivelled and raisin-like they will produce the world's finest sweet wine.

Left: Château d'Yquem – the building dates back to the twelfth century and the Renaissance. The grapes are left to attain the perfect degree of noble rot before picking.

attacked by a kind of mildew, *la pourriture noble*, or the noble rot. This is, in fact, a peculiar mould called *Botrytis cinerea*, a fungus which pierces the skin of the ripe grapes, takes off some of the water in the grape, but leaves the sugar. The sugar, in turn, is converted to alcohol during fermentation and, because it is in a greater concentration, the wines are extremely good and sweet.

Throughout the châteaux of Sauternes this principle is developed in the viniculture. The grapes are processed according to the château and the price received for the wine. For instance, during the vintage at the world-famous Château d'Yquem, which is the first great growth of Sauternes and the sweet wines throughout France, the pickers are sent through the vineyard daily with sharp scissors, snipping out only the grapes which have become wrinkled and overripe since the previous picking. These individual grapes are then gathered and pressed. The pickings occur up to nine or ten times in some years, until nothing remains on the bunch. The wine is of great character, tremendous and unique sweetness, and with very high alcoholic content, sometimes rising to 15°. It is necessarily expensive and only Yquem can afford to make the wines exactly in this fashion. Notwithstanding, there are many fine châteaux in these districts making splendid wine at a lower cost by harvesting the grapes in bunches when they are overripe. Among the fine wines in the *commune* of Sauternes are Château Guiraud, Château d'Arche-Lafaurie, Château Filhot (a daughter château to Yquem), and in nearby Bommes are Château La Tour-Blanche, Clos Haut-Peyraguey, Château Rabaud-Promis; and in Barsac, the famous Châteaux Coutet, Climens, Doisy-Daëne and Caillou, besides many others. In Preignac there is the Château de Suduiraut and in Fargues, Château Rieussec, both making good wines.

The fashion, however, is tending away from the older sweetness and it is interesting to see in the last two years that the great Château d'Yquem has found it necessary to make and bottle dry 'Sauternes'. Well, it isn't all that dry and its AC is Bordeaux Supérieur rather than Sauternes, but it is certainly a fine wine. There is one thing to emphasise with these luscious sweet wines of Bordeaux: the best of them cannot be drunk with anything other than dessert, that is, not with any pleasure. Some drink it with *foie gras*, but not myself. Some of the Barsacs, I suppose, can be served with fish, but by and large these are certainly dessert wines and should be kept as such. I remember being given in New York a rather special meal by a kind host who wished to give me the best of everything, and he served Château d'Yquem right through the meal from the melon, through the fish, through the roast and the sweet. It was not a pleasant experience.

The vintage at Château d'Yquem. The nobly rotten grapes are carefully selected in the vineyard; they arrive at the chais *in small tubs; the stalks are removed and the grapes pressed. Right: Monsieur Guy Latrille employs the old-fashioned method of treading the grapes before they are mechanically pressed. In good years the grapes are so shrivelled that it takes one vine to produce a glass of Yquem.*

The *commune* of Sainte-Croix-du-Mont is chiefly notable for the luscious white wines not unlike those of Barsac and Cérons, and is reasonably proud of its produce. The district is *appellation contrôlée*, but the wine is not imported into England to any great extent, except under a general *appellation*. There are a few very good châteaux, such as Loubens, Lamarque, Laurette, Grand-Peyrot and the Domaine de Morange. They all produce fat, luscious wines and the local wine control stipulates a minimum 13° of alcohol, although this is often exceeded in a good year.

The next district downstream is Loupiac, on the right bank of the Garonne opposite Barsac. Again the wine is all fruity and luscious, that is, about the same as Sainte-Croix-du-Mont, and the principal vineyards are Château de Ricaud, Château du Cros and Château Pontac.

Far right: The final picking at Château d'Yquem. Only local people are employed as vendangeurs as it needs an experienced eye to know when the grapes are ready.

Sauternes vintages

1961 Good, but much less good than for claret. A small crop of elegant wines, but lacking the quality of a great vintage.

1962 An excellent vintage for Sauternes. Long-lasting fine wines, some of which will still be good in five years.

1963 As for reds, a disaster for Sauternes. Very little made.

1964 A very moderate year.

1965 Another disastrous year. Dreadful weather and rot.

1966 A good year, but wines rather variable and lacking in fatness.

1967 An excellent vintage for Sauternes. An even better year than 1962, producing firm, ripe, rich wines. Some will last another five years.

1968 A disastrous year; virtually no Sauternes.

1969 A moderately good year, but wines variable. A good sunny October for the vintage.

1970 A good year for Sauternes. Glorious, long sunny autumn, but a bit dry for noble rot! Wines rather light weight. Drink up.

1971 Another good year with a fine autumn. Some attractive wines, longer-lasting than the 1970s.

1972 A poor vintage. Very little Sauternes made. No Yquem.

1973 A moderate light vintage. Drink now.

1974 Even worse for Sauternes than for reds. Cold and wet.

1975 A moderate to good vintage, not as good as for reds.

1976 A potentially great vintage with some excellent classic Sauternes. Rich, concentrated, luscious wines.

1977 A very poor vintage and very little Sauternes.

1978 A moderate to good vintage. Insufficiently humid autumn for much noble rot. Honeyed, fruity wines but not luscious. A year for early drinking.

1979 A good vintage. Abundant crop and good humid conditions for noble rot. Lightish wines for early drinking.

1980 A good to very good vintage, much better than for reds. A small crop of stylish wines from fully ripe fruit with good noble rot. Worth keeping.

1981 A good but variable vintage. A very small crop, not enough noble rot, but some elegant wines.

1982 A disastrous year for Sauternes because of the continual rain in October. Crop ruined.

1983 An excellent vintage. Plenty of good wines.

1984 A moderate vintage, some good light wines.

1985 A very good vintage after autumn heatwave.

1986 Good quality wines: may be better than '85.

La Mission Haut-Brion produces some the finest red wines of the Graves.

Right: Semillon grapes in a Barsac vineyard. It is the main variety for Sauternes and Barsac as it is particularly susceptible to noble rot (see page 69).

The good years

Good years for sweet white wines are not quite the same as for red wines. The harvest takes place later and different weather conditions are required for a successful vintage. To make really good sweet white wines, it is necessary to have a long warm autumn, but with just enough gentle rain to provide the humidity required for the growth of noble rot. In the case of these rich Sauternes and sweet wines it is true to say that they do not last nearly so long. On one occasion I drank Château d'Yquem as old as 1869, but it was no great experience and an 1898 was a definite loss. On the other hand, 1921, which was an exceptionally good year for white wines throughout France and Germany, is still good, although it is well past its peak. The 1923 wines were very good, and 1924 and 1929 coincided with the clarets in that they were really good years, although not as good as 1921. Other good years were 1934 and 1945, and of course 1949 was an excellent year, but I doubt its availability today, except through Christie's or Sotheby's auction rooms. Then nothing noteworthy occurred until 1961, which was not quite up to the standard of the reds, and 1962 was better. Although a moderate year in Bordeaux, 1967 was a really excellent one for the sweet white wines of Sauternes and Barsac and very good wines were made in 1970 and 1971, too. Both 1975 and 1976 were good years, but nothing much has happened since then. I am advised that 1982 will be a 'wine of the century' year in Bordeaux, but it will not be a great Sauternes year because rain set in before the grapes became over-ripe. I was there, so I know!

The little white wines of Bordeaux

Premières Côtes de Bordeaux, Entre-Deux-Mers, St-Macaire, Ste-Foy Bordeaux and Graves de Vayres are all made in the comparatively rich ground between the Dordogne and the Garonne rivers. The region is the largest of the Bordeaux vineyards and it is probably one of the most picturesque in the Gironde. It is rolling country, furrowed by green valleys and small streams, which flow into the Garonne or Dordogne, and the slopes of the hills as far as the eye can see are covered in well-cultivated vines. Here are grown most of the white and many of the red wines that go to make up the straight, moderately priced Bordeaux.

There are vintage and château-bottled wines in these districts but, in this market, the wine is made and marketed to be sold mainly for what it is and not for what it might have been had it come from a mile or so to the north or south and grown on rather different soil. I strongly recommend these Bordeaux wines and I hope you will ask your wine supplier to sell you a bottle or two to try. They will not cost much.

Burgundy

Right: The undulating vineyards and village of Moulin-à-Vent in the Beaujolais.

The greatest wines of Burgundy come from the vineyards of the *département* of the Côte d'Or, which lie terraced along hills to the west of the road from Chagny in the south, north through Beaune and Nuits-St-Georges up to Dijon. Below Chagny and west of Chalon-sur-Saône are the less important wines of the Côte Chalonnaise, and lower still are the much larger wine-growing areas of the Mâconnais and the world-famous and sometimes notorious Beaujolais. To the north-west of Dijon and in a little pocket by itself lies Chablis, where is

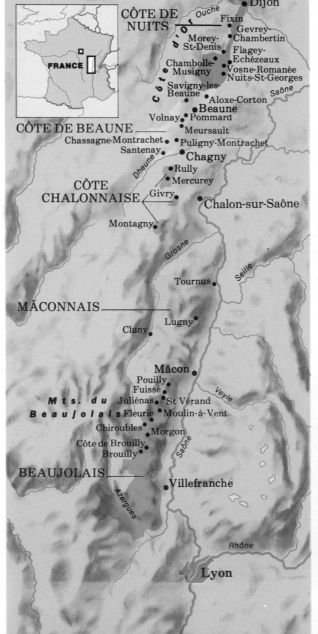

Above: Vintage time; the harvesters with the traditional baskets for carrying the grapes at Louis Latour's cellars in Beaune.

Right: Picking the Pinot Noir grapes in Louis Latour's vineyards on the Côte de Beaune.

instead of white wine. Whether or not the red wine will ever make a particularly good sparkling wine is, of course, another matter.

So let us start our tour of the Burgundian vineyards at Chagny, travel up to Dijon, then go across to Chablis and down again to Chagny, from whence we can look at the Côte Chalonnaise, the Mâconnais and Beaujolais.

Côte d'Or

Chagny marks the southern end of the Côte d'Or, which gets its name, some say, from the liquid gold derived from its fabulous vineyards which lie on the western slopes on long terraces, or, others say, from the glory of the leaves as they turn gold in the vineyards in the autumn. The Côte is divided into two, the Côte de Beaune in the south and the Côte de Nuits in the north.

Côte de Beaune

The southern vineyards of the Côte de Beaune are a little to the west of Chagny, and Santenay is the first village of any merit. Good red wine is made here and there is one vineyard, Les Gravières, of special note. Otherwise the wines are really first-class Burgundy. North of Santenay are Puligny and Chassagne, which include probably the greatest of all French white wines, the *grand cru* of Montrachet. As in the case of Clos de Vougeot, the Montrachet vineyards are very small (the famous Le Montrachet, although only 7.5 hectares/18 acres, is split between eleven *vignerons* according to André Simon). The whole vineyard cannot produce more than 2,500 cases a year, and so it is indeed a very rare, much sought-after wine. There is a vineyard with the gallant name of Le Chevalier-Montrachet and lower on the slopes of the hill La Demoiselle Montrachet (now known as Cailleret), and perhaps it is not surprising that what I think is the best wine of Montrachet, the Bâtard, comes in between the two. Among the *premiers crus* in this district is Les Pucelles, which is in itself a wine of tremendous character. But, undoubtedly, the Montrachets rank with the greatest white wines in the world and in saying this I mean no disrespect to the next *commune,* Meursault. This little town is known for its many excellent whites of *premier cru* status and has a pleasant small hotel. It is surrounded by vineyards in which about twice as much white wine as red is produced, and the red is generally marketed under the label of neighbouring Volnay. Again the vineyards are chopped up and it is difficult to find any particular one of them to recommend (there are no *grands crus*) but, since all are of the best, we are faced with no difficult problem. Personally, I am very fond of Les Genevrières, but this too is split up among a few *vignerons.* Another well-known vineyard is the Goutte d'Or.

White Burgundy vintages

1962 An excellent vintage. A small crop of classic wines, mostly at their peak around 1970.
1963 A moderate to poor vintage, but better than for reds.
1964 A good to very good vintage. Ripe rich wines, heavy in style. Basically without long-lasting qualities.
1965 A disastrous vintage. No good wines.
1966 A very good vintage. Fine, well-structured wines of great elegance. Longer-lasting than the 1964s.
1967 Another very good vintage, somewhat overlooked.
1968 A very poor vintage. Few drinkable wines.
1969 A very good vintage. Reliable, well-constructed and long-lasting wines.
1970 A good vintage but variable. Some quite rich wines but they tended to lack acidity and were for early drinking.
1971 An excellent vintage of classic, long-lasting wines.
1972 A moderate vintage. Wines rather unexciting.
1973 A very good vintage. Lovely delicate wines. Drink up.
1974 A moderate to poor vintage of unattractive thin wines.
1975 A poor vintage. Some good wines, now past their best.
1976 A good vintage. A ripe crop resulted from the excessive heat, with rich fat wines high in alcohol but relatively short-lived.
1977 A poor vintage of miserable wines.
1978 A very good to excellent vintage, particularly for Chablis. Firm, ripe well-balanced wines. Drink now.
1979 Another very good vintage. A large quantity of elegant, fruity wines. Drink now.
1980 A moderate vintage. Drink now.
1981 A good vintage, best in Chablis and the Mâconnais. Wines for early drinking.
1982 A very good vintage, particularly in Chablis. A large crop of rich, fat wines.
1983 A variable vintage, so choose with care.
1984 A moderate vintage, should be drunk young.
1985 A good vintage of soft wines good to drink now.
1986 Attractive but low in acidity: drink soon.
1987 Patchy, select carefully. Some good wines.

Monthélie, to the north, is a small village entirely given up to vine growing, making a small number of red wines, none outstanding but all good. Yet nearer to Beaune are Volnay and Pommard, both names to conjure with among Burgundies. They are fine wines and mostly red. Les Epenots and Rugiens are the best known of the Pommards, and Les Caillerets, Les Champans and Les Angles are the best known of the Volnays. The Santenots vineyards are partly in Volnay and partly in Meursault, but are generally associated with the former. Also sought after is the wine of the small vineyard Clos de Ducs made by the proprietor the Marquis d'Angerville, but it is hard to find.

Beaune

Beaune, the lovely walled city which is the commercial centre of the Côte de Beaune vineyards, deserves a chapter to itself. It is a place of great historic and considerable architectural interest and obviously not without a deal of gastronomic interest, too. Many wines are made in the immediate vicinity of the town. The vineyard of Grèves has a particular corner named La Vigne de L'Enfant Jésus (Bouchard Père et Fils) and the very good wines produced here have been sold under that name for

A selection of recommended Burgundy wines is listed below. The price of Burgundy depends partly on the appellation of the wine and partly on the domaine/grower or négociant but tend to be high and rising. Most grands crus (in italics) are very expensive, premiers crus are moderately expensive. The symbol ☆☆ indicates a wine very expensive in its class.

Côte de Nuits

The northern part of the Côte d'Or. Red wines of greatly varying style. Look for a good vintage and a good grower.
IMPORTANT GROWERS AND NEGOCIANTS: Ets Bertagna, Clair-Daü, Drouhin-Laroze, Domaine Dujac, Gérard Elmerich, Louis Gouroux, Domaine Grivelet, Grivot, Louis Latour, Morin, Jacques Prieur, Domaine de la Romanée-Conti, Domaine de Varoilles, Charles Viénot, Louis Jadot, Chanson.

Commune	Vineyards
Fixin	Hervelets, Clos du Chapitre, Clos de la Perrière.
Gevrey-Chambertin	*Chambertin, Chambertin Clos-de-Bèze.* Clos St-Jacques, Cazetiers.
Morey St-Denis	*Bonnes-Mares, Clos St-Denis.*
Chambolle-Musigny	*Musigny,* Charmes, Amoureuses.
Vougeot	*Clos de Vougeot.*
Vosne-Romanée	*Romanée-Conti* ☆☆, *La Tâche* ☆☆, *Richebourg, Romanée St-Vivant, Grands-Echézeaux, Echézeaux.* Les Malconsorts, Beaux Monts, Suchots.
Nuits St-Georges	Murgers, Porrets, Cailles, Les St-Georges, Les Vaucrains.

Côte de Beaune, red

The southern part of the Côte d'Or is centred on Beaune.
IMPORTANT GROWERS: Bonneau du Martray, Bouchard Père et Fils, Joseph Drouhin, Louis Jadot, Jacques Prieur, Charles Viénot, Hospices de Beaune, Chanson.

Commune	Vineyards
Ladoix-Serrigny	
Aloxe-Corton	*Corton, Corton-Bressandes, Corton Clos du Roi, Clos de la Vigne au Saint, Corton-Maréchaudes.*
Pernand-Vergelesses	Ile des Vergelesses.
Savigny-lès-Beaune	Dominode, Marconnets.
Beaune	Vignes-Franches, Marconnets, Bressandes, Fèvres, Grèves, Teurons, Clos des Mouches.
Pommard	Rugiens, Epenots.
Volnay	Caillerets, Champans, Santenots.
Monthélie	
Auxey-Duresses	
Chassagne-Montrachet	Morgeots, Clos St-Jean.
Santenay	Gravières.

Côte de Beaune, white

Includes the famous Montrachet, the most expensive white Burgundy. More colour than Chablis; Chardonnay aroma. In good years, rich and full on the palate with balancing acidity.
IMPORTANT GROWERS: Robert Ampeau, Bonneau du Martray, Bouchard Père et Fils, Delagrange-Bachelet, Joseph Drouhin, Louis Latour, Jacques Prieur, Ramonet-Prudhon, Ropiteau.

Commune	Vineyards
Aloxe-Corton	*Corton-Charlemagne.*
Auxey-Duresses	
Meursault	Caillerets, Perrières, Genevrières, Goutte d'Or.
Puligny-Montrachet	*Montrachet, Chevalier-Montrachet,* Cailleret.
Chassagne-Montrachet	*Montrachet, Bâtard-Montrachet,* Boudriottes. La Maltroie.

Top: Smiling vendangeur *with his baskets of Chardonnay grapes.*

Above: Baskets filled with Pinot Noir grapes, destined to become fine red Burgundy.

Right: The vineyards of Louis Latour in the Côte de Beaune. Their estate totals 46 hectares between Chambertin and Chevalier Montrachet.

the last 200 years. The principal vineyards are Clos de la Mousse, Clos des Mouches, Les Bressandes, Les Champimonts, Les Fèvres, Les Grèves and Les Marconnets – nearly all red wine, although some white is made at Clos des Mouches.

The great interest in Beaune lies in its famous hospital and the wine auction, which takes place on the third Sunday of November each year. The Hospices de Beaune was founded in 1443 by Nicolas Rolin and from time to time in the succeeding centuries grateful patrons and patients have donated or left to the Hospices vineyards all over the Côte de Beaune. These vineyards are assiduously cultivated, and excellent wine is made and sold every year at the auction. The wines, or *cuvées*, are named after their donors: thus from Aloxe-Corton there are *cuvées* named after Charlotte Dumay and Dr Peste; from Beaune itself we have the original benefaction of Nicolas Rolin and Guigone de Salins and many others. Among the white wines, Goureau and Jéhan Humblot come from Meursault, and indeed many of the great wine-growing villages of the Côte de Beaune are represented.

In the Hospices de Beaune the auction takes place by candle – that is to say, the candle is lit and a pin inserted part of the way down through the wick; while the candle is burning the bidding goes on and it is the last bidder before the flame gutters and goes out who obtains the wine. Prices are universally high and it must be difficult in some cases for the wine merchants to get their money back, but they certainly do themselves no harm by selling these excellent Burgundies.

After leaving Beaune, going towards Nuits-St-Georges, we pass through Savigny-lès-Beaune, which contains well-known and excellent vineyards like Les Marconnets, Les Vergelesses and La Dominode. The best wines are grown on the eastern slopes of the hills to the west of the road. After Savigny come the famous *grand cru* vineyards of the hill of Corton in Aloxe-Corton, among which are found some excellent wines, especially from the vineyard of Le Corton itself. I have extremely fond memories of a little bin of Clos de la Vigne au Saint (a vineyard on the hill of Corton owned entirely by Louis Latour) of the remarkable vintage of 1919. The last bottle was drunk a few years ago, and every bottle seemed better than the last. Les Perrières, one of the village wines, is also very good, and the famous *grand cru* Charlemagne vineyard is well known and rather bigger than most. There are red Cortons as well, but the *appellation* of Corton-Charlemagne is restricted to white wines. Château Corton Grancey is one of the best reds.

Côte de Nuits
Nuits-St-Georges, the centre of the Côte de Nuits, is a tiny little town in the middle of the

vineyards and most, if not all, of its occupants depend entirely for their prosperity on the vines. The wines, although there are no *grand cru* vineyards, are almost universally good and if some of them are not as great as the giants of Vosne-Romanée I shall be well content if I never have anything less. Among the Nuits-St-Georges Burgundies I have one or two favourites, including especially Vaucrains, which is nearly as good as the best in Burgundy. It is a wine of great fragrance and it is full without being over-bodied. Murgers is another good vineyard and Porrets another. Probably Les Saint-Georges is the best known and a very good one it is too.

As we have travelled towards Dijon our steps have taken us through the temple of the great wines of Burgundy, and now as we enter Vosne-Romanée we are practically at the high altar. Here are the great and magical names of many *grands crus*;

The magnificent courtyard and colourful roof of the Hospices de Beaune, home of the famous annual wine auction.

Opposite: The village and vineyards of Chambolle Musigny. Its best known wine is Bonnes Mares and it is twinned with Sonoma in California!

including Romanée-Conti, La Romanée, La Tâche and Richebourg, the home of Les Verroilles, which is sold under the name of Richebourg. The whole of these five vineyards makes about seventy-nine casks in an average year and La Romanée only five and a half casks. I suppose the best Burgundy I have ever drunk was a La Tâche, again a tiny vineyard of only a few acres, but it was an odd year: 1933. The most important grower here is the Domaine de la Romanée-Conti, who take great care and get great prices for their marvellous wines. They are sole owners of La Romanée-Conti and La Tâche and part owners of Richebourg, Romanée-St-Vivant, Grands-Echézeaux, Echézeaux and Montrachet.

From Vosne-Romanée we travel to Flagey-Echézeaux, where the vineyards are not quite so famous but make wonderful wine, especially Les Grands-Echézeaux and Les Echézeaux du Dessus. The wines of this village have a right to the *appellation* Vosne-Romanée.

We are about to enter the walls of the Clos de Vougeot itself. This is a famous *grand cru* vineyard of nearly eighty different owners within walls surrounding 50.5 hectares (125 acres). The historic Château of Vougeot dominates the vineyard from the north-western corner and it is all that remains of the Abbey of Vougeot, built in the thirteenth or fourteenth century. Many are the stories that are told about it, and it is extremely interesting and very well worth a visit. It is now the headquarters of the *Chevaliers du Tastevin,* a rather theatrical organisation made up of *vignerons,* shippers and people interested in wine. Since the chief function of the order is the *dégustations* of fine Burgundian wine and food, it certainly does a lot of good, to the

Chevaliers, to its members and to the Château of Vougeot itself. The original, enormous wine presses can still be seen in the courtyard.

In such a large vineyard it is inevitable that the quality of the soil, and therefore the wine, varies. The wine used to be classified in three grades, but it is no longer. It is necessary, therefore, to know something of your shipper and in this you must trust your wine supplier, who will buy from those of the forty-odd proprietors who make the best wine. Drouhin-Laroze, Clair-Daü, Drouhin, Morin and Grivot are names you can trust and there are many others, but with Clos de Vougeot you must be careful. Above all beware the 'stretched', faked wine labelled 'Clos de Vougeot' and sold in dimly lit restaurants: labels can be printed quite cheaply!

The next village is Chambolle-Musigny and here again are some of the great wines with some very charming names. The *grand cru* wines are Le Musigny and, a favourite of mine, Les Bonnes-Mares, which always seems to be perfectly balanced, round and altogether delicious. Among the *premiers crus,* the vineyard with the charming name of Les Amoureuses cannot help but be good and Charmes is in the same class. Part of the Bonnes-Mares is in the next village of Morey-St-Denis, but this part does not make nearly so much wine as that in Chambolle-Musigny. The other *grand cru* wines of Morey-St-Denis are Clos de Tart, owned by Madame Mommessin, who takes great trouble with her wine, Clos de la Roche and Clos St-Denis, most of which are obtainable domaine bottled. There are some nineteen or twenty other vineyards making excellent wine, but not in the same quantity.

Gevrey-Chambertin contains the great vineyard of Chambertin, reputedly Napoleon's favourite wine, although this is by no means proved. By all accounts, Napoleon was not a great gastronome and paid little attention to what he ate and drank, but he certainly demanded the best and I suppose that Chambertin might well come under that heading. There are two vineyards entitled to be called Chambertin: Chambertin itself and Chambertin Clos-de-Bèze, which is a part of it. No others can be called Chambertin legally, but seven further *grands crus* are allowed to use the name as a suffix thus: Chapelle-Chambertin, Charmes-Chambertin, Griotte-Chambertin, Latricières-Chambertin, Mazys-Chambertin, Mazoyères-Chambertin, Ruchottes-Chambertin, all excellent wines. Among the many *premiers crus,* Clos St-Jacques and Cazetiers are to be particularly recommended. It should be remembered that, in spite of the many *appellations,* the quantity of wine made in Chambertin is very small indeed, although not so small as in the Vosne-Romanée vineyards.

Next is the village of Fixin, and the great

Below: Vineyards and château in the village of Gevrey Chambertin. It is the largest village appellation of the Côte de Nuits.

vineyards of the Côte d'Or come to an end there for not many vineyards in Fixin produce wine of superlative quality. Clos de la Perrière is only 5 hectares (12 acres) in extent, but the wine is much better than many of the more notable names in some of the preceding villages. There are two other good *premier cru* vineyards of repute, Clos du Chapitre and Les Hérvelets.

These great Burgundies which I have just described to you are comparable in quality with the great wines of Bordeaux, but greater care must be taken in their selection and purchase. Never was there a greater need for a reputable and inspired wine merchant than with Burgundy and, at the risk of becoming repetitious, I must emphasise this.

Chablis
Chablis comes from a little pocket of vines around the tiny town of Chablis, which lies about 134 kilometres (84 miles) to the north-west of Dijon and gives its name to one of the cleanest, driest and most attractive of the French white wines. If it does not aspire to the fatness and arrogance of the great Montrachets or Meursaults, it is still extremely fine, dry and pleasant to drink. In the higher grades, it has a good deal of character and is in very considerable demand all over the world. The wine is, I suppose, a perfect partner with fish of any kind and I personally sometimes use it as an aperitif.

There are a few vineyards of importance from which wine is sold with the vineyards' labels and these include, among the *grands crus*, Les Clos, Valmur, Grenouilles, Vaudésir, Preuses and, now less familiar than it was, La Moutonne. La Moutonne is within the vineyards of Vaudésir and Les Preuses, which long ago belonged to the monks of Pontigny. For many years it was used as a brand name by the then owners, the Long-Depaquit family, who also owned vines in other vineyards. However, following a *procés* in the French courts, the name of La Moutonne in Chablis may not be used for any other wine except that coming from the Moutonne vineyards. *Premier cru* vineyards include Fourchaume, Monts de Milieu and Montée de Tonnerre. Nearly all Chablis is either bottled at the domaine or in shippers' cellars in Beaune. The co-operative plays an important role and handles about a quarter of the production.

Côte Chalonnaise, Mâconnais and Beaujolais
South from Chagny is the country of the Côte Chalonnaise wines, north-west from Chalon-sur-Saône. These wines are, not unnaturally, rather like the wines from Beaune to the north, but lighter. The wines are made both white and red, and of these the red seems to be rather better, although I remember that years ago I used to buy an excellent white Côte Chalonnaise at quite a moderate price,

Above: The vintage on the undulating slopes of the Chablis vineyards.

Opposite: The village of Pouilly in the Mâconnais, reputed to produce the best white wines of the region, gave its name to Pouilly-Fuissé.

Red Burgundy vintages

1963	A poor vintage with very few good wines. Indifferent weather and a very late harvest.
1964	An excellent vintage; lovely, soft, ripe and rich wines. Drought reduced the size of the crop.
1965	Very poor; worse than 1963. A very wet year with virtually no sun.
1966	A very good year. Firm, stylish wines.
1967	A moderately good vintage, but variable. Lightish wines, most of which should have been drunk.
1968	A poor year. Very thin wines, the result of a very wet July and August.
1969	An excellent vintage with lovely rich, classic wines. Most wines best drunk now.
1970	A good vintage. Variable weather but plenty of sun resulting in a large crop of rich, fine wines.
1971	An outstanding vintage of long-lasting big fruity wines. The best wines will keep another ten years.
1972	A good vintage generally underrated. Well-structured, firm, but rather lean wines. Drink within five years.
1973	A rather moderate vintage. A large crop of light wines. Most now past their best.
1974	A very moderate vintage of dull wines. Drink up.
1975	A poor vintage. Few good wines. Drink now.
1976	A very good vintage with classic deep rich wines. Longer-lasting wines, the best of which will still be good in five years.
1977	A poor vintage. Too much rain swelled the crop. Few good wines, but most unlikely to improve. Drink now.
1978	An excellent vintage. Consistent well-balanced wines, for drinking over the next five years.
1979	A good vintage. A large harvest of medium-weight elegant wines. Drink now.
1980	A moderate vintage.
1981	A poor vintage. A very small crop of thin wines.
1982	Potentially good. Choose with care.
1983	An excellent year. The best wines are expected to have a long life.
1984	Better than expected wines from grapes not fully ripe.
1985	A good vintage which will produce some excellent wines. Very expensive.
1986	Good, but some growers did better than others. Choose with care.
1987	Variable, some useful wines.

which gave me great pleasure as a change from Chablis. The vineyards of Rully, Mercurey and Givry produce excellent wine of a moderate quality which is fairly moderate in price, and Mercurey, the best of the reds, gives its name to the wines of two or three other *communes* in the same district. Montagny also produces quite a good wine. But none of these is in any way great and they correspond roughly to the wines of Bourg and Blaye in Bordeaux compared to Médoc.

The Mâconnais, bordered by Cluny in the west, Tournus on the River Saône in the north-east and Mâcon itself in the south, is a sizeable vineyard area producing large quantities of ordinary red and white wines, as well as its more famous whites. The vine-clad hills stretch in chains from north to south, but the area is less densely planted than that of Beaujolais. Chardonnay is the predominant variety, followed by Gamay and far behind these two, the Pinot Noir. Production is largely in the hands of the sixteen co-operatives. Much of the wine is sold as Bourgogne *rouge* or Bourgogne *blanc,* Bourgogne Grand Ordinaire or Passetoutgrains (a wine from a blend of Pinot Noir and Gamay) or Bourgogne Aligoté. The Aligoté grape is inferior to the Chardonnay but the wines can make a pleasant aperitif, provided they are served very cold. Mâcon also produces much of the sparkling wine Cremant de Bourgogne. Apart from the basic Mâcon *appellation* and Mâcon Supérieur, forty-three villages in the south, of which the best known are Lugny and Viré, are entitled to call their wine Mâcon-Villages.

The most famous white wine of Mâcon is Pouilly-Fuissé, which can be very good, as can the excellent St-Véran, which is now deservedly popular and it tends to be less expensive. Pouilly-Fuissé

A selection of recommended Burgundy wines is listed below. The prices of Chablis and Côte d'Or wines depend partly on the appellation and partly on the grower. Most grands crus vineyard wines (in italics) are very expensive and premiers crus moderately expensive. With one or two exceptions, the wines of the Côte Chalonnaise, Mâcon and Beaujolais are all reasonably priced.

Chablis

White wines only, slightly austere. Very pale in colour; fine on the nose. (Four appellations, in ascending order: Petit Chablis, Chablis, Chablis *premier cru*, Chablis *grand cru*.)
IMPORTANT GROWERS/SHIPPERS: Louis Michel, François Raveneau, René Dauvissat, Henri Laroche and William Fèvre.

Commune	Vineyards
Chablis	*Vaudésir, Les Clos, Grenouilles.* Fourchaume, Monts de Milieu, Montée de Tonnerre.

Côte Chalonnaise

Red wines: Made from the same grape as the Côte d'Or wines. Should be good value. Best commune, Mercurey; also Givry.
White wines: Good, well-balanced and dry, particularly Montagny.
The Côte is one of the main centres for the production of sparkling Burgundy (Bourgogne Mousseux).
GROWERS: Delorme-Meulien, Protheau, René Ninot Rigaud.

Mâcon

Less expensive than the Côte d'Or wines. Ordinary reds and some quite good crisp and dry whites, particularly Pouilly-Fuissé, Pouilly-Vinzelles, St-Véran and Mâcon-Lugny Genièvres. (Appellations: Mâcon, Mâcon Supérieur, Mâcon with village names and variations; St-Véran, Pouilly-Fuissé, Pouilly-Loché and Pouilly-Vinzelles.)

Beaujolais

Very agreeable in style from the very young, slightly *pétillant* Beaujolais *nouveau* to the *grands crus*, quite different with reasonable colour and body, and good Gamay bouquet. Avoid simple 'Beaujolais' unless from a well-known shipper. (Appellations: Beaujolais, Beaujolais Supérieur, Beaujolais Villages and the *grands crus*, e.g. St-Amour.)
GROWERS: Georges Duboeuf, Thorin, Piat, Chanson, Loron.
Grands crus. St-Amour, Chénas, Chiroubles, Fleurie, Côte de Brouilly, Moulin-à-Vent.

Vintage scenes in the Beaujolais: vines in their autumn colours; traditional and modern containers for the grapes.

Beaujolais vintages

1981   A good to very good vintage. Beaujolais much better than the Côte d'Or.
1982   A good vintage. Drink up.
1983   An excellent vintage. Most should be drunk by now.
1984   A moderate vintage with some very good wines.
1985   An excellent vintage. Ripe wines good to drink now with *crus* worth keeping.
1986   A good vintage: the *cru* wines will be fine at 3-4 years old.
1987   Moderate, not for keeping.

compares more favourably with the best white Burgundies than Mâcon or Beaujolais can with the greater red Burgundies. There is a good deal of competition in this and Pouilly has had the names of other villages tacked on to it, but the *appellation* Pouilly-Fuissé is now protected and the wine is more and more being sold under vineyard or estate names. In the past I have drunk some excellent domaine-bottled Pouilly-Fuissé from Le Clos at Pouilly and from the Château de Fuissé at Fuissé. It is interesting to see how this wine has developed from one which was practically unknown to the general public outside France at least before the Second World War.

What shall one say of *le beaujolais*? It is so famous and the wine is so good. Its names are lovely: Fleurie, St Amour, Juliénas, Moulin-à-Vent, and who has not heard of Clochemerle-in-the-Beaujolais? It is the wine of Paris, which city alone was said to consume twice its annual output! It is the wine of laughter and good living and if you can get honest Beaujolais, it is all these things. It is never a great wine, it is jolly good and is sold at a reasonable price, if that can be said today. Some of the wine, when it is bottled at a château, and there are one or two even in Beaujolais, can be remarkably good. Once I was fortunate enough to have some magnums of 1947 Moulin-à-Vent, bottled at the Château of the Clos du Grand Carquelin by Monsieur Thorin, which were not so very far behind some of the great Burgundies. Nevertheless, Beaujolais should be drunk and enjoyed for what it is – the wine that can be made well, bottled early and drunk quickly. There is a lot of it made and there will be plenty more where it came from, and if it is sometimes mixed with other wines by a disreputable supplier, let us never deal with such and put our trust in those who will deal fairly.

Of recent years it has become fashionable, for some reason which I cannot tell, to drink Beaujolais in the year in which it is made. This wine is imported to arrive in November and is usually advertised with such *réclame* that people flock to buy it and pay over the odds for it. Let us not doubt that it is good Beaujolais, but on the other hand let us be equally certain that it is not the real thing.

The Rhône Valley

Right: The vineyards of Châteauneuf-du-Pape, with the ruined château in the background. The large stones, characteristic of the Châteauneuf vineyards, are called galets.

The vineyards of the Rhône Valley may be said to start just south of Vienne below the confluence of the Rhône and the River Saône. They start with the Côte Rôtie, through Condrieu, Château Grillet, to Hermitage and on past Montelimar, then down to Avignon nearby, where are the vineyards of Châteauneuf-du-Pape, and across the river to Tavel, famous for its rosé wines. All these wines have considerable character and are fairly high in alcohol, 13° or 14° is not unusual, and they have considerable staying power. They are, for the most

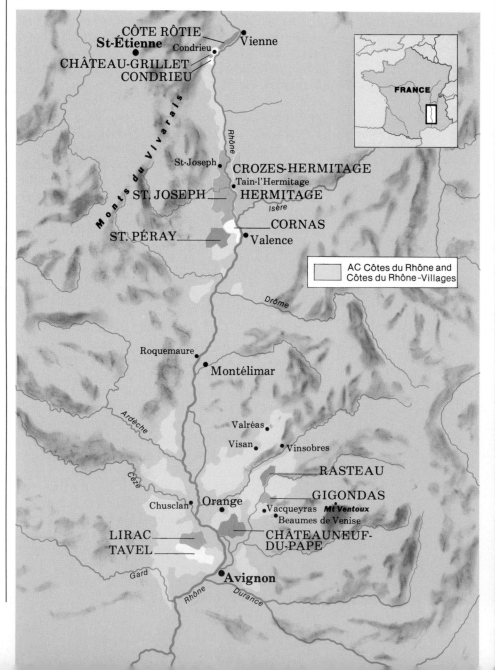

CÔTE RÔTIE
St-Étienne
Condrieu
Vienne
CHÂTEAU-GRILLET
CONDRIEU

Monts du Vivarais

Rhône

St-Joseph
CROZES-HERMITAGE
Tain-l'Hermitage
ST. JOSEPH
HERMITAGE
Isère
CORNAS
ST. PÉRAY
Valence

FRANCE

AC Côtes du Rhône and
Côtes du Rhône-Villages

Drôme

Roquemaure
Montélimar

Ardeche

Valréas
Visan
Vinsobres

RASTEAU

Cèze

GIGONDAS
Chusclan
Orange
Vacqueyras
Mt Ventoux
Beaumes de Venise
LIRAC
CHÂTEAUNEUF-
TAVEL
DU-PAPE
Gard
Avignon
Rhône
Durance

Rhône appellations contrôlées

Côtes du Rhône. Basic generic appellation for the area. Good robust reds. Whites tend to be a bit heavy. Light red-coloured rosés; good carafe wines.

Côtes du Rhône-Villages. A blend of wines from within the seventeen communities entitled to the appellation (Beaumes-de-Venise, Cairanne, Chusclan, Laudun, Rasteau, Roaix, Rochegude, Rousset-les-Vignes, Sablet, St-Gervais, St-Maurice-sur-Eygues, St-Pantaléon-les-Vignes, Séguret, Vacqueyras, Valréas, Vinsobres, Visan); or, if from one village only, with village name, e.g. Côtes-du-Rhône Cairanne.

Basic district appellations, Côte Rôtie, Hermitage, etc. ACs for the individual districts producing the finest wines. All more expensive than the preceding appellations.

Vins délimités de qualité supérieure

Côtes du Luberon VDQS, Côtes du Vivarais VDQS. Ordinary wines, but from reliable shippers can be very good value.

part, grown on the west bank of the Rhône, but some of the best of them are grown on the granite and stony slopes above Hermitage on the east bank. The red wines of the Côte Rôtie, the northernmost vineyards, are of pleasant character and made from the Syrah grape and sometimes with the addition of white Viognier grapes as well. Côte Rôtie is perhaps only 3 kilometres (2 miles) long, after which Condrieu and its adjoining *communes* make a good white, or rather golden wine, some of it of very good quality but only in small quantities. It is made entirely from Viognier grapes. Just to the south is Château Grillet, a vineyard of rather less than 1 hectare (2½ acres) in extent. It makes some of the best white wine, again from Viognier grapes, of the very special dry quality much valued by some connoisseurs although not to everybody's taste. Also, it is very hard to come by – and expensive. Again, these white wines are heavy and heady, and with never less than 11° of alcohol.

Anybody who has travelled the famous *route bleu* to the south of France will have seen the Hermitage vineyards on the great bluffs overlooking the Rhône, and for a mile or two along the road. It is inconceivable that vines can be grown on such steep slopes, and when I first saw the *vendange* in this district I could hardly believe that men could hump the great tubs down the slopes to the waiting tumbrils and tractors ready to take the grapes for pressing. They seem to enjoy it, however, these big men who come charging down the hillside like mountain goats, and I am told they have developed tremendous leg muscles as a result of this, which isn't difficult to believe. I would not like to get in their way when they are under a full load.

Both white and black grapes are grown here

(Marsanne, Roussanne and Syrah), and if I prefer the red wines to the white, this is purely a personal preference. You will not escape the names of the *vignerons* as they are painted all over the hillside, and there are plenty of opportunities along the road for a *dégustation,* some of which I hope you will take, but remember that the wine is much stronger than it seems to the taste, especially if you are thirsty. A visit to the cellars of one of the shippers, like Paul Jaboulet Aîné, would be well worth while. Vintage years do not matter much with this wine. It is sufficiently near the south to be reasonably hot nearly every year, and in any case the *vignerons* are extremely skilful in the art of making adjustments to nature. But it just isn't that sort of wine. It is a very, very good wine without pretensions, and while it can be bought under its years, and undoubtedly some are a little better than others, I do not think it matters very much. I doubt you will find the neck label of a bad year anyway. The wines of Crozes-Hermitage are particularly noteworthy.

Along the banks of the northern Rhône are the wine *communes* of St-Joseph, Cornas and St-Péray, and then there is a gap before the vineyards of the southern Côtes du Rhône.

Farther down the Rhône, just north of lovely Avignon, are the famous vineyards of Châteauneuf-du-Pape, once under the ownership of the Popes of Avignon during the time of the great schism in the fourteenth and fifteenth centuries. Here the wines are slightly lighter in colour, but no less strong, and

The prices of Rhône wines have risen fast and they are no longer such good value for money. The rare white Château Grillet, is very expensive and Condrieu too is scarce and commands high prices. Three-star wines (★★★) are modestly expensive, two-star wines (★★) are reasonably priced and one-star wines (★) are inexpensive.

Northern Côtes du Rhône
The following wines are all *appellation contrôlée.*
Côte Rôtie. ★★★ Small appellation for red. Two sections, Côte Blonde and Côte Brune; most wines a blend of the two. Deep colour; fine bouquet; rich, full-bodied and elegant.
GROWERS/SHIPPERS: Guigal, Duplessy, Vidal-Fleury, Chapoutier, Jaboulet Aîné.
Condrieu. ★★★★ White. Very pale in colour; delicate in flavour, yet full-bodied and sometimes earthy.
GROWERS/SHIPPERS: Vernay, Dumazet.

Château Grillet. ★★★★ White. The smallest and only single-château appellation in France. Deeper in colour; complex, fruity-floral bouquet; full-bodied. Scarce and expensive.
Hermitage. ★★★ Red and white. Robust reds: deep in colour; rich, fruity and soft on the nose; high in alcohol. Whites: medium yellow; strong, rich and round.
GROWERS/SHIPPERS: Jaboulet Aîné, Guigal, Chapoutier, Chave.
Crozes-Hermitage. ★★ Red and white. Similar to Hermitage but lighter in style; less powerful.
GROWERS/SHIPPERS: as for Hermitage.
St-Joseph. ★★ Known for its reds: deep in colour; medium-bodied and fruity. Lighter and with less complexity than Hermitage.
Whites: similar in character to Hermitage but much less fine.
GROWERS/SHIPPERS: Chapoutier, Chave, Délas.

Cornas. ★★ Different soil and hot climate result in the deepest-coloured, fullest wines of the Rhône.
GROWERS/SHIPPERS: Clape, de Barjac.
St-Peray. ★—★★ *Méthode champenoise* sparkling white. Medium-yellow or golden colour; individual earthy bouquet; strong, grapy, typical Côtes-du-Rhône taste.
GROWERS/SHIPPERS: Milliand, Dubourg, Chaboud, Vérilhac.

Opposite: The steep terraces of the Côte Rôtie were first built by the Romans.

Right: View into a grower's courtyard in the village of Châteauneuf-du-Pape. Oak barrels are used by many growers for ageing their wine.

The majority of the wines of the Rhône are reasonably priced and good value for money. Among the reds, some of the domaine-bottled Châteauneuf-du-Papes tend to be more expensive and the vins doux naturels will also cost a little extra. Three-star wines (★★★) are moderately expensive, two-star wines (★★) are reasonably priced and one-star wines (★) are inexpensive.

Southern Côtes du Rhône

The following wines are all *appellation contrôlée* unless otherwise indicated.

Châteauneuf-du-Pape. ★★–★★★ Reds (and a very little white). Very varied: medium to deep colour; at best, herbal bouquet; medium weight, fruity and powerful. Best wines from individual domaines.
GROWERS: Domaines Mont-Redon, Beaurenard, Châteaux Fortia, des Fine Roches, Clos de L'Oratoire des Papes, Père Anselme (shippers).

Gigondas. ★★ A fairly recent AC for reds (and rosés). Reds: deep in colour; rich and fruity on the nose; full-bodied wines. Excellent.
GROWERS/SHIPPERS: Meffre, Roux, Archimbaud, Burle.

Tavel. ★★ Rosé: onion skin, orange-pink colour; fresh fruity nose; clean fresh tangy palate with good acidity and finish. The best French rosé.
GROWERS: Bernard, Maby, Caves Coopératives des Grands Crus de Tavel.

Lirac. ★–★★ Red, white and rosé; known for the latter. Similar to its neighbour Tavel, but less well known.
GROWERS: Verda, Bernard, Rousseau.

Muscat de Beaumes de Venise. ★★ *Vin doux naturel* from Muscat grapes: golden to nut brown in colour; muscaty, raisiny bouquet; luscious sweet, grapy palate; not too heavy. Can be excellent dessert wine. (Reds as well sold under Côtes du Rhône-Villages label.)
GROWERS/SHIPPERS: Castaud, Rey, Vidal-Fleury.

Rasteau. ★★ *Vin doux naturel* from Grenache grapes: golden-brown, raisiny bouquet, heavy, heady and sweet, but can be good. (Good reds as well, Côtes du Rhône-Villages.)
GROWERS/SHIPPERS: Bressy, Charavin, Caves des Vignerons.

Clairette de Die. ★–★★ Sparkling white, either *brut* (*méthode champenoise*), fairly pale in colour and neutral in character, or *tradition* or *demi-sec* (made by natural methods) which has more individuality and a muscaty, more interesting flavour, with considerable richness and roundness.
GROWERS/SHIPPERS: Buffardel, Cave Coopérative de Die, Salabelle.

Coteaux du Tricastin. ★–★★ Reds from vineyards around Donzère. Good honest wines: deep colour, fruity and appealing on the nose; medium weight and well-balanced on the palate. Also some white.
GROWERS/SHIPPERS: Caves Coopératives des Coteaux du Tricastin, Pierre Labeye.

Côtes du Ventoux. ★–★★ Red, white and rosé from vineyards on the slopes of Mont Ventoux. Reds tend to be lighter than Côtes du Rhône and lower in alcohol: excellent for quaffing. About twenty-five per cent rosé, but very little white.
GROWERS: Malcolm Swan, Caves Coopératives des Coteaux du Mont Ventoux.

Côtes du Vivarais VDQS. ★–★★ Red, white and rosé from scattered villages in the Ardèche. Light, refreshing, easy to drink. Serve cold and consume young. Reds better than whites or rosés.
GROWERS/SHIPPERS: Caves Coopératives d'Orgnac L'Aven, Dubourg, Serlavert.

Côtes du Luberon VDQS. ★–★★ Mainly whites; some reds and rosés.

undoubtedly the popularity of this delicious wine is due to its quality as much as to the romance of its name and age. These are wines which it pays to keep, as the best of them will improve and continue to improve for a decade or so. Look for single-estate wines, such as Domaine de Mont-Redon or Château Fortia, but do not expect them to be cheap.

Across the river at Tavel probably the greatest rosé wines in the world are made. It is a comparatively small community growing red and white

grapes of different varieties and in the finest of Tavel wines no fewer than five different varieties of grape may be used. One I know about and saw being made (and, of course, tasted) was made from three black and two white grapes, to a formula that had been handed down to the *vigneron* by his father, and by his father's father. I do not suppose it matters very much if the formula has altered a little, but the resulting wine is certainly unique both in its onion-skin colour and its distinctive dry flavour. A little to

Picking the grapes on the Côte Rôtie, one of the steepest vineyards of the Rhône Valley.

Rhône vintages

1961 An excellent vintage for both white and red, north and south. The best reds good for another five years.
1962 A good to very good year.
1963 A poor to very poor year. Insubstantial wines.
1964 An excellent vintage. Drink up.
1965 A poor vintage. Some reasonable wines.
1966 A very good vintage throughout the Rhône. Deep-coloured, rich and well-balanced reds which can still be good. Whites now past their best.
1967 A very good vintage, but lighter in the north.
1968 A moderate vintage which should have been drunk.
1969 An excellent vintage for Côte Rôtie. Drink up.
1970 A very good vintage of robust, tannic, slow-developing reds. Good for five years. Excellent in Châteauneuf.
1971 An excellent vintage, especially in the north. Tremendous colour and depth. For drinking now and over the next five years.
1972 Excellent in Hermitage and at Château Grillet, good at Châteauneuf-du-Pape and disappointing at Côte Rôtie.
1973 A very good year for Hermitage, less good elsewhere.
1974 Another abundant vintage of light wines, quite good in Châteauneuf-du-Pape. Wines need drinking.
1975 A much smaller harvest, but a mediocre light vintage.
1976 Generally an excellent vintage, comparable to 1961. Châteauneuf-du-Pape harvest spoilt by September rain, but some very good wines. A vintage generally to enjoy for at least five years.
1977 A good vintage in the south, but a mediocre year in the north. Drink up.
1978 An exceptional year, excellent wines throughout. Most wines have a long life ahead.
1979 A very good vintage, generally better in the north than the south, but Côte Rôtie disappointing. Ready to drink now.
1980 Another very good year, unlike in the rest of France. Soft and charming wines for early drinking.
1981 A moderately good vintage for reds, very good for whites. A cold start to the year resulted in a small crop of disappointing wines for early drinking. Côte Rôtie good.
1982 A very good to excellent vintage, better in the north than the south. Some excellent whites. A very dry summer and a good early harvest.
1983 An exceptional vintage in the north. Reds should last for twenty years.
1984 Elegant wines, maturing early.
1985 A very good vintage. Scarcity of Côte Rôtie will mean higher prices.
1986 A classic vintage, hot weather made intense wines. Keep the best: they will age well.
1987 Better here than in northerly regions, but not outstanding.

the north of Tavel is Lirac, which makes similar rosés as well as reds and whites, and includes in its *appellation* the villages of Roquemaure, St-Laurent-des-Arbres and St-Geniès-de-Comolas. Further north is Chusclan, but wines from here must be sold as Côtes du Rhône or Côtes du Rhône-Villages. These latter wines, mostly red, can be excellent and other villages entitled to the *appellation* include Cairanne, Vacqueyras, Valréas, Vinsobres and Visan.

Almost all the wines of the lower Rhône are best drunk cold. Excellent wines are made at Gigondas. Also to be mentioned are the luscious sweet wines like Muscat de Beaumes de Venise, splendid when drunk with soft fruit and best drunk young.

The Loire Valley

Above: Picking the grapes in a Loire vineyard.

Opposite: The imposing château de Luynes, near Tours, dates back to the thirteenth century and is still occupied by the descendants of the Constable de Luynes. It is an example of the many lovely sights that can be enjoyed during a tour of the Loire vineyards.

I suppose it could be claimed that the vineyards of the Loire constitute the loveliest vineyards in the world. From Sancerre to the sea, the great river flows steadily past low hills, magnificent scenery and great turreted châteaux. A great deal of wine is made along these hills, which in October flame in reds, yellows and browns. Alas, none of it is very great wine. The soil is perhaps a little too rich and, while the Loire like everywhere else produces its good and bad years, there is not a great deal of difference between them and the date on the bottle is not really important. The range and variety of wines are extraordinary, and while different districts tend to produce the same kind of wine they do vary very much indeed over the course of the river. Here follows a list of Loire wines, from St-Nazaire at the mouth of the river through Nantes to Angers and going up the Sarthe a little and the Loire, back through Saumur, which is noted for its sparkling wine, to Chinon along the Vienne, then through Tours and Vouvray and along to Pouilly-sur-Loire and Sancerre, and across to Quincy on the Cher.

The wine from around Nantes is Muscadet; going east, south of Angers are grown the grapes from which the Anjou wine is made; from slightly west of Angers on the north banks of the river comes Coteaux de la Loire. On the lovely hills to the south of the Loire itself between Angers and Saumur are the Coteaux du Layon wines and, all round Saumur, you have first of all Saumur wine and Coteaux de Saumur. Between Saumur and Tours there are the Bourgueil and Chinon wines (very strong red wines, these); on the hills a little to the north and all

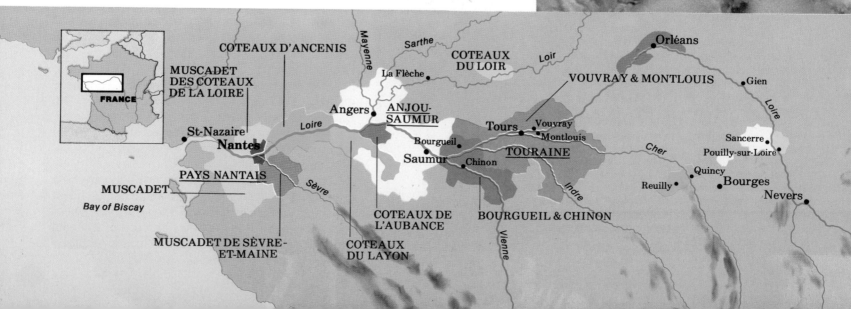

Top: An old wine press in a cellar in Bourgueil.

Above: Chenin Blanc grapes, the main white grapes of the Central Loire, in the morning dew.

Right: Aerial view of the Château de Chenonceaux, one of the most beautiful of all the Loire châteaux.

around Tours, Coteaux de Touraine; but Vouvray is made near Vouvray and a little to the east there is Montlouis. Then there is a very long gap, as the lovely Loire wanders through the country until we reach Sancerre on the west bank and Pouilly-sur-Loire on the east bank, both of which make the distinctive wines of this area, including the excellent Pouilly-Fumé. Farther to the west again on the Cher River tributary are made the wines of Reuilly and Quincy. Here we have something like sixteen wines all made along the river Loire and its tributaries. All have their particular character and all are very drinkable. Almost everywhere, however, the wine must be drunk young – that is to say before its third or fourth year. This is not to say it will not keep, but it will not keep very well.

In Saumur and round about there is a very considerable sparkling-wine industry, and sparkling

Saumur is very well known in Britain, some of it under the trade name of Golden Guinea. In some cases, that is in the best, the wine is made by the *méthode champenoise* and can be very good of its kind. However, the climate is too gentle and the soil too rich, although similar to the soil of Champagne, and the wine cannot compare any more than the best red wine from the Loire can be said really to compare with the châteaux of the Médoc. I buy from my local wine merchant a Saumur sparkler – Bouvet-Ladubay – which is excellent for my annual garden party. A good deal of sparkling wine is made by the vat method, and this is sold quite cheaply – it is sound and very pleasant as an aperitif.

I am not going to try to describe all these wines because I shall run out of superlatives and you will, I hope, have noticed by now that I try to avoid what I call wine jargon. There are some words that come happily to the tongue and describe wine very well, pretension is one of them. Well, these little wines of the Loire (I don't think the growers themselves would claim very much more than this) are all delicious in their way, and quite unpretentious. The best advice I can give is that you should lose no opportunity of trying them out. Drink them as beverage wines, white, red or some of the extremely good rosé made along the Loire. Drink them for what they are: do not expect miracles, for you won't get any. Expect, however, some good wine. Among the very best is Pouilly-Fumé made at the upper end of the river. This is extremely good and made from the Sauvignon grape. It should not be confused with Pouilly-Fuissé of Burgundy, which is quite different. At the other end, near Nantes, can be found the excellent, slightly sharpish, most refreshing white wine called Muscadet, a wine which I much enjoy on a hot summer morning as an aperitif. All white and rosé Anjou Loire wines should be drunk cold. Keep them in the refrigerator as long as you like.

Above all, give yourself the tremendous pleasure, if you can, of tasting these wines in their native haunts. There you will drink them at their very best and in marvellous surroundings. In recent years the *vignerons* of the Loire have taken tremendous trouble to improve their wines for the export market and some of them, like those prepared by the late M. Vacheron of Sancerre for the International Exhibition Co-operative Wine Society, are superb. I would also recommend you to try, if you get the chance, some wine of the Château de Panay at Saumur, which is very good. But these wines are produced essentially as fine wines for the export market and prepared for travel. The little local wines are different, and you may be disappointed if you bring some home to remind you of an enjoyable trip. No wine of this class is ever quite the same drink outside its own manor.

Loire appellations contrôlées

The Loire Valley divides into four regions: Nantes (Muscadet), Anjou Saumur, Touraine and the Central Vineyards, but there is no basic appellation for the entire area. Various district ACs and smaller ones within them; VDQS wines intermingled.

All Loire wines are reasonably priced, although of course some domaine-bottled Sancerre and the sweet wines of Anjou are more expensive than basic appellation wines.

Nantes region
Muscadet AC. White wine, pale in colour; not much nose; neutral flavour, bone dry, some roundness. Refreshing served cold.
GROWERS: J. Aulanier, Donatien-Bahuaud, Chéreaux.
Gros Plant VDQS. Very dry white wine. Less expensive.
Coteaux d'Ancenis VDQS. Interesting rosés.

Anjou Saumur
Anjou and Saumur ACs. Basic generic ACs for large quantities of ordinary whites and sweetish, pretty rosés.
Two good co-operatives: Vignerons de Saumur at St-Cyr-en-Bourg, and Les Caves de la Loire at Brissac.
Saumur Mousseux AC. Sparkling Saumur. Large industry producing straightforward sparkling wines.
GROWERS: Gratien et Meyer, Ackerman-Laurance.
Coteaux du Layon AC. Superior white wines. Includes the excellent sweet wines of Bonnezeaux and Quarts de Chaume. Pale yellow colour; sweetish palate, fruity with high acidity.
GROWERS: Fourlinnie, Pascal Laffourcade, Lalanne.
Coteaux de la Loire AC. Region includes AC Savennières, the best vineyards of which are La Roche aux Moines and La Coulée de Serrant (Mme Joly). Pale colour; honey and flowers bouquet; dry, full-bodied and crisp on the palate; marked acidity.
GROWERS: M. Giraud, Bizard, Mme Joly.
Coteaux de l'Aubance and Coteaux de Saumur. Two more smaller ACs within Anjou.
Saumur Champigny AC. Small district producing red wines from Cabernet Franc grapes. Light in colour; very fruity and sharpish.
GROWERS: Couly Dutheil.

Touraine
Touraine AC. Basic generic AC for the region's ordinary reds, whites and rosés. Labelled with grape variety, e.g. Sauvignon de Touraine. Good value. Appellations sometimes followed by village name, e.g. Azay-le-Rideaux.
GROWERS: Confrérie de Vignerons de Oisly et Thésée.
Chinon, Bourgueil and St-Nicolas de Bourgueil AC. Three ACs for reds, the best of the Loire. May be served chilled.
GROWERS: P. Maitre, R. Desbourdes, C. Jouget, Angelliaume.
Vouvray and Montlouis AC. Two similar ACs for whites. The best are the sweetest, produced only in exceptional vintages. Pale yellow colour; excellent balancing acidity. Long lasting, mellowing with age. Also sparkling wines.
GROWERS: M. Brédif, A. Foreau, Berger, J-P Leblois (Montlouis).
Coteaux du Loire AC and Jasnières AC. Vineyards north of Tours; light, dry whites.
Vins de Haut Poitou VDQS and Vins de Thouarsais VDQS. Good whites, e.g. Sauvignon, an inexpensive alternative to Sancerre.
GROWERS: Co-operative at Neuville-de-Poitou.

Central vineyards
Sancerre AC. Best-known white of the Loire. Pale colour; firm, crisp, fruity palate, lively with good acidity. At best delicate in flavour and elegant. Relatively expensive. Also red and rosé.
GROWERS: Vacheron, Caves des Vins de Sancerre.
Pouilly Blanc Fumé AC. Across the river from Sancerre, similar wines. Sometimes more generous. Often as expensive.
GROWERS: de Ladoucette, Renaud-Bossuat.
Pouilly-sur-Loire AC. Same district as Pouilly Blanc Fumé, but for wines from a different grape. Less important.
Reuilly, Quincy, Menetou-Salon AC. Declining vineyard areas; similar wines to Sancerre.
St-Pourcain-sur-Sioule VDQS. Vineyards farther south near the Auvergne. Red, rosé and white. Interesting and good value.

Champagne

Bollinger label – RD means récemment dégorgé.

Below: A monument to Dom Pérignon, the cellarmaster of the Abbey of Hautvillers, who did so much to make Champagne the drink we know today.

Right: Autumnal view of the Champagne vineyards, with elementary devices for frightening the birds.

It is fashionable in some circles to call Champagne overrated, but nothing could be further from the truth. What I suppose people mean when they call Champagne overrated is that they find it too expensive or that it doesn't agree with them, or that they consider it ostentatious, or something else, but overrated Champagne certainly is not. It is the prince of wines and fully worthy of our attention. It can mean also that its denigrators are talking about cheap 'Champagne', which may well be overrated, especially if it happens to be somebody or other's private *cuvée* at twenty-five per cent less than usual price. It may come from the Champagne district and may even be made by *méthode champenoise*, from the second or third pressings of the grapes, but more likely it is made by a shortened process and in glass tanks instead of bottles, which is not the *méthode champenoise*.

Champagne is made from grapes grown in the Champagne district, a large area south of Rheims, with Epernay as its centre. It covers three distinct districts, the Montagne de Reims to the south and east of Rheims, the Vallée de la Marne, its vineyards stretching like a great tapestry across the hillsides, and, south of Epernay, the Côte des Blancs, with magnificent views of the plain. There are also some less important areas, the valley of the Cubry and the Petite Montagne and, much further

Above: Chardonnay (top) and Pinot Noir; the two main grape varieties of Champagne.

Right: The vintage in the vineyards below Hautvillers. The traditional wicker baskets, or mannequins, *are used to carry grapes to the press-house. Every care is taken not to damage the grapes.*

south, more vineyards in the *département* of Aube. The topsoil is thin and chalky and the subsoil is poor enough, but it is this poor chalk soil which is vital to the production of Champagne. Only wine which is made in this district may be called Champagne, and a case in the English law courts decided this point against the Spanish wine firm who were selling Spanish sparkling wine as Spanish Champagne. If we study the pleadings in this law case, we shall get very near to the reason why Champagne is what it is and worthy of being singled out for special treatment. Counsel for the Champagne Association said the making of Champagne as such, although not in sparkling form, had gone on for more than 2,000 years. It was grown on special soil – that is to say, one only suitable for the making of this wine – and with variations in climatic conditions that also make for special qualities and flavours. Nowhere else in the world could such a wine be reproduced, hence the necessity to protect purchasers who may well be misled by a name on a label into believing that the wine in the bottle would be something like the real Champagne. Many witnesses were called, among them wine-making experts, wine shippers, writers about wine, connoisseurs and so on, and in the end the learned judge decided once and for all that Champagne could only be made in Champagne.

For centuries, the wine of Champagne has been made and marketed. In the Middle Ages it was called Sillery, which is one of the principal vine-growing villages on the Montagne de Reims. Because the climate is variable and they are very much the most northern vineyards in France, the grapes will not always ripen fully and it is for this reason that not every year is a vintage year – usually only about one year in three. The ordinary Champagne bought under some famous label is therefore a blend of wines from various years; and also a blend of the wine pressed from grapes of any one of a dozen villages, quite unlike Bordeaux and Burgundy, where it is usual to buy great wines bottled at a vineyard that might be as small as three or four acres, like La Tâche in Vosne-Romanée.

The Champagne system is for the shipper to buy what grapes he needs, over and above those he grows himself, from the 11,000-plus smallholders of Champagne. The grapes are taken to a central *pressoir*, which may or may not belong to the shipper, and are then pressed three times. The first pressing is obviously the best one, and is called the *vin de cuvée*; the second pressing can never make first-class wine and constitutes second-pressing wine or *vin de taille*. The third, of course, is very poor stuff indeed and only used for the cheapest classes of wine, which are sold at very low prices. What is left after all these pressings – that is, the husks and the stalks and the pips, and very dry they are – is distilled into the famous *marc de Cham-*

pagne, which at its best is really good and at its worst is reminiscent of liquid razor blades.

To return to our first pressing of grapes: after the first fermentation, which in the case of a strong wine may only take twenty-four to thirty-six hours, the wine is run off into casks and shipped off to the cellars of the shipper, who cherishes it through its second fermentation in bottle and until it becomes Champagne. Most of the shippers will have bought grapes for their own presses, but the process will be the same. The casks rest in the courtyard for a long time and buzz away in quite heavy secondary fermentation although, I suppose, this is really a continuation of the first. Listening at the bung-hole you will hear a sound like a swarm of bees inside the barrel. The wine stays in its cask for perhaps a year until it is ready for bottling, when it is on its way to becoming Champagne.

Dom Pérignon, the famous monk of the Abbey of Hautvillers, just outside Epernay, is generally credited as being the father of Champagne as we know it, but this is only partly true. Dom Pérignon was for over forty years the cellarer of the Abbey and became a very great expert on the local wine. He could judge it, he could make it well, and he did both, but he did not invent Champagne. There

Veuve Clicquot was one of the great ladies of Champagne.

Dégorgement à la volée, still practised for larger and unusual bottle sizes.

A tractor enjambeur *designed to straddle the rows of vines.*

shippers knew not where to turn. I have been told that two of the great water towers characteristic of France everywhere were filled with the wine for storage purposes (this may be apocryphal!), and there were wine tanks at every siding full of the wine of Champagne. The vintage was quite good and this tremendous crop of 1970 enhanced both the quality and the quantity of Champagne for many years. I am now credibly informed that stocks are still short, such is the demand, even with the world recession. As a postscript to this point, I would mention that when I was in Champagne in 1961, with André Simon, and he was writing his book on the *History of Champagne* (Ebury Press, 1962), the price of the grapes alone bought from the grower at the *pressoir* worked out at 8 shillings, or 40p, *per bottle* of wine made from them. This is only for the raw material before pressing, blending, cellaring, bottling, or marketing, overheads, profit, packing, shipping and so on can be accounted for. Of course, lower qualities are much cheaper and only in the very best Champagne will a very large percentage of *catégorie hors classé* grapes be included, but it is bound to be expensive, like all first-class wine. Most reputable wine suppliers have their own private *cuvée* which most people know as 'party wine'. It is fair to say it is not always first quality, although probably excellent value for money.

It should be remembered that Champagne is at its very best when it is between seven to ten years old. After that, other than in very exceptional years like 1921, which stayed with us for twenty years, it will not keep. The best wines are now 1982 and 1983, both hot years, and the excellent 1979 if you can still find it. There are many old Champagnes, but they are mere curiosities rather than anything else. Pommery found in the cellars a few years ago an old bin of 1898 Champagne which had been overlooked and in fact had never been disgorged. This was disgorged and liqueured slightly and wired up in 1953 or '54, I think, and proved to be in excellent condition, if somewhat dark in colour and without the edge to it which is the chief joy of Champagne. But it was delicious and still sparkling. The wine of 1986, incidentally, is considered to be absolutely splendid in quantity and quality.

This is the best place to say something of pink Champagne. There is no reason why sparkling wine should not be pink or red: it merely means that black grape skins are left in the vat for twenty-four hours or so during the first fermentation until the pigment in the skin starts to dissolve and colours the grape juice which is being turned into wine. It used to be fashionable to serve pink Champagne to the ladies, and sometimes with dessert, but there is no great point in it. It cannot possibly be any better than the pale golden 'straight' Champagne. But if you like pretty colours you can have a pretty wine.

Champagne labels – a
vintage from Mercier and the
de luxe labels of Moët &
Chandon and Laurent
Perrier.

Left: The lovely vineyards of
Champagne.

Alsace

Above: The Gewürztraminer grapes that make Alsace's most characteristic wine. They take on a pinkish hue when ripe.

Right: A grower's courtyard at Riquewihr, with bins ready for the vintage.

Looking down on the village of Kientzheim in the mist.

The vines of Alsace grow on the eastern slopes of the Vosges mountains just west of the Rhine, and a very wonderful part of France this is: the fairy castles on the crags, the deep blue-green mistiness of the mountains from which may be seen the full sweep of the mighty Rhine. According to André Simon, there are four hundred and forty parishes in Alsace making wine and some 30,000 *vignerons* engaged in it, which surprises me considerably because there is comparatively little Alsace wine available in the United Kingdom. Some three-quarters of it, or about 1,090,000 hectolitres (about 24,000,000 gallons) is sold in France, and the remainder is sold for export. The wine itself is a heady wine of considerable character and not to be drunk lightly. It is by no means a little wine and has a good deal of the character of German wine in it. The same Riesling, Sylvaner and other grapes are grown in Alsace as are grown in the German vineyards along the Rhine only a few miles after the Alsatian vineyards stop. In any case, Alsace was in German occupation from 1870 until 1918 (and again from 1940 until 1944).

Vine growing and wine making is quite a considerable industry in this area and it is best seen in places such as Riquewihr, a small medieval walled town where the vines grow up and into the town itself. Every single person is directly or indirectly engaged in wine making and has been for many, many centuries. The town remains unchanged and unfaked; there has been no restoration and it has

merely been kept in good order while the *vignerons* have concentrated, year in, year out, on their beloved wine. It is one of the only towns in this part of Alsace that escaped destruction at the end of the Second World War. I recommend Riquewihr as being the best place to observe Alsatian wines made in both the ancient and the modern manners. If you poke round the back streets and the cobbled alleys during the *vendange* you will see grapes brought in from the vineyards outside the town walls being pressed in the ancient presses, some of them hundreds of years old, by small growers who make their own wine. On the other hand, if you go to Hugel or the Château de Riquewihr, which is now owned by a famous wine-making firm, Dopff and Irion, you will see wine made by the most modern methods and you will be allowed to taste the wine and enjoy it. You may have a simple meal in one of the restaurants, and if you are wise you will take away one or two bottles of the wine as being the best kind of souvenir. This can be an altogether memorable experience.

Open the door of a famous *vigneron* in a courtyard just off the main street and near his great wine press you will find this inscription: *'Des voix mystérieuses soufflent à notre vin en gestation des histoires vieilles et éternellement jeunes.'* ('To our wine as it comes to birth mysterious voices breathe stories old and everlastingly young.') This is the true spirit of Riquewihr. Hardly less interesting, but smaller, is another wine village west of Colmar, Husseren-les-Châteaux (there are three ruined châteaux overlooking the vineyards). A refreshing stop for *dégustation* may be made at the cellars Kuentz-Bas, who make excellent wines.

The vines themselves are trained on wires stretched between 2-metre (7-foot) poles, almost as high as hops in England, and the wine is classified according to the grapes from which it is made: Sylvaner, Muscat, Pinot, Riesling, and Gewürztraminer. Then they make wines of different character according to the grape. Sylvaner, for instance, makes a light, fresh wine not very suitable for keeping and with very little bouquet, but it can be quite delicious and it is, as a rule, rather less expensive. On the other hand, the Muscat makes a heavy wine, not altogether to our taste perhaps, and not so sweet as you might expect from the name.

By and large, Alsace wines are dry and do not run to sweetness as some of the German or Bordeaux wines, although there are some very splendid examples in good years. The Pinot grape, of which two white varieties are grown in Alsace, Pinot Blanc and Pinot Gris, makes wine more in character with the white Burgundies and some of them can be very good indeed, although I never heard of a Pinot Gris being used for Burgundy. The red Burgundian

grape, Pinot Noir, is also grown in Alsace and is used to make a light, fruity wine, but this is not very important. The Riesling, as in Germany, produces perhaps the best wine, for it is a noble grape and it is the Riesling which is largely grown in the district around Riquewihr and Ribeauvillé. Gewürztraminer and the Traminer, two names for the same grape, are smaller and rounder than the Riesling, and make the finest wine. They ripen earlier than the others, and in a good year, when allowed to stay on the vines, produce the only really sweet wine from Alsace. It is in the smaller vineyards, reserved by the larger *vignerons* for the special grapes, that the Gewürztraminer grapes will be grown and made into the very best wine. Generally speaking, the best years for Alsatian wine are bound to be the same as for the Rhine and Moselle.

Alsace wines, generally speaking, are reasonably priced. Riesling, Gewürztraminer and Muscat will cost a little more than the other grape varieties. The sweeter wines of exceptional vintages are more expensive.

Alsace appellations contrôlées

Alsace, or Alsace followed by the grape variety.
Gewürztraminer, Riesling, Pinot Gris or Tokay d'Alsace, Muscat, Pinot Blanc, Sylvaner, Pinot Noir.
Vin d'Alsace Edelzwicker. A wine from more than one of the grapes listed above.
Alsace Grand Cru. A superior appellation for certain designated vineyards.
Crémant d'Alsace. Sparkling wines, *méthode champenoise.* Neutral flavour, soft.

Alsace wines

Dry, full-bodied spicy whites, often slightly *spritzig.* Sweetish wines produced in exceptional vintages such as 1976, e.g. *réserve spéciale, grande réserve, vendange tardive* and Hugel's *séléction des grains nobles.*
GROWERS: Hugel, Trimbach, Dopff and Irion, Dopff au Moulin, Kuentz-Bas, Schlumberger, Gustave Lorentz, Preiss-Henny, Laugel, Gisselbrecht.
Riesling. The wine the Alsatians are most proud of. Pale yellow colour; spicy Riesling bouquet; fruity with high acidity; very lively and elegant.
Gewürztraminer. Heavily perfumed; softer spicy palate; less acidity than Riesling.
Muscat. Aromatic grapy nose; medium weight with a delicate grapy flavour. Lighter than Gewürztraminer and some think more charming.
Pinot Blanc. Spicy nose; rounded and more neutral flavour. Easy to drink.
Tokay (Pinot Gris or Ruländer). Positive bouquet of the grape; medium weight with very spicy fat flavour.
Sylvaner. Less distinctive bouquet, slightly earthy, less spicy; light and fresh to taste. Drink young. Less expensive.
Pinot Noir. Light-coloured fruity red wines of Burgundian style. Not very serious.

Above: A typical vintage scene – and so back to the cellars for pressing.

Right: Hillside vineyards outside Riquewihr, characteristic of the undulating Alsace countryside.

Opposite: Vintage time at Riquewihr. The church of this picturesque village towers out of the autumn mist.

The little wines of France

Picpoul, one of the white grapes of the Midi.

Good wine is made all over France except in seven *départements*. Consequently, there are hundreds, if not thousands, of wines that we have not touched upon in the preceding pages. Neither can we, because they are not of any great importance in relation to the great wines, and in the vast majority of cases they do not get beyond the confines of the nearest town and sometimes village, or even farmhouse. On the other hand, these are the wines we can afford to drink as average wines. 'Plonk' in fact.

Languedoc and Roussillon (the Midi)

There are vast quantities of wine made outside the districts we have already mentioned and the most prolific district is that of Languedoc and Roussillon (the Midi), which is a vast area stretching roughly from Carcassonne to the Mediterranean and wedged between the foothills of the Pyrenees and the Massif Central. Here is produced most of the good, dull wine so useful for blending with even inferior wine from elsewhere and which can be seen along the railways in tanker trains or on the roads in tanker juggernauts and bought as the *vin rouge ordinaire* throughout thousands and thousands of *alimentations* in France, at the lowest possible price. The soil is rich, the grapes are big, and the area makes a vast quantity of wine. It is dull, fruity and heady and in its natural state is not always rough. This is the true wine of the Midi which has sustained urban France for centuries. It is quite unremarkable but is not to be despised.

There are, however, a few pockets where very good wine of a different kind is made, especially sweeter wine, for the Muscat grape is grown very successfully in the Mediterranean areas, especially in the Côtes du Haut-Roussillon, near Banyuls and Perpignan, immediately north of the Spanish frontier. Many towns and villages here are making excellent, sweet or, shall we say, super-sweet fortified wine from Muscat, Grenache and Malvoisie grapes, like the Muscat de Frontignan, or the Muscat de Lunel.

The Jura

I am not at all sure that it is fair to call the Jura a little wine of France. This is a very strong white wine, sharpish to our taste and altogether masculine in character. Warner Allen has devoted more than a chapter to this wine in his excellent book *White*

Right: Dramatic, almost alpine scenery of vines and a village in the Jura.

Some recommended little wines of France are listed below. Most of these wines are inexpensive or reasonably priced.

South-west France

The following wines are all *appellation contrôlée*.

Bergerac, Côtes de Bergerac. Red and white wines similar to Bordeaux, including appellations of Monbazillac (sweet white wine, but dry on the nose), Pécharmant and Montravel.
Blanquette de Limoux. Sparkling white from vineyards near Carcassonne. Better than average. Some still wine as well.
Cahors. Deep red wines of character, full-bodied and long lasting.
Côtes de Buzet. Red, white and rosé from vineyards bordering the Garonne. Lighter than Bordeaux in style; same grapes.
Côtes de Duras. Red and white wines from Bordeaux grapes and others from vineyards south-east of Bordeaux. Good value.
Gaillac. White and sparkling wines from the Tarn valley. Good, crisp white wines; Bordeaux grapes. Also reds and rosés.
Jurançon. Sweet and dry whites from vineyards near Pau.
Madiran. Good red wines from vineyards near to Armagnac.
Pacherenc du Vic Bilh. White wines made near Madiran.

The Midi

Large area producing inexpensive *ordinaires*.

Red wines: The best are easy to drink, light and fruity, more acceptable than the whites. At worst, they are dull and coarse.
AC Fitou (small area within Corbières), Collioure (tiny region on Spanish border). **VDQS** Costières du Gard, Coteaux du Languedoc, Corbières, Minervois, Côtes du Roussillon, Côtes du Roussillon-Villages.
White wines: Unexciting and generally neutral in flavour, dull.
AC Clairette du Languedoc. Clairette de Bellegarde.
VDQS Picpoul de Pinet.

Vins doux naturels. Fortified dessert wines or *vins doux naturels*: golden to nut brown, sweet and raisiny to taste but with tangy acidity to balance. Good aperitif wines if chilled.
AC Muscat de Beaumes-de-Venise, Rasteau (see Côtes du Rhône), Muscat de Lunel, Muscat de Frontignan, Banyuls.

The Jura

Little-known reds, ordinary whites and rosés and sparkling wines. Inexpensive, unless you are looking for old vintages of Château-Chalon (★★★). Two special types of wine:
Vin jaune. Made from late-harvested grapes. Yellow or golden in colour; nutty on the nose; dry, full-bodied, high in alcohol and similar to old sherry. Long-lived. Made in the best vintages only.
Vin de paille. Made from dried grapes. Yellow in colour; sweet with a concentrated and raisiny flavour. Production now reduced.

Côtes de Jura AC. Ordinary wines; red, white, rosé and sparkling, including *vin de paille*.
Arbois AC. Probably the best Jura whites; also reds and rosés.
Château-Chalon AC. The most famous Jura wine (from several communes).
L'Etoile AC. Good whites, dry and straw-flavoured. Includes some *vin jaune*, e.g. rare Château d'Arlay. Also sparkling wines.

Haute-Savoie

Known for its sparkling wines. Also produces still wines.

Savoie, Mousseux de Savoie, Pétillant de Savoie, Roussette de Savoie ACs. Basic appellations for the area.
Seyssel AC. Still white wines.
Seyssel Mousseux AC. Sparkling wines.
Crépy AC. White, dry and aromatic, sometimes semi-sparkling.
Vins de Bugey VDQS. Reds, whites, rosés, and sparkling wines.

Provence

Côtes de Provence AC. The most general appellation for the area. Dull whites, pretty rosés and light fruity reds, drunk locally.
Coteaux d'Aix en Provence VDQS. Reds, whites and rosés. All good luncheon wines, some rather better, e.g. Ch. Vignelaure.
Palette AC. Good whites, e.g. Château Simone.
Bandol AC. Probably the best provençal red.
Cassis AC. The best white of Provence. Can be a bit heavy.
Bellet AC. Reds, whites and rosés. Quite good.

Wines and Cognac (Constable & Company, 1952), but I doubt many of us can share his enthusiasm, although it is true that the famous Château-Chalon is one of the classic and rarest wines in France. It is not made at the château but in a number of small vineyards in the Jura. It has an affinity with the finest of fine dry sherry. It can be kept for years and years and years. Some people say it ought not to be opened until fifteen or twenty years have passed it by, but better still, thirty or forty. It is not a wine you will meet often outside France. But if you are travelling through France to Switzerland, stop at Dôme, the birthplace of Louis Pasteur, and there you will be able to buy a bottle of Château Chalon.

Provence

The *vignobles* of Provence lie between Draguignan in the north-east, Aix in the west and La Ciotat to St-Tropez in the south, and from them come red, white and rosé wines, all rather heady and nearly all best drunk in Provence, and why not? The best of

Above: Vines on the hillsides; there are other crops on the valley floor and trees on the hilltops which are both unsuitable for vines.

Left: Weighing the grapes. Small farmers are paid according to the weight and sugar content of their grapes.

them are put up in very graceful, waisted bottles, sometimes with enormous birth certificates tied to the necks. The red wine is one of the few which takes no harm from being chilled – this is a matter of taste – but the rosé and white must be very cold. Vintage years do not count for much with Provençal wines. Some of them may be found rather harsh to our tastes but quite delicious – in Provence.

South-west France

Not very far from Albi and about 56 kilometres (35 miles) from Toulouse is the town of Jurançon, from whence the local wines have very strong historical associations. I do not know whether you will like them in their own country – they tend to be over-sweet to our taste, although some excellent dry Jurançon is made. You are unlikely to come across them elsewhere.

Many good, sound little wines are grown along the Dordogne, the most famous is made at Monbazillac. It is a sweetish white wine from the Sémillon grape. A good many dry and even elegant wines are made near Bergerac, the home of Cyrano of that ilk, but they should be drunk *en route* or whenever you go to Lascaux or tour this delightful country. You will find vineyards in vine-growing villages such as St Foy-des-Vignes and St Laurent-des-Vignes up and down the Dordogne and you will mostly buy only the local wine in the towns and villages. The rather richer wines of Cahors, Côtes de Buzet and Côte de Duras make a good inexpensive substitute for Bordeaux. A fair, inexpensive, white wine is made in Gaillac.

The range of the wines of France is quite frankly enormous, and the only advice I can give is: when in France drink the local wine for the experience, buy yourself a bottle of excellent wine if you can afford it (and fine wines are dearer in France than they are in Britain and America), and enjoy them all. It may be that you will get a bad bottle (and there is one such name that I cannot quote here for risk of a libel action that is a household word in my family for all that is bad in wine), and take it as you find it, and you will do very well.

Brandy

Above: Vintage time in Cognac; loading the lorry.

Brandy is distilled from wine; that is to say, the grapes are pressed in the ordinary way, the wine is fermented and after the first fermentation it is stored in barrels and later distilled into brandy. *Eau de vie* or *marc,* on the other hand, is certainly not brandy, for this is distilled from the husks, pips and stalks of the grapes when every single drop of juice has been pressed, not once or twice, but thrice. This has a place in the literature of wine and drinking, but not in the same breath as brandy.

The finest brandy is made in or near Cognac, east of La Rochelle, and at Armagnac, which is near the northern Pyrenees, to the south-east of Bordeaux. The finest Armagnac is generally considered to be very nearly as good as the best Cognac, and I will not argue the case here. I am myself extremely satisfied with a good Cognac and the best Armagnac.

Cognac

The wine that is the basic ingredient of Cognac is made from the St-Emilion grape, which is a white grape of no special character except that it makes the wine from which may be distilled the most superb spirit. Cognac itself is a comparatively small area divided by regulations into several classifications. The best brandy is considered to be made in the area round Cognac itself on the south bank of the Charente and is called the *Grande Champagne* because the chalky soil has an affinity with the chalky soil of Champagne. To the north of the Charente is an area that is known as the *Petite Champagne,* of which Jarnac is the centre. There is another area called the *Petite Champagne* south of the *Grande Champagne.* Immediately round the Champagne areas are the *fins bois* and *bons bois*; those districts which grow fine grapes specially suited to Cognac, but which perhaps are not quite so good as the *Champagne* districts. Farther to the west along the coast between the mouth of the River Gironde and La Rochelle are the *bois ordinaires,* where simply good, brandy-making grapes are grown. The grapes are pressed, made into wine and, in the next spring, distilled into brandy.

The raw spirit when first distilled is not drinkable by ordinary standards. The farmers who grow the grapes, press them, make the wine and distil it, but they cannot afford to keep it, so they take it to Cognac and sell the spirit to the big brandy shippers,

The undulating hills of the Charentais countryside between Cognac and Segonzac in the heart of the Grande Champagne.

The distillery at the Domaine de Dagnaud.

supplier or in the cellar of a friend, a bottle labelled *Hine 1914, landed 1915, bottled 1942 or 1943* then that bottle, if it be a genuine label, will contain the truly great brandy. But you may well die without ever having this opportunity.

There are other brandies that are rarely seen, such as old brown brandy, which was very popular in the second half of the last century and, if you are lucky enough to come by a bottle, it is interesting to drink. The brandies that you buy in the ordinary course of events from the great brandy people like Martell, Hennessy, Hine, Remy Martin, Bisquit, Courvoisier and so on, are classified first of all by the ordinary three stars which usually indicates that the brandy is at least seven years old, and then as follows:

VSO or very superior old
Usually brandies from twelve to seventeen years.

VSOP or very superior old pale
Brandies from eighteen to twenty-five years old, most of which are certainly not pale, though they ought to be.

VVSOP or very, very superior old pale
Brandies from twenty-five to forty years old.

Other house marks like Hennessy's XO, which is the equivalent of VVSOP, and Martell's Cordon Bleu (much the same), are all very good indeed and you may rely on the name of the great brandy houses to keep up their reputation for quality.

Armagnac

Most of the things that are true about Cognac are equally true about Armagnac except, of course, the wine is made from different grapes. It is again something of a village or farm industry in that the *vigneron* will distil his own brandy, but there are no houses of the size of the vast Martell and Hennessy or even the medium-size Cognac houses. It is therefore quite possible occasionally to come upon a very special bottle of Armagnac, although this must not be confused with some of the enormous Methuselahs of Armagnac (and indeed Cognac) brought to diners mounted on gun carriages and other contraptions by *restaurateurs*. Armagnac at its best can be very good indeed.

I suppose there is more humbug over old brandy than almost any other class of wine. Suffice it to say that I once saw in a mirror in one of the greatest restaurants in London a waiter filling up the VSOP bottle from a three star, which I suppose was his own special form of blending. Taste is the only thing that can save you from fraud, other than dealing with only people of integrity, whether they be wine merchants or restaurants. I have never returned to the particular restaurant where this happened.

who have vast cellars and blending vats. The casks of new brandy are tasted, stored, and when the time comes the spirit is blended with older brandies to make the best possible combination according to the market and the price.

It is true to say that about ninety-nine per cent of all brandies are blends of different years. There are, however, old vintage Cognacs but the ancient date on the bottle, such as 1849, 1865, 1878, certainly does not refer to the age of the entire contents of the bottle. The casks have obviously been kept topped up with younger brandies over the years and some of the old Cognac may well have been needed to improve younger blends. Under the new laws which control the export of brandy from France it is no longer permissible to put a date on brandy unless it is authentically the brandy made of the wine of a given year, and so we may expect to see rather less vintage Cognac in the future. The finest brandies are not the oldest and they are called in the trade 'early landed brandies', and they are all but impossible to obtain outside the trade, except at auction. If you should ever see, at your reputable wine

Marc

Once upon a time (I last saw them in 1953) in villages of France, especially in Burgundy and along the Rhône Valley, at the time of the *vendange,* weird, Heath Robinson arrangements could be seen, that had great coppers and a chimney stack on wheels, rather like traction engines. They stood in the market squares. To these contraptions the local *vignerons* would come after they had pressed their wine, with the husks, the pips and the stalks that had survived several heavy pressings. This residue, which had the consistency you might expect of stalks, pips and husks with no moisture, was brought in tumbrils or on tractors and a receipt was given for so many kilos by the man in charge of this portable still.

The tumbrils were unloaded in the middle of the square, the *vignerons* departed with a receipt and came back in a few days, after the husks had been fermented and distilled, to collect the correct number of litres of the product of the distillation which is called *marc.* Onto the heap were tipped the contents of many tumbrils and gradually the pile got larger while the distillers worked away boiling it up. Dogs and goats seemed to like the smell of the grape-skins. I have seen them walk all over it, munching a little here and there. Dogs usually just sniffed and cocked a leg, and I am credibly informed that this added considerably to the flavour. Gradually the heap went down, and gradually the large demijohns of *marc* were handed out to their owners. I once asked the distiller whether I could taste the raw *marc* as it came from the retort and he smiled and poured a little into an old jam tin – one sip was enough, for to drink raw *marc* is like drinking broken glass. Such then is the nature of *marc* and it cannot, by its nature, be very much. It can be kept to a great age, and in the course of time it loses a great deal of its astringency and fire. The best of it, which is sold in shops, *Marc de Champagne, Marc de Bourgogne,* etc., while never *very* good, certainly smells nice and is usually made, I believe, from second pressings to make it drinkable. In the case of a great château, a little *marc* may be made after a very light first pressing for their own use and for special and special and favoured guests.

So we depart from France as we should do, savouring, I hope with pleasure, the finest wines and I hope accompanied by the best food.

In this book we shall not pass this way again, but I hope in real life you will do as I have done for many years and hope to do while my life lasts, that is to travel quietly through the little yellow roads of France, taking my wine and pleasure at local inns drinking local wine. Perhaps, now and again, on Saints' days and special occasions, you will have some great and noble wines, which are the incomparable wines of France.

Above: The house of Courvoisier at Jarnac on the banks of the Charente. They are the only important Cognac house not in the town of Cognac.

Left: Removing the marc from the press.

GERMANY

Right: Schloss Bernkastel towers above the town and vineyards of Bernkastel. It is one of the many hilltop castles of the Moselle.

Wines made in Germany along the Rhine and its tributaries the Nahe, the Main, the Neckar and the Ahr, together with the Moselle with its tributaries the Saar and the Ruwer, are nearly all white wines and some of the greatest at that. The red wines, from Baden and the Ahr, are relatively unimportant; they are consumed in Germany and rarely exported.

The white wines are of excellent, and in some cases of quite superb, quality. The three principal grapes used in their making are: the Müller-Thurgau grape, which makes over a quarter of the wine; the Riesling, which is one of the noblest white grapes in the world, with late-ripening, small berries, and which is responsible also for about a

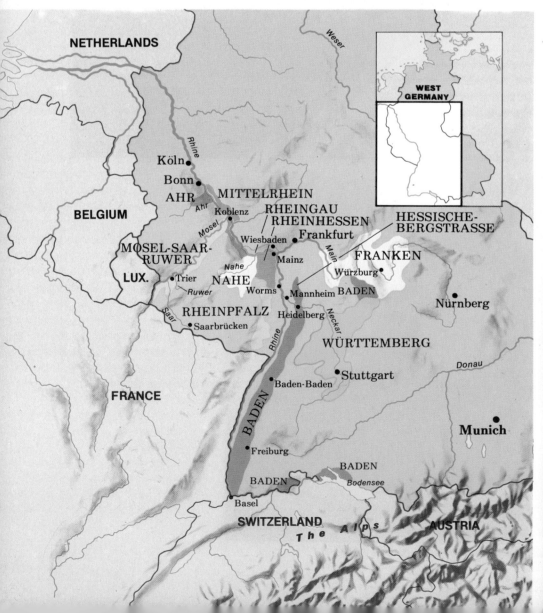

Vintage time at Johannisberg in the Rheingau. The grapes are emptied directly into a tanker for easy transportation to the winery.

quarter of the best wine production; and the Sylvaner, which is a middle-sized, juicy grape making mild, non-acidic wine, and which makes about a fifth of the country's total production. There are five or six other grapes that have their virtues, but are unimportant in this context, none of them making more than about three per cent of the whole.

Some of the wines from Germany are made from vines that are the most northerly in Europe and it is not every year that the grapes ripen sufficiently well to make really sweet wine, although most German wines are slightly sweet. The wines go through the whole range of flavours from sharpness to ultrasweetness but mostly they have a certain sweet

Ripe Sylvaner grapes with autumn leaves. Sylvaner is at its best in the dry Steinwein *of Franconia.*

edge to them and are all the better for it. In bad years it has been possible to correct a crop that has had to be harvested before it was fully ripe in a slightly artificial manner, by using sugar to avoid disappointment. *Chaptalization*, although strictly limited, is legal, except in the case of top-quality wine, or *Prädikatsweine*.

German wine regulations are probably the strictest in the world. A new set of rules, now under consideration, will call for day-to-day control for the better wines. Wine makers must make daily harvest declarations within seven days of picking. The vintner making wines of quality will be given, in addition to an AP number (see opposite), one official seal for each bottle awarded this number. Thus wines with AP numbers but without the official cap seal will not be sold as quality wines. These rules are meeting some opposition.

The principal German wine regions, or *Anbaugebieten*, which all come under the German supervising wine laws, are listed at the top of the following page. Smaller delimited areas are *Bereiche* (of which there are usually several within each *Anbaugebiet*), then come the names of the vine-growing communities and villages, followed by the *Grosslagen* (collective sites) and the *Einzellagen* (individual vineyards and sites), which must be a minimum of 5 hectares (12.4 acres) in size. Before the 1971 law, the 20,000 or so German wine producers were using no less than 25,000 site names; now only about 2,500 are legally recognised.

The German wine regions

Ahr	Rheinhessen
Hessische-Bergstrasse	Rheinpfalz
Mittelrhein	Franken
Mosel-Saar-Ruwer	Württemberg
Nahe	Baden
Rheingau	

The classic wines all come from the low hills through which the Rhine flows and the steeper hills along the Moselle. Touristically, there could be no better trip than to drive from, say, Saarburg or Trier on the Moselle, along the river, through the lovely hills where the vineyards fall straight down to the river, as far as Enkirch. From there cross the hills to Lorch on the Rhine and drive down through Bingen and Mainz to Worms, or even farther south. The scenery is delightful, the romantic castles of the Rhine occasionally in view, the people are friendly and the wine, which is in plentiful supply, delicious, and indeed cheap by modern standards.

In discussing German wine, however, it is necessary to know something of the extraordinary refinement to which the German wine grower has brought his art and to understand something also of the odd polysyllabic words appearing on the labels of the bottles. They are most important in so far as they refer to the contents of the bottle. Some German wines can be literally the most expensive in the world; they can also be comparatively cheap and wonderful value. In the current stock of a London wine merchant there is a *Trockenbeerenauslese* wine made by the great Moselle wine grower, J. J. Prüm. This is no less than £146.36p per bottle. Add VAT to it at fifteen per cent and this will give you some idea of the heights that German wine has reached. In order to find out why this is, we must learn something of the German wine nomenclature and labelling.

The ordinary wine of the country – that is, the wine of any village or vineyard – will be called in the first place by the name of the village and the wine region. Let us take one of the best known of the Moselle wines, Bernkastel. The common wine of this area will be called Bernkasteler, then if it is from a particular vineyard like the famous Doktor vineyard it will be called Bernkasteler Doktor, so the second name on the label is the name of the vineyard. It is usual to follow this with the date, which might be 1971. This would be followed by what is called an *Amtliche Prüfungsnummer,* or AP number, that is to say, after the description of the wine there will be a number like (AP) Nr. 2576 967 1172. This means that the wine has undergone a taste test carried out by experts from the wine industry; the last two digits indicating the year in which the AP number was authorised. The experts mark the wine on a 20-point system, taking in

The picturesque church of Piesport reflects into the waters of the Moselle. The vineyards of the village rise in steep hillsides behind.

colour, clarity, bouquet and taste, which are all individually marked. Only if the wine achieves a minimum prescribed score in all categories is it allowed to carry the coveted quality grade on its label and receive the official examination number as authentification. This information will appear on all labels of QbA and QmP wines.

Then we come to some rather special classes. The basic category is that of *Kabinett* quality, then comes *Spätlese* from late-picked grapes, followed by the sweeter *Auslese* wines made from selected ripe bunches. Above this come *Beerenauslese* wines, superb dessert wines made from singly selected overripe grapes. Finally we get to the great *Trockenbeerenauslese*, which is made only in the hottest years from very, very overripe even

Traditional work in a cellar in Hattenheim. The wine is run off, or racked off, its lees into a clean barrel.

raisin-like grapes, picked singly, and upon which the *pourriture noble (Edelfäule)* has already formed. Some growers are said to take only the juice pressed out of the rotten grapes by the weight of the equally rotten grapes resting on them; at least this would explain the price of the wine. *Kabinett* is the bottom rung of the top-quality ladder. *Weingut* indicates that it comes from the person named on the label, but does not necessarily mean that the wine is bottled at the named place. It may indeed have been bottled anywhere in the world, and be none the worse for that. (Most good German wine is, however, bottled in Germany because of the procedure at the time of bottling of submitting

samples to the government offices, in order to obtain the AP numbers.) Certain classes of wine used traditionally have been eliminated by the more recent wine laws but may be found on older bottles. These are: *Goldbeerenauslese, feine, feinste, hochfeinste, Naturwein, Wachstum, Originalabfüllung, Schlossabzug, Fass no., Fuder no.,* St Nikolaus wine, etc.

In recent years, the wines of Germany have been drunk younger and this is largely due to new technical processes of filtering, racking and fining which expedite the slow natural process. Some people, including the greatest experts, think that great wines cannot properly be made this way, and I think it improbable that the greatest wines are, but it is certainly true that the vast majority of German wine is made in hygienically impeccable press-houses and fermenting vats by the most modern processes. The wine is absolutely delicious, and provided you do not keep it for too long (there would appear to be little point in this except for *Auslese* and higher qualities), I think it can only be helped by modern aids in its making. Since it is now fashionable for German wines to be drunk in the year after, and certainly within three years, of making, there is little cause for concern.

The general procedure in Germany is for the grower to make his own wine and the standard barrel in which the wine is contained is called the *Fuder* on the Moselle and some parts of the Palatinate. It corresponds roughly to the tun and contains 1,000 litres (220 gallons). On the Rhine, the barrel

Wine label terms

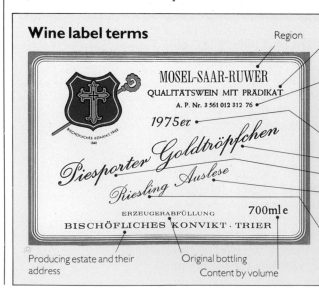

Region

Qualitätswein mit Prädikat (QmP): the highest quality category.

Amtliche Prüfungsnummer. All QbA and QmP wines have an AP No. on the label to show they have been officially tasted and approved.

Vintage

Goldtröpfchen is the vineyard

Piesport is the village name

Auslese is the QmP designation and indicates a good quality sweet wine made from selected bunches of very ripe grapes.

Riesling is the traditional grape variety used for the finest Moselles.

Producing estate and their address

Original bottling

Content by volume

MOSEL-SAAR-RUWER
QUALITÄTSWEIN MIT PRÄDIKAT
A. P. Nr. 3 561 012 312 76
1975er
Piesporter Goldtröpfchen
Riesling Auslese
700ml e
ERZEUGERABFÜLLUNG
BISCHÖFLICHES KONVIKT · TRIER

The steep slopes of the Bernkastel Doktor vineyard, the most famous vineyard of Bernkastel.

is called a *Stück*, and contains 1,200 litres (264 gallons). The *Fuderen* or *Stücken* of wine are then laid by in a cellar and auctions take place throughout the wine-growing districts during the winter months. Some of the wine is bought and sold through brokers, by the great wine-shipping firms in Bernkastel, Mainz, Worms, Bingen and in various larger wine villages in the middle of the vineyards. Sometimes a *Fuder* of especially good wine is kept by the grower for a year or two and sold at a much higher price.

German wine starts life as the palest of pale gold and as it gets older it gets darker. On the last occasion I had the privilege of drinking a 1921 *Trockenbeerenauslese* it had become as dark as *oloroso* sherry, and the edge had gone off its sweetness, but it was still very good.

1971 German wine law

EEC regulations and German wine law stipulate the methods and procedures (including the kind of preservatives) that may be used in the making of wine.

There are basically five categories of wine (described below) which are grouped under two main headings: quality wine and table wine. Unlike France, any German vineyard, whether great or small, may produce both types of wine. The law specifies the minimum sugar content (or must weight) required for each officially recognized quality wine.

Qualitätswein mit Prädikat (QmP). Quality wine with predicate, i.e. superior wines, unsugared, with officially controlled quality designations or predicates, which are, in ascending order of sweetness: *Kabinett, Spätlese, Auslese, Beerenauslese, Trockenbeerenauslese*; also *Eiswein* (see glossary of terms, on page 125).

Qualitätswein bestimmte Anbaugebiete (QbA). Quality wines produced in specific regions. Must be from a single *Anbaugebiet* (see below).

Landwein. A new (1982) designation for superior table wine made from grape juice containing more sugar (leading to more alcohol) than ordinary table wines. Dryish: either *trocken* or *halbtrocken*.

Deutscher Tafelwein (DTW). Wine has to be made from one hundred per cent German grapes and from one *Weinbaugebiet*. Label may show a village name.

Tafelwein. The most basic appellation for table wine. Must be from a single EEC wine-growing zone but not necessarily one hundred per cent German. No village or site names; *Bereich*, or district, names only.

Geographical Divisions

Weinbaugebiete. Areas for the production of table wine (*Tafelwein*, DTW and *Landwein*): Rhein, Mosel, Main, Neckar, Oberrhein.

Anbaugebiete. Specific regions within the five *Weinbaugebiete* for the cultivation of quality wines (QbA or QmP):

Bereich. A district within an *Anbaugebiet* where similar wines are produced. A *Bereich* name on a label always appears with the word 'Bereich', e.g. *Bereich Nierstein* or *Nierstein Bereich* (NB not 'Niersteiner', which is a wine from the village of Nierstein). Other commonly used *Bereich* names: *Bereich Bernkastel* and *Bereich Johannisberg*.

Grosslage. A 'great' site or collection of neighbouring sites producing similar wines, generally including vineyards of several villages. The name of any village within the *Grosslage* can be used for the wines, e.g. *Niersteiner Gutes Domtal*, which could actually come from the nearby village of Dexheim. Other commonly used *Grosslage* names:

Zeller Schwarze Katz, Piesporter Michelsberg, Bernkasteler Kurfürstlay, Bernkasteler Badstube, Binger Schlosskapelle, Rüdesheimer Rosengarten, Johannisberger Erntebringer, Rüdesheimer Burgweg, Niersteiner Auflangen, Oppenheimer Krötenbrunnen, Forster Mariengarten.

Lage or Einzellage. A site or single site. A smaller unit but sometimes covering the vineyards of more than one village. Minimum size of 5 hectares (12.4 acres) (some exceptions).

Ortsteil or Ort. Suburb. Small villages or single estates which have been tacked onto other villages: e.g. Schloss Vollrads is now an Ortsteil of Winkel, though the label may still state simply 'Schloss Vollrads'.

The wines of Germany

The price of German wines depends largely upon their quality designation, although estate-bottled wines from the top properties on the Moselle and in the Rheingau naturally command a premium. Wines can be classed approximately as follows: ★★★★ Trockenbeerenauslese *(very expensive);* ★★★ Beerenauslese, Eiswein *(moderately expensive);* ★★ Auslese, Spätlese *(reasonably priced);* ★ Kabinett, QbA, Tafelwein *(inexpensive).*

Rheingau

White wines almost entirely from Riesling grapes. Superb bouquet; good body, firm, lots of fruit. Very fine, well-balanced and long-lasting wines.
GROWERS: Deinhard, von Mumm, Schloss Eltz, Schloss Johannisberg (von Metternich), Schloss Reinhartshausen, Schloss Vollrads (Matuschka-Greiffenclau), von Schönborn, von Simmern, Staatsweingüter, Geh.-Rat. Julius Wegeler Erben.

Mosel-Saar-Ruwer

Fine white wines from Riesling grapes. Very pale greenish in colour when young; particularly mouth-watering and fruity on the nose; often *spritzig* (a slight liveliness) on the palate. Light and refreshing. In the best years, high acidity, successfully balances sweetness. Excellent *Beerenauslese* and *Trockenbeerenauslese* in good vintages.
GROWERS: Bischöfliches Priesterseminar, Deinhard, Hohe Domkirche, von Kesselstatt, Licht-Bergweiler, J. J. Prüm, Zach Bergweiler Prüm Erben, von Schorlemer, Staatliche Domäne, H. Thanisch, Vereinigte Hospitien, von Schubert, Egon Müller, Friedrich Wilhelm Gymnasium.

Nahe

The finer wines from Riesling grapes. Less intense and softer than Moselles, lighter than Rheingau wines. More ordinary wines from Sylvaner and Müller-Thurgau grapes.
GROWERS: Anheuser, Ludwig Herf, von Plettenberg, Staatliche Domäne.

Rheinhessen

Easy, attractive, soft, ripe, fruity wines, the best from Riesling grapes. Much ordinary wine from Sylvaner and Müller-Thurgau vines.
GROWERS: A. Balbach, Dr R. Senfter, F. K. Schmitt.

Rheinpfalz (Palatinate)

Borders Alsace to the south and produces deeper, fuller wines, more grapy and aromatic, the emphasis on bouquet. Rather delicious. Lots of different grape varieties.
GROWERS: von Buhl, Dr Bürklin-Wolf.

Ahr

Produces fifty-five per cent red wines, light in colour and sharpish. Ordinary white, high in acidity. Little exported.

Franconia (Franken)

Wines high in extract with an earthy or flinty flavour. Mostly dry. Quality wines sold in *Bocksbeutel* or flagons. Many different grape varieties.
GROWERS: Bavarian Domain, Staatsweingut Hofkellerei, Juliusspital, Bürgerspital.

Württemberg

Over fifty per cent red wines and mostly consumed locally. Many grape varieties. Weissherbst (rosé) a speciality.

Baden

The driest and sunniest German wine district. Mostly white wines: fragrant on the nose; full and charming with low acidity on the palate. Dryish. Excellent wines now being exported from the co-operative, Zentralkellerei Badischer Winzergenossenschaften, at Breisach. Many different grapes; Ruländer a speciality. Also Weissherbst (rosé).

German vintages

1963 Disappointing. Some satisfactory light wines.
1964 Medium to good, fruity wines.
1965 A very bad year.
1966 Good quality; fruity and balanced.
1967 Moderate quality but some very good Rheinhesse wines.
1968 Disappointing. Very few useful wines.
1969 Fine vintage, particularly in the Moselle.
1970 An underrated vintage, best in Nahe and Palatinate.
1971 Very good, fruity wines in all districts.
1972 A large quantity of indifferent, although useful, wines.
1973 Attractive, dryish wines.
1974 Similar to 1974.
1975 Excellent wines; elegant, well-balanced, long-lived; particularly fine Moselle-Saar-Ruwer wines.
1976 Excellent wines, richer and heavier than the 1975s.
1977 Disappointing. Most wines in QbA category.
1978 Similar to 1977, but even smaller quantity produced.
1979 Moderately good but some very good Riesling wines.
1980 A very disappointing year though a few acceptable Rheinhesse wines.
1981 Moderately good; most successful areas were Rheingau, Nahe and Middle Moselle.
1982 Large quantity of wine. Drink up.
1983 Very good vintage. Keep Auslese.
1984 But for QbA wines.
1985 Very good quality, promising Riesling.
1986 QbAs have good acidity, few QmP wines.
1987 Moderate. Mostly QbA.

NOTE: On the whole, German wines should be drunk young, i.e., in less than ten years, often much less. However, wines of *Auslese* quality up to the great *Trockenbeerenauslese*, from a fine estate on the Saar or the Ruwer, and particularly of a good vintage, will not necessarily have reached maturity even ten years after the vintage. These wines could still go on improving and their lifespan may be fifteen to twenty years.

A vineyard worker at Graben on the Moselle stops for a break, and a glass of Moselle wine.

Glossary of wine terms

Abfüller. Bottler, i.e. *not* estate bottled.

Affentaler. Red wine from around Neuweier in Baden from Spätburgunder grapes. No village or site names allowed on the label but can be DTW or quality wine.

Amtliche Prüfungsnummer (AP Nr). An eleven-digit number supplied by the government for each bottling of quality wine. Must appear on the label of every bottle.

Aus eigenem Lesegut. 'From our own harvest', i.e. estate bottled.

Auslese. Third-quality QmP, from selected ripe bunches. Varies from grower to grower and according to vintage, but should be sweeter and richer than *Spätlese.* More expensive. Pre-1971 vintage, some Estates used (at their discretion) further sub-divisions of *feine* and *feinste Auslese.*

Bacchus. White grape. New crossing Sylvaner × Riesling × Müller-Thurgau. Similar to Müller-Thurgau but superior in quality. Attractive flowery wines with a hint of Muscat.

Beerenauslese. Second-quality QmP from singly selected grapes affected by *Edelfäule (Botrytis cinerea).* Deeper yellow colour; rich, honeyed and ripe on the nose; sweet, rich, grapy palate. Expensive dessert wine.

Deutscher Prädikatssekt. Quality sparkling German wine.

Deutscher Sekt. Sparkling wine produced in Germany. Base wine may come from elsewhere.

Edelfäule. *Botrytis cinerea (pourriture noble),* the beneficial mould which attacks the grapes, essential for the production of very sweet wines.

Ehrentrudis. Weissherbst from *Bereich* Kaiserstuhl-Tuniberg in Baden. QbA or QmP.

Eiswein. QmP from grapes frozen on the vine when picked and with the necessary sugar level for *Beerenauslese* quality. Sweet, concentrated flavour, high acidity and often a dry, tangy finish. Expensive and overrated.

Erzeuger Abfüllung. Estate bottled.

Faber. White grape, Pinot Blanc × Müller-Thurgau. Attractive full-bodied fruity wine.

Flaschengärung. Equivalent of *méthode Champenoise.*

Gewürztraminer. Pinkish-white grape. White wines, highly aromatic. Rheinpfalz, Rheinhessen.

Gutedel. Red or white grapes. Mild, agreeable white wine. Baden.

Halbtrocken. Medium-dry.

Herb. Brut, dry.

Huxelrebe. White grape, Gutedel × Courtillier Musque. Light, flavoury wines with pungent Muscat flavour.

Kabinett. Fifth-quality QmP, from musts of a higher sugar content than QbA. Natural wines of guaranteed quality. Not very sweet and not expensive.

Kerner. White grape, Trollinger × Riesling. Light- or medium-bodied elegant white wines; slightly Muscaty bouquet. Fresh, clean and delicate.

Liebfraumilch. QbA from Riesling, Sylvaner or Müller-Thurgau grapes grown in the Rheingau, Rheinhessen, Rheinpfalz or Nahe.

Morio-Muskat. Highly scented white grape, Sylvaner × Pinot Blanc. Very strong Muscat bouquet. Rheinpfalz and Rheinhessen.

Müller-Thurgau. The most widely grown white grape of Germany. Mild, fragrant wines, harmonious and pleasant, to be drunk while young and fresh.

Naturrein. Pre-1971, denotes a wine without any added sugar.

Optima. White grape, Sylvaner-Riesling and Müller-Thurgau cross. Lovely fragrant wines.

Ortega. White grape, Müller-Thurgau × Riesling. Wine low in acidity with a fine bouquet. Useful for blending. Early-ripening and sweet.

Perle. Pinkish grape, Gewürztraminer × Müller-Thurgau. Mild, fragrant, slightly Muscaty wines.

Perlwein. Any wine containing a little carbon dioxide but not fully sparkling.

Portugieser. Red grape. Light-coloured mild red wines. Ahr, Rheinhessen, Palatinate and Württemberg.

Qualitätsschaumwein. Quality sparkling wine. One hundred per cent German. Impregnation method not allowed.

Reichensteiner. White grape, Müller-Thurgau cross. Fair quality, rather neutral. Nice fragrant bouquet.

Riesling. The principal white grape making the finest and longest-living wines. All regions, but predominates in the Rheingau, Mosel-Saar-Ruwer and Mittelrhein.

Rotling. DTW or QbA wine from a blend of red and white wine.

Ruländer. (Pinot Gris or Tokay d'Alsace) Red grape making aromatic white wines with low acidity. Baden (Kaiserstuhl) and Franconia.

Schaumwein. Lowest category sparkling wine. Neither necessarily German nor produced in Germany.

Scheurebe. White grape, Sylvaner × Riesling. Fragrant, peachy bouquet, strong flavour, reminiscent of blackcurrants. Rheinhessen, Rheinpfalz and Franconia.

Schillerwein. QbA Rotling from Württemberg only. Pale red.

Spätburgunder. (Pinot Noir) Red grape. Light Burgundy-style wines. Some wines sweetish. Ahr, Baden and Württemberg.

Spätlese. Fourth-quality QmP, from selected overripe bunches. Varies according to origin and vintage but generally sweeter and fuller than *Kabinett.* Pre-1971 vintage, some Estates used (at their discretion) further sub-divisions of *feine* and *feinste Spätlese.*

Steinwein. The name by which Franconian wines are known but, by law, a wine labelled 'Stein' may only come from Wurzburger Stein.

Sylvaner. Widely planted white grape. Good ordinary wines. Rheinhessen, Rheinpfalz, Nahe and Franconia.

Trocken. Dry.

Trockenbeerenauslese. Top-quality QmP from singly selected grapes, shrivelled by *Edelfäule.* Bright rich yellow colour, deepening with age; intense raisiny nose; luscious and rich in the mouth, high in sugar, low in alcohol. Needs high acidity to be successful. Very expensive sweet dessert wine.

Trollinger. Red grape. Light red neutral wines, low in acidity and for early drinking. Württemberg.

Weisser Burgunder. (Pinot Blanc) Light, mild, rounded wines.

Weissherbst. QbA rosé from one grape variety; speciality of Kaiserstuhl.

The Rhine

Above: 50°N passes through the estate of Schloss Johannisberg.

Right: Schloss Vollrads, one of the finest estates of the Rheingau.

Far right: The grape harvest.

Rhine wines are sometimes called Hock and this is derived from Hochheim, which is roughly between Frankfurt and Wiesbaden, and contains fine vineyards. In the early years of Queen Victoria's reign very little Rhenish wine was sent to England, but with the advent of the Prince Consort a few *Stücken* were shipped, and became very popular. Queen Victoria, who had decided preferences in most things, thought that the best of it came from Hochheim and, as is usual when the Crown expresses its opinion, this wine became tremendously popular. Hochheim could not produce enough of it, so it gradually gave its name to the wine generally from that part of the Rhine which is called Rheingau and which does, in fact, produce the greatest of all Hocks. The German wine regulations, which, if anything, are stricter than the French, would not allow any wine other than that from Hochheim to be labelled under that name. So we have the Rhine wines, and those of its tributary the Nahe, known as Hock, and the wines of the Moselle and its tributaries, the Ruwer and the Saar, which are called

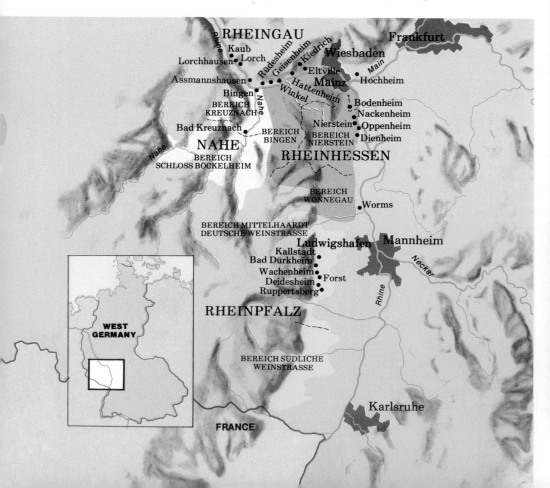

Moselles, and if you want to get a reputation for knowing the difference between them, remember that the Rhine wines, or Hocks, are always sold in brown bottles and Moselles are always sold in green bottles. To make an impression, just observe the colour of the bottle from which the wine is being served. In point of fact, there is quite a difference between the two wines, which, with a little cultivation, you will soon become proficient in noticing. The Moselle wines are a little more light and charming or, as the Germans say, *spritzig*, which means sprightly, but which does not mean sparkling – it means the wine is lively. The great German Hocks have a certain dignity. They are serious wines and the little Moselles chuck them neatly under the chin and run away laughing.

Rheingau

The first of the great Rhine wine districts is the Rheingau – that is to say, the vineyards on the north bank of the Rhine between Lorch and Mainz. There are one or two small vineyards or wine towns on the south bank, but the main ones are on the north. Here we have the classic Schloss Johannisberg, which is still in the von Metternich family and has been for nearly two hundred years, and, what may be even greater, Schloss Vollrads. Both of these famous vineyards make and bottle their own wine, Schloss Johannisberg under Prince von Metternich and Vollrads under Graf Matuschka-Greiffenclau. There are many other vineyards doing the same,

Schloss Johannisberg rises above its vineyards. There are breathtaking views of the Rhine from its terraces.

The Rhine at Oberwesel. A Rhine steamer plies its way down the river; the vineyards rise steeply in the background.

but generally the wine is made and sold by the smaller growers at auction or by private bargain.

The Rheingau really starts with Lorchhausen, comes down to Kaub, which is somewhat inland from the river, then to Lorch, which marks the beginning of the great vineyards: Assmannshausen with its red wine; and Rüdesheim, which has developed into something like a Rhine wine resort – Brighton on the Rhine. Good hotels are found in Rüdesheim, and indeed all along the Rhine. There is always plenty to see with the great life of the Rhine, its steamers, its enormous barges, its pleasure-boats plying busily up and down, and the vineyards and forests at the back of the hills to visit. Above all, there is the famous Drosselgasse, or 'the street of the thrushes', in Rüdesheim. This is a comparatively short and narrow street lined on both sides with enormous German wine cellars that have wonderful bands. During the vintage festival singing and dancing go on all the time, while pretty waitresses rush backwards and forwards with the wine. There is a good deal of competition between the Germans who drink the wine. As one bottle is disposed of and another brought, the empty ones remain in the middle of the table, and towards morning, when the night is far spent, there is sometimes very little of the table left showing. After Rüdesheim come

Geisenheim and Winkel, Mittelheim, Oestrich, Hattenheim and Erbach, while farther up the Rhine are Hallgarten, Eltville, Kiedrich, Martinsthal and Rauenthal. These are all famous names and each of them has many equally famous vineyards. From this district come some of the greatest wines in Germany and, of their kind, some of the greatest in the world.

Rheinhessen

Along the Rhine between Bingen and Worms are the original vineyards of the Rheinhessen in a great horseshoe made by the Rhine and the Nahe. This area contains many famous names that you may have pondered over on the complicated labels, such as Bodenheim, Dienheim, Bingen, Nierstein, Oppenheim and Nackenheim.

Many famous wine houses have their head-quarters in the lovely city of Worms near where the Rhine maidens still guard the Nibelungen treasure, which was thrown into the river. Worms is insepar-able from Liebfraumilch, about which so many stories are told. The true story of Liebfraumilch is not unlike that of Hock, only very much older. Just as Hock derives from the town of Hochheim, so the Liebfraumilch derives from the Church of Our Lady in Worms, which, in the Middle Ages, was a monas-tery whose monks were extremely good makers of wine, rather like Dom Pérignon at Hautvillers. The monks cultivated their vines (which grow right up to the walls of the church itself) and such was their industry and expertise that over the years the wine made by the monks became famous throughout the length and breadth of the land, and of course it was called *Liebfraumilch*, which simply means 'the milk of the Church of Our Lady'. Like Hock, soon there was not nearly enough wine from the vineyards of the Church of Our Lady to supply the demand. Consequently, the local growers and exporters soon matched the wine, or tried to, with wine of a similar standard and dubbed it all Liebfraumilch. And so it still goes everywhere to the uttermost ends of the earth as being a popular and rather sweet wine of moderate price and one which can be drunk with most things.

The true Liebfraumilch is still made and can still be bought, but it is called Liebfrauenstift, which means literally the 'Church foundation'. It is of excellent quality. Only three vintners, one of whom is Langenbach, have vineyards in the Liebfrauen-stift; no others may so describe their wine. The vineyards are cultivated with great care and the wine made from the grapes grown there is ex-tremely rare and hard to come by – there is so very little of it. It is supremely delicate and charming; so delicate that I do not think it should be drunk with food at all, but purely on its own merit with nothing more than a dry biscuit.

View of the vineyards of Deidesheim in the Palatinate.

Rheinpfalz (Palatinate)

The third great wine district of the Rhine proper is the Rheinpfalz or Palatinate. This is south of Worms and the low-lying hills to the west, and contains famous names like Bad Dürkheim, Deidesheim, Forst, Wachenheim, Ruppertsberg, Kallstadt and so on. The Palatinate has been developed for wine growing since Roman times and particularly under the electoral princes of the Palatinate during the heyday of the Holy Roman Empire. Indeed, further extensions of the vineyards had to be stopped because of over-production and the consequent lowering of quality. Actually the Palatinate still produces a greater quantity of wine than any of the other Rhine vineyards or wine-growing provinces. The climate is milder than in the more northern areas. The soil is suitable and, considered as a whole, produces good, clean wines of above aver-age quality. The wine is very reasonable in price and one may always find the exception of a remarkable *Stück* from one of the great vineyards.

Nahe

Finally the wines of the Nahe almost provide a link between Rhine and Moselle both in geography and style. The Nahe Valley stretches south and then west from Bingen and centres on Bad Kreuznach. The wines have a characteristic flowery appeal.

The Moselle, Saar and Ruwer

The most famous vineyard of Wehlen on the Moselle takes its name from the sundial, or sonnenuhr, *on the vineyard wall.*

Where the Luxembourg vineyards leave off, the German vineyards begin, starting at Wasserbillig, going on through Trier, through places with such famous names as Piesport to Bernkastel, and finishing, as far as fine wines are concerned, somewhere near Enkirch, but with a good many vineyards between there and the confluence of the Moselle with the Rhine at Koblenz. There are many long-established and well-known estates in these towns and also several district co-operatives. The fresh and elegant wines they produce should be drunk young, although the fine Rieslings need a little time to give their best.

The particular characteristics of these Moselles were commented on with considerable approval by that wine-loving Roman Ausonius (of Château Ausone in St-Emilion), who lived in the Roman town of Trier for some years and who not only drank and enjoyed the wine but wrote poetry about it. I personally find it extremely difficult to distinguish a wine of one village from another. If they are well made, they are delicious, and they are usually well made. Some are better than others, and some are considerably more expensive. You cannot expect,

and of course this is true of many other wines besides Moselle, to buy the finest wines cheaply, but you can, with Moselle, buy an extremely good wine at a reasonable price.

Probably the most famous vineyard along the Moselle is the Doktor vineyard at Bernkastel. Like most Moselle vineyards, it is on very, very steep, slaty, gritty slopes, which make difficulties for the pickers at the time of the vintage. The grapes are gathered with great care and, when the weather permits, great vintages are made. The Doktor vineyard is sometimes thought to be named after its original proprietor, Dr Thanisch, who by supreme cultivation and application brought it to its well-deserved fame, but this appears to be something of a vinous legend. Certainly the vineyard is *partly* owned by the descendants of Dr Thanisch; there are now three or more wine growers. Some of the stories told about this very famous vineyard are to

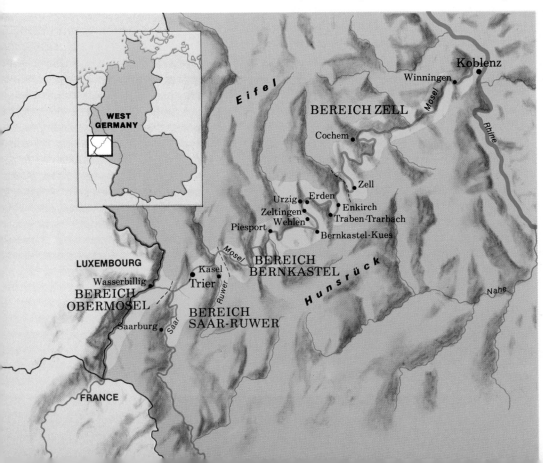

The village of Niederemmel with the vines of Piesporter Gunterslay. The vineyards of Niederemmel are incorporated with those of Piesport across the river.

Below: Planting young vines on the Moselle. The gradients are steep and the soil hard slate, so it is an unenviable task.

be found in *Moselle* by the late Otto Loeb and Terence Prittie (Faber & Faber, 1972).

From Bernkastel, it is not very far to Wehlen, renowned for its famous Sonnenuhr vineyard, partly owned by J. J. Prüm, where some of the finest wines of the Moselle are made. Downstream of the town are Zeltingen, Uerzig, Erden and Traben Trarbach, with the most glorious scenery, an occasional castle and always the Moselle winding round and round through the steep vineyards. Here you may, in one of the many small riverside restaurants, which are not pretentious or expensive, have a delicious light lunch of trout, caught that morning in the Moselle, washed down by the *ordinaire* of the district, which is more likely to be *extraordinaire* under these conditions. In great years the wines of the Saar and Ruwer may surpass all others in Germany thanks to their elegance and balance, which they owe to their higher acidity.

Other German wines

Above: Deinhard & Co. are famous Koblenz merchants and growers, with estates in many different areas.

Right: The picturesque village of Mayschloss in the Ahr, the area that produces Germany's best red wines.

Below: Fermentation tanks in Deinhard's cellars. Modern methods favour stainless steel; each vat has the name of the vineyard.

The Wines of the Middle Rhine are made north of the Rheingau above Koblenz and west of the Ahr. They are generally good, clean, ordinary wines which are better than they used to be. Acceptable wines are made in Baden and Württemberg and most of the German red wines are grown here. They are not particularly remarkable but seem quite receivable, especially if drunk where they are made. A good deal of local red wine is made round Lake Constance and this is nearly all sold in or near Germany and rarely met with abroad. I said as much to that indomitable Frenchman André Simon many years ago, to which he replied, laconically, 'The rarer the better.'

The only other considerable wine district in Germany is the Franconia area. The wine is popularly known as *Steinwein*. It is made rather to the east of the Rhine in the Main Valley, the district round Würzburg due east of Mainz and on the River Main. *Steinwein in Bocksbeutel* is very well known in most parts of the world. The *Bocksbeutel* is a squat flagon which has always been the vessel for the white wines of Franconia. The wine itself is earthy, strong and very good, but sometimes a little sharpish. I cannot go as far as the late Morton Shand, who says in *A Book of Wine* (1900), now alas long out of print:

'There is a sort of family resemblance between all German wines which may be called,

for lack of a better phrase, a sort of vernal floweriness. This characteristic Steinwein possesses in a greater degree than any of its fellows. It has a bland elusive flavour like the smell of a dewy posy of wild flowers, fresh picked by fairy fingers from lush early morning pastures in which the scents, now meadow sweet and ferns, seem to predominate in turn.'

I knew Morton Shand at the end of his life and I greatly respect his memory and his writings, but I must say that when it comes to *Steinwein in Bocksbeutel*, and I have had very many, I cannot say more than that it is an extremely good wine. I hope that you are curious enough to check him on it.

The origin of the *Bocksbeutel* itself is lost in antiquity and to quote Shand again:

'It is a silly kind of bottle, difficult to ship, easy to break, it cannot be binned with any kind of facility, but it is a splendid vehicle for carrying the rather lush heraldic labels of Franconia.'

It seems that any attempt to alter the shape of the bottle has been bitterly fought and indeed defeated by the local growers. Well, it may be truly said that there is good wine even in a bad bottle. The red wines of Franconia, which are unremarkable, are sold in normal slim 'German' bottles.

Sekt and sparkling wine

There is no special district, like Champagne in France, in which all the grapes are used for making sparkling wine. Under the 1920 Peace Treaty, the Germans were forbidden by law to call their sparkling wine Champagne and they have not done so since. Along the length of the Rhine there are very good wine firms who make brands of sparkling wine, which is called Sekt, from selected wine. Some of this is made by the *méthode champenoise*. Researchers have found that the Germans were making sparkling wine before Dom Pérignon in Champagne, and it has developed in Germany over the centuries into quite a major industry. Sekt is made by two methods, by the *méthode champenoise*, and, in the case of the much cheaper *Schaumwein*, by vat storage. Sometimes, alas!, impregnation of carbonic acid gas produces the desired sparkle. The cheaper wines, whatever the label may say, should be avoided, for they are neither good to drink nor interesting in any way. The label is often pretentious (and this, of course, is true in France too), but the contents are not amazing. The true Sekt however will, if served properly, reach a very high standard and, while it is not Champagne, it has a good deal of character of its own. I should also mention sparkling Moselle, which has a pleasant grape character. There are many well-known brands of Sekt, and among the best are:

Deinhard & Co; Kupferberg; Henkell; Matheus Müller; Söhnlein and Langenbach.

ITALY

Right: Vineyards in the Marche near Ancona. Verdicchio dei Castelli di Jesi is the best wine.

The vine grows everywhere in sunny Italy and wherever the vine grows wine is made. Mostly it is very good wine. There are places in Italy where rough wine is sold at a rough price, but by and large one can drink good wine at a reasonable price anywhere. Outside of Italy, it is among the cheaper wines of quality and in my view excellent value and rarely disappointing. Sometimes it is a bit heavy to our tastes but nonetheless very drinkable.

Most Italian wines are honest and although it is illegal to *chaptalize* anywhere in Italy, the addition of concentrated must, often from similar locally

produced grapes and at levels of from five to fifteen per cent, is permitted depending on the particular wine. However, the sun shines strongly during the Italian summers and ripens the grapes well and little added sugar is needed, if any. Both black and white grapes flourish and red and gold wines are traditional in their districts.

Italy is now the greatest wine producer in the world and in 1981 produced considerably more than France. Wine is of supreme importance to the Italian economy so it needs to be not only good but respected, and for this reason the government has set up a system of controls and checks, the fulcrum of which are the DOC and DOCG categories of wines.

DOC's envisaged function was to establish in geographic, tasting and chemical terms the traditional character of a given wine, but the quality aspect, although always implicit, was never actually put into words in the laws; with each DOCG regulation the quality emphasis is explicit (see opposite).

There is a further classification required legally for certain wines. The addition of *classico* means that the wine has been made from grapes grown in the original production heartland before the DOC area was extended. Apart from Chianti, other wines with *classico* sectors are Orvieto, Soave,

Valpolicella and Bardolino. Santa Maddalena in German-speaking Alto Adige is another one, but here *classico* is translated as *klassisches Ursprungsgebiet*. The words *metodo classico* on a label indicate a sparkling wine made by the Champagne method.

The term *superiore* means the wine is higher in alcoholic strength than the legal minimum; *not* higher in quality. The term *riserva* means that the wine has been aged for a prescribed extra period of time, often in wood. The minimum for Chianti is three years, while for Barolo it is four years.

Much experimentation takes place in Italy and many of the most respected growers know that they can produce wines of intrinsic high quality outside the DOC regulations and indeed outside the DOC areas. The best example of the latter is Sassicaia, made from a claret grape on the coast south of Leghorn where no DOC laws are deemed worth the creating. Yet the wine is outstanding by any standards – 'perhaps Italy's best red' says Hugh Johnson – expensive and a *vino da tavola*, since EEC law requires all wines to have a category and since no DOC or DOCG area exists to enclose it. Hence the term *vino da tavola* may mean supermarket wholesomes or high-quality individual wines; one can tell only from its price.

Above: Traditional equipment used for keeping the vineyards in good order throughout the year.

Below: After the vintage the colourful modern bins used for collecting the grapes are stacked up to dry.

Left: Vineyards near Dudda in the Chianti region. Cypresses are as much a part of the Tuscan countryside as vines.

Opposite: Walking home in the early evening through vineyards in Veneto.

Italian wine law

The aim in Italian legislation is to stabilise the *character* of a wine in addition to its *location* of production. This means that, for DOC and DOCG, both grapes and proportions used are *compulsory*, whereas legislation in other countries nominate *eligible* grapes, not all of which need be used.

Denominazione di Origine Controllata e Garantita (DOCG). The honours list, roughly similar to the basic idea behind Germany's *Qualitätswein mit Prädikat*. It has the same structure as DOC (see below) but the quality aspect is emphasised with rigorous tasting panel controls. Only five top quality areas have been guaranteed in this category so far – Barolo, Barbaresco, Brunello di Montalcino, Vino Nobile di Montepulciano and Chianti.

Denominazione di Origine Controllata (DOC). Similar to France's *Appellation Contrôlée*. For each wine name the law stipulates grape-types and proportions to be used, geographic location of production, yield per hectare, minimum alcoholic strength, minimum periods of maturation, etc. *Chaptalization* is not permitted. If permitted production per hectare is exceeded the entire crop for intended DOC is invalidated (in comparison with AC in France where only excess is declassified).

Vini Tipici This is a wine typical or representative of a given area. Legislation is now being finalised and, when in force, will regulate wines from specific grapes and areas as with DOC but to less stringent degree. Equivalent to French *Vins de Pays*.

Vino da Tavola con Indicazione Geografica. Table wine (see below) produced within a zone demarcated by law.

Vino da Tavola. Table wine, but a term to be treated with caution. In most cases the simplest category, embracing all wines not eligible for those above. No compulsory grape or area specification. Most is modest, wholesome and inexpensive, but the term also covers many high-quality, often expensive, more individualistic wines from producers who choose not to be bound by DOC regulations.

Wine label terms

Name of estate

Type of wine: Chianti *Classico* indicates a wine from the centre, which is the best part of the Chianti zone.

The quality status of the wine: DOC

Original bottling at the estate's cellars

Name and address of proprietor

Content by volume

Alcohol content by volume

Vintage

Above: Carboys of Valpolicella in the cellars of Masi, one of the best producers of the Veneto.

Piedmont (Piemonte)

In Piedmont, over the border from France, are made perhaps the greatest wines that come from Italy. Barolo, Barbaresco and Gattinara are all wines that can hold up their heads against the classic growths of France and Germany and which will live to a great age and improve with time. I myself have drunk Gattinara more than thirty years old which showed no sign of fading. These wines are made from the Nebbiolo grape and, as Michelin would say, worth a considerable detour to sample, although your wine supplier will probably save you the trouble and expense, and be very pleased to do so. I never visit Italy without drinking Gattinara and praising God to be alive to do so, and when at home, I occasionally have a bottle of Barolo or Barbaresco or one of the other Nebbiolo grape wines (such as Carema, Fara, Ghemme, Sizzano, etc.) to keep my palate and memory lively.

The quality of the Piedmont vineyard is indicated by its thirty-seven separate DOCs; some Italian regions have only one. Many of these delimit good everyday wines, including some from the same grape grown in different locations, e.g. Barbera d'Asti, Barbera d'Alba, etc. Other good reds in Piedmont are those made from the Dolcetto grape, the high-quality, brilliant Bonarda and the light, sweet Malvasia (also rosé). Among the recently greatly improved whites are Cortese di Gavi and Arneis. Moscato is sweet and its DOC spumante from Asti is extremely well known (see page 147).

Lombardy

In north-west Lombardy the Nebbiolo grape is grown (known as the Chiavennasca) and used in Valtellina wines. They come across as lighter versions of Barolo from neighbouring Piedmont and need less time to come round to optimum maturity. The geographic sub-denominations of Sassella, Grumello, Valgella and Inferno (!) are particularly noteworthy. DOC Oltrepò Pavese covers seven styles of wine, from fresh whites like Riesling and Pinot (plus an excellent fresh red Bonarda) to tannic and deepish reds. The distinguished Frecciarossa wines are now included in DOC Oltrepò Pavese under different grape headings.

Trentino-Alto Adige

The people of the Alto Adige, the northern part of this autonomous region which abuts onto Austria, are German-speaking and prefer to use the alternative name Südtirol, South Tyrol, for their beautiful part of the world. They make wines of an understated, classical and often austere style, using grape types whose names are familiar to English-speaking consumers – Riesling, Cabernet, Gewürztraminer, Merlot, etc – and in bottle liveries wholly German in appearance.

White wines predominate and have excellent balance, crispness and acidity not often expected of Italian wines. Although many of the grapes used are associated with Alsace, Alto Adige wines are less dry. The Gewürztraminer grape is thought to have originated near the little Alpine village of Tramin (Termeno). The reds are also well made but often misunderstood. The Cabernet is not made simply to ape claret: the usual style is fuller, rounder and younger, if anything more akin to Loire Cabernet.

The most important grape particular to the region is red Schiava (Vernatsch)·from which come Santa Maddalena and Caldaro. The former, said to have been Mussolini's favourite, can be a wine of impressive depth and complexity. The Trentino area uses similar grapes although the Teroldego is native and yields an interesting if tannic red.

Veneto

One of the most famous white wines of Italy is Soave; delicate, light and made in the district of Soave between Verona and Vicenza. It is sold in most of the northern Italian cities (and in most civilised places in the world), and is extremely well balanced, dry and flavourful. It has a light straw colour. Must made from semi-dried Soave grapes also makes a good dessert wine. This is called Recioto di Soave, which means very simply that the wine is made from the outside grapes of the bunch, which are left to shrivel, thereby developing more sugar. The wine is therefore richer in alcohol and attains an attractive raisiny sweetness.

The red Veneto counterpart to Soave is Valpolicella, a lightish, approachable wine which is never completely dry. It is one of Italy's top export wines. Semi-dried Valpolicella grapes are also used to produce two different styles of Recioto wine. Recioto Amarone is dry and powerful (minimum 14° alcohol by volume) but also velvet-smooth and fine. 'Amarone' refers to the slightly bitter tang that is part of the complex finish of the wine. Recioto della Valpolicella is a dessert wine that can reach a really startling alcoholic content of 16° but without being in any way over-sweet or ultra-heavy. Frankly I think it is fantastic wine but I would not like to drink a bottle of it. It is also among the more expensive of Italian wines outside its country of origin but well worth it. I would not recommend drinking it as an aperitif or table wine but probably as an alternative to port or Madeira. Bardolino, from the same grapes as Valpolicella, plus the Negrara, is predictably similar to it and preferred by some. Certainly 'straight' Bardolino often has the edge for flavour on 'straight' Valpolicella, while the latter's *classico* wine usually turns the tables.

French grapes like Cabernet and Merlot as vinified in the Piave and Pramaggiore are interesting and worth seeking out.

Opposite: The vineyards of Soave, seen from the hilltop village, with those of Valpolicella in the far distance.

Some recommended wines from the provinces of Piedmont, Lombardy and Trentino-Alto Adige are briefly described below. Most Italian wines are reasonably priced and the star coding is used here as an indication of the quality of the wine: (★★★★) exceptional; (★★★) very good; (★★) good. Stars refer only to wines and growers specified.

Piedmont

Region of north-west Italy regarded as top producing area of quality wines. Barolo, Barbaresco and other fine Nebbiolo reds are produced here as are dry whites, fruity young reds and sweet dessert wines.

Barolo ★★★—★★★★ Dry red. Deep, tarry, concentrated and tannic.
GROWERS: Borgogno, Franco Fiorina, Prunotto.

Barbaresco ★★★—★★★★ Dry red. Not as austere or robust as Barolo; often reaches impressive elegance without losing its positive personality.
GROWERS: Gaja, Rinaldi, Pio Cesare.
NOTE: The following dry red wines have similar broad characteristics to the above and derive from various proportions of Nebbiolo but different production areas within Piedmont.

Gattinara ★★★★ Good depth and very fine finish.
GROWERS: Mario Antoniolo, Le Colline.

Boca ★★★ Sometimes less than 50% Nebbiolo, yet always has the distinctive tarry smoothness.
GROWER: Lorenzo Bertolo.

Sizzano ★★★ Less tannic or austere than Barolo.
GROWERS: C. S. Sizzano e Ghemme.

Ghemme ★★★ Medium-bodied, complex yet rounded.
GROWER: Agostino Brugo.

Caramino ★★★ Best when over seven years old.
GROWER: Luigi Dessilani.

Carema ★★★★ Distinguished. Lighter and finer than Barolo, but with lasting finish.
GROWER: Luigi Ferrando.

Gavi dei Gavi ★★★★ Splendid dry white, very elegant and balanced. Tiny production.
GROWER: La Scolca.

Dolcetto ★★ Dryish red, mouth-filling, fruity, Beaujolais-like. (Many good producing houses.)

Lombardy

In northern Italy, a region which receives wine-growing influences from all around. Frothy light reds, Germanic-styled whites and Barolo stand-ins – they are all here and more.

Clastidium ★★★★ Rare aromatic dry white, aged in wood, from Pino Grigio and Pinot Nero grapes.
GROWER: Angelo Ballabio.

Sassella Valtellina Superiore ★★★ Velvety, warming, well-balanced dry red from Chiavennasca (Nebbiolo) grapes. Lighter (but not light!) and less tannic than Barolo.
GROWER: Nera.

Oltrepò Pavese Frecciarossa ★★★ Very fine individualistic dry red.
GROWER: Odero.

Oltrepò Pavese Riesling Frecciarossa ★★★ The elegant, dry white counterpart to the above. Splendidly assertive.
GROWER: Odero.

Trentino-Alto Adige

A region in north-east Italy where wine-production is of an extremely high standard but it divides into: a) easily understood reds (Marzemino. Santa Maddalena, some Merlot) and whites (Riesling, Müller-Thurgau, Pinot Grigio), and b) other reds (Teroldego, Cabernet, Caldaro, Lagrein) and whites (Gewürztraminer) for which one must acquire the taste.

Foianeghe ★★★ Another Cabernet/Merlot blend in this Südtirol mould which is concentrated and powerful in flavour with pronounced fruity assertiveness.
GROWER: Conti Bossi Fedrigotti.

Gewürztraminer ★★★ Less dry and with fuller aroma and general style than in Alsace.
GROWERS: Hofstätter, Wilhelm Walch.

Emilia Romagna

Lambrusco di Sorbara, made from the Lambrusco grape grown in vineyards in the province of Modena, is brilliant red in colour and characteristic in flavour, but it can be sweetish and very fruity. It has a *frizzante* (or *pétillant*) quality and foams at the brim. It is supposed to be good with fat foods, and it is appreciated by most people who like their wine on the sweet side.

There are three other Lambrusco DOCs and numerous non-DOC wines, many of which are available in the UK, and several dry versions are starting to appear here.

Sangiovese di Romagna comes from the hills of Romagna. It is a wine with body plus a dry flavour and it has a reputation for keeping well. Its highly drinkable white partner is Trebbiano di Romagna, which has well-balanced fruit and acidity. Albana di Romagna Secco is a deep golden-yellow wine of the same district, very agreeable to those who like their wine dry. It is velvety and altogether a pleasing wine. There is a sweeter quality (*amabile*) which is suitable for drinking with a dessert. Albana di Romagna is currently under examination for promotion to DOCG ranking.

A red worthy of note is Gutturnio dei Colli Piacentini, from Barbera and Bonarda vines. It is a smooth, elegant, positively flavoured wine and one wonders why this grape combination has not been tried more often by producers elsewhere.

Friuli-Venezia Giulia

Friuli's wines are broadly similar to most of those of adjacent Trentino-Alto Adige and many of the grapes used are the same. Although the region is Italian-speaking, it is legal for label information to appear in Slovenian as well as Italian – the border with Yugoslavia is very close. Again the whites are better-known – Tocai, Pinot Grigio, Verduzzo – although a greater volume of red is actually produced. Cabernet and Merlot have an engaging, youthful, fruity style. The native Refosco also is often made this way but some producers make a deeper, more resonant wine which is absolutely splendid.

Picolit, Friuli's famed dessert wine, is extremely expensive because it is notoriously difficult to produce. Some production is achieved, however, although only in Colli Orientali is it DOC.

Liguria

This is the beautiful boomerang-shaped stretch of coast which curves west from Tuscany towards France. Cinque Terre (the Five Lands) is the name of one of the two DOCs but it is better known for the dramatic location of the vineyards. Terraced on Moselle-like cliffs which dive downwards into the Mediterranean, the vines take a lot of husbanding.

Above: A cellarman at Biondi Santi opening bottles of Brunello di Montalcino. Biondi Santi make the finest Brunello of all.

Italian vintages (north)

1965	Very varied. Soave excellent; Umbria and Marche good to excellent; Piedmont good. Avoid Lombardy and north-east. Others mediocre.
1966	Soave excellent; rest of Veneto good; north-east mainly good; non-Classico Chianti mediocre. Most others good to excellent.
1967	Mainly good to excellent. Some exceptional reds.
1968	Good to excellent. Some exceptional in Umbria and Marche; mediocre in north-east and Lombardy.
1969	Very good; some exceptional. Chianti Classico excellent.
1970	Mainly excellent; some exceptional. Friuli, however, mediocre.
1971	Good to excellent; some exceptional. In Tuscany and Emilia-Romagna high-quality reds variable.
1972	Mainly mediocre, but some excellent in north-east and Tuscany. Avoid Piedmont, Lombardy and Brunello di Montalcino.
1973	Some good to excellent in south of zone but otherwise much mediocre wine produced, including in Chianti.
1974	Mainly good to excellent, although Lombardy and some Tuscans disappointing with Marche below par.
1975	Excellent in north-east and south of zone. Some good Valtellina, otherwise patchy.
1976	Very wide variation, particularly in north-east. Excellent in Veneto; good Oltrepò Pavese and Albana di Romagna; mediocre in Tuscany, Emilia-Romagna, Umbria and Marche.
1977	Difficult year. Excellent in Veneto and southern belt of zone; Valtellina poor. Otherwise a cross-section depending on locality.
1978	Mainly good to excellent. Some exceptional in Piedmont, Lombardy and Chianti Classico. Some disappointing reds in Trentino.
1979	Excellent in Piedmont, Veneto, Tuscany, Emilia-Romagna, Umbria and Marche. Good to very good in Lombardy and north-east, although latter's whites had problems.
1980	Mainly good. Very good in Piedmont and south Lombardy; good in Veneto; Orvieto modest.
1981	Brunello di Montalcino exceptional; excellent Soave, Bardolino and Verdicchio. Mainly good throughout the zone but varied in the north-east. Non-Classico Chianti mediocre.
1982	Mainly excellent. Many reds exceptional. Whites with good body, excellent fruit and balance.
1983	Mainly very good, excellent in Veneto.
1984	Variable year, very good in Veneto, fair in Tuscany.
1985	Mainly excellent, some exceptional.
1986	Good to excellent.
1987	Moderate.

No road serves the entire vineyard area and it is said that some of the terraces are accessible only by boat. Sweet Cinqueterre is called Sciacchetrà, which sounds less like a denomination and more like a sneeze. The other DOC is red Rossese di Dolce-aqua, variable according to who makes it, but which numbers Napoleon among its past admirers.

Tuscany (Toscana)

The best-known wine of Italy in the English market is Chianti, the great wine of Tuscany, which is made from grapes grown in the hills around Arezzo, Florence and Pisa. The best Chianti is (according to legend) reputed to be made to a more or less secret formula. It is said to contain three different kinds of grapes, which is true, and also a certain herb, which may not be true, and you can believe it if you want to. It is also said that unless this herb occurs in the district of origin, good Chianti cannot be made.

The Chianti Classico, made only in the districts lying between Florence and Siena, may have a distinguishing external sign of a black cockerel on the neck label. Chianti at its best, drunk, shall we say, in Pisa, Florence or Siena, may be a mature, complex, high-quality, vintage wine or a young, clean, heady wine made by the zest-giving *governo* process – either way, in my view, quite delicious. (The *governo* system is part of the process used for making young Chianti, although it is less common now. Must from grapes which have been semi-dried is added to the wine and this induces a new fermentation. The result is an added richness and a slight 'prickle' in the wine.) Two famous consortia of growers do much to maintain production standards well above the legal minima. The Consorzio Chianti Classico (Black Cockerel) tends the centrally located wine of that name, and the Consorzio Chianti Putto (Cherub) fosters wine from six other separately designated Chianti regions. Many of the constituent producers make both a simple quaffing Chianti for drinking young, often but not necessarily in the famous flasks, and a finer, more interesting vintage wine. There is a growing tendency among growers these days to improve the quality even more by non-inclusion of the traditionally permitted white grapes.

Below: The stunning scenery of the Ligurian coast with its steep terraces is the home of Cinqueterre, a little-known fragrant white wine.

Above: Traditional bins for carrying grapes stacked up in a vineyard.

Right: Dramatic views looking north from the town of San Gimignano, with the vineyards of vernaccia di San Gimignano on rugged hillsides.

People do not associate Chianti and Italian wines generally with any special keeping qualities, but I can vouch that they can keep for a very long while. I acquired some years ago a bin of Barone Ricasoli Chianti of 1921, which had become mellow with age and in its fifty-first year had a breed and distinction which would not dishonour a good Médoc or Burgundy. The romantic story of Ricasoli and Chianti is delightfully told in Cyril Ray's splendid work on Italian wines *The New Book of Italian Wines* (Sidgwick and Jackson, 1982).

The 'noble wine' of Montepulciano, now DOCG category, is a rich garnet colour and all the better for a few years' keeping, when it develops a very good bouquet. There are outstanding examples from Poderi Boscarelli and Fassati.

Brunello di Montalcino is a dark red, rather dry wine of strong flavour which is altogether to be recommended.

Moscadello is an aromatic Muscat wine, rather sweet to our taste but a good dessert wine, with a bright golden colour.

Montecarlo wines are both dry and excellent in their class. They are made from grapes grown on the hills of Valdinievole. They are splendid with fish, and all the better for a year or two in cask.

Vernaccia di San Gimignano is made from Vernaccia grapes and comes from the beautiful mountain town of San Gimignano with its myriad towers, each one trying to be higher than the next. An altogether unforgettable experience is to sit outside a café on an evening in May in the square of San Gimignano, with the towers all around, and drink this velvety, straw-coloured wine.

There are several types of wine made in Elba. The white is light, straw coloured and has rather a strong bouquet. It is a very clean wine of considerable character. The traditional style of red wine, almost black in colour with a strong bouquet, is rather sweet for a red wine. It is made from Aleatico grapes and is only really relevant if you are there on holiday. Modern reds, however, are vinified to be lighter and dry; they are made from the Sangioveto grape, which is a variation of Chianti's Sangiovese.

Vino Santo Toscano is made in several parts of Tuscany from overripe grapes. It is rather sweet, delicately perfumed and, with age, makes an excellent dessert wine.

Umbria

The famous white wine of Orvieto rivals the red Chiantis, and it is worth taking the trouble to find *classico* versions. *Secco* (dry) and *abboccato* (medium-sweet) are the usual styles. It is extremely well balanced and clean, and is best drunk in an open-air restaurant overlooking the hills, somewhere near the Villa Borghese.

Lungarotti produce red Rubesco, smooth and mouth-filling, and a good white, both of which qualify as DOC Torgiano. They have done some experimentation in recent years with French grapes and good-quality Cabernet Sauvignon and Chardonnay wines are now in full production.

Latium (Lazio)

South-east of Rome near the Alban Hills are the Castelli Romani. These little hill towns nestle amid not very high peaks. Once they were fortified, but now are surrounded by their vineyards. My idea of heaven is to sit on a summer's day on the terrace of a restaurant looking down on the perfect circle of Lake Nemi drinking the local wine, which is probably made from grapes from the vineyard stretching down below the restaurant to the water's edge. I do not think the wines are exported and I doubt if they will travel, but they are delicious.

Probably the best-known wine from Latium is Frascati, the town of which is very close to Rome. Mainly from Malvasia and Trebbiano grapes, it traditionally has *secco* (dry), *amabile* (medium-sweet) and *cannellino* (sweet) styles although the first two are more widespread. The quality has improved noticeably over the last few years.

I suppose everybody knows the story of Est! Est!! Est!!! of Montefiascone, but in case not, here it is. Bishop Fugger of Bavaria, on a visit to Rome in AD 1110, sent his steward before him to mark the place where he should eat and where he should stay overnight, and particularly to note the inns with the best wine. The steward went his way, marking the inn of his choice with '*est*', that is 'Here is good wine' (*vinum bonum est*). And so all went well until the steward came to Montefiascone, and there the wine was so marvellous, he wrote emphatically in large characters, '*Est! Est!! Est!!!*' It is a very excellent wine indeed, with a very high reputation which I am not quite sure it fully deserves. But don't make any mistake about it, it is excellent, if rather sweet, and made from Trebbiano and Malvasia grapes. The Bishop, by the way, is reputed to have gone no further and stayed drinking his Est! Est!! Est!!! until the day he died.

Aleatico is the red wine of the Gradoli district. It has purple bubbles winking at the brim, and it is in fact quite sweet. Marino, white and from a similar grape mix to Frascati, is attractive, dryish and worth looking out for.

Some recommended wines from the northern provinces are briefly described below. Most Italian wines are reasonably priced and the star coding is used here as an indication of the quality of the wine: (★★★★) exceptional; (★★★) very good; (★★) good. Stars refer only to wines and growers specified.

Veneto

North-eastern region known for low-priced Soave.
Campo Fiorin ★★★ Rounded dry red with body and pleasing tartness.
GROWER: Az. Agric. Masi.
Soave ★★★★ If only all Soave were like this…!
GROWER: Pieropan.
Recioto Amarone ★★★ Tangy dry red from grapes of Valpolicella. Full and velvety with attractive finishing tartness.
GROWERS: Masi, Santa Sofia.
Venegazzù ★★★ Interesting dry red with distinctive style and good fruit from four claret grapes, including Malbec.
GROWER: Conti Loredan Gasparini.

Emilia-Romagna

North-Italian region distinguished by its rich cuisine and known for its four DOC Lambrusco *frizzanti*.
Albana di Romagna ★★★ The *secco* version is a clean, well-balanced white with a pleasing background tartness.
GROWER: Pasolini dall'Onda.
Gutturnio dei Colli Piacentini ★★ Dry red from mainly Barbera grapes. Extremely smooth with good flavour and balance.
GROWER: Castello di Prato Ottesola.

Friuli-Venezia Giulia

Region in north-east Italy with high standards of production.
Pinot Grigio Grave del Friuli ★★ Dry white with good draw and fruit. Good positive finish.
GROWER: Morassutti.
Picolit Colli Orientali ★★★★ Famous white dessert wine with distinctive aroma and flavour behind the honey.
GROWER: E. Collavini.
Verduzzo Colli Orientali Amabile ★★★ Extremely good balance and gratifyingly rounded for a light white.
GROWER: Ronchi di Fornaz.

An old-fashioned filter using calico bags in the cellars of Falcini.

Some recommended wines from the central Italian provinces are briefly described below. Most Italian wines are reasonably priced and the star coding is used here as an indication of the quality of the wine: (★★★★) exceptional; (★★★) very good; (★★) good. Stars refer only to wines and growers specified.

Tuscany
Within this west-Italian region much high-quality wine is underrated because of the familiarity of the name Chianti. All styles, red and white, dry to sweet, are produced throughout Tuscany and the very best are outstanding while remaining relatively unknown in the outside world.

Brunello di Montalcino ★★★★ Vaunted by many as Italy's best dry red. Capacity to mature akin to that of first-growth clarets and when well-developed is silky, spare and long-lasting.
GROWERS: Biondi-Santi, Castelgiocondo.

Carmignano ★★★★ Elegant, succulent, dry red from Chianti grape-mix plus Cabernet.
GROWER: Tenuta di Capezzana.

Chianti Classico Castello di Volpaia ★★★ Assured, stylish, dry red with backbone and insistent concentrated fruit flavour.
GROWER: Volpaia.

Chianti Putto Rufina Nipozzano ★★★ Nipozzano is a soft, full dry red which shows that *Classico* does not have it all.
GROWER: Frescobaldi.

Sassicaia ★★★★ Concentrated, complex, almost spicy depth of flavour. Rounded but elegant. From Cabernet Sauvignon.
GROWER: Marchesi Incisa della Rocchetta.

Tignanello ★★★★ Wood-aged, dry red from Chianti grapes plus 10% Cabernet. Complex, polished and impressive.
GROWER: Marchesi Antinori.

Vino Nobile di Montepulciano ★★★—★★★★ Spare dry red with medium body and gently tannic, tarry finesse.
GROWER: Fassati.

Umbria
This central-Italian region has been summed up as: 'one producer (Lungarotti) and one wine (Orvieto) although the former does not produce the latter'. The company is certainly restlessly innovative and, for me, in a class by itself. All three wines below are theirs.

Rubesco Riserva ★★★★ Full, generous and devoid of sharpness or toughness. Attractive dry red.

Cabernet Sauvignon di Miralduolo ★★★ Tight, deep, rounded and chewy. Splendid dry red.

San Giorgio ★★★ A most impressive dry red. Smooth, well-knit and bountiful.

Latium
The west-central region around Rome is better known for the white wines among its eighteen DOCs. Unjustifiably overshadowed are a clutch of extremely worthy ★★ reds.

Cesanese del Piglio ★★ Slightly tannic dry red, but otherwise soft and nicely rounded.
GROWER: La Selva.

Torre Ercolana ★★★★ Interesting, polished, dry red, also from Cesanese, and including claret grapes. Tiny production and expensive.
GROWER: Colacicchi.

Abruzzi
East-central region now coming into its own in quality wine production. Reds are full and exuberant; whites are much lighter and often quite ordinary.

Montepulciano d'Abruzzo ★★★ Velvety red with positive style and dry flavour.
GROWERS: Edoardo Valentini, Emidio Pepe.

The Marches
East Italian region producing honest, straightforward whites and reds – needs to talk more about its wines in the market-place. Best known for its two Verdicchio wines and some good reds.

Rosso Cònero ★★★ Deepish, worthy, dry red from Montepulciano grapes.
GROWER: Umani Ronchi.

Abruzzi and Molise
Even in Italy the Abruzzi region is a world apart, separated from Rome by the Appenines, where brown bears still roam free in the wild. Abruzzi still has only two DOCs and its satellite Molise also has two. Montepulciano d'Abruzzo is a warming velvety red that deserves a lot of success, not least for its being as yet inexpensive.

The Marches (Marche)
Verdicchio is the best-known name from this coastal region east of Umbria, although it figures in two separate DOCs. That of the Castelli di Jesi is almost universal while Verdicchio di Matelica – predictably similar in style – is rare. A sparkling Verdicchio is also made and Vernaccia di Serrapetrona is a sparkling red. Rosso Cònero is a red from the identical grape-mix to that of Abruzzi's DOC Montepulciano but the style is younger and more tangy. Rosso Piceno uses the same grapes as Cònero but in different proportions

Campania
The wines of Falerno are famous for their keeping quality. The Roman poet Horace reputedly cried aloud, 'O for Falernian wine an hundred years old.' Falerno is a rival claimant with the wine of Capua for descent from Horace. It is made just north of Naples in the fantastic district known as the Campi Flegrei, the Greeks' Phlegrean Fields, and in the districts of Formia and Mondragone. Strong, and deep ruby red in colour, it is very good indeed. I have never tasted Falerno wine 'an hundred years old', but I would like to.

Italy is not over-burdened with outstanding whites and the southern half of the country is often dismissed as unproductive of anything other than cutting wines. However, Fiano, from hill-girt Avellino, stands out as an elegant and very distinctive dry white. Greco di Tufo is another fine dry white grown nearby. Fiano and Greco are the grapes and Avellino and Tufo the nearest towns – this pattern is logical and hence widespread in Italian wine nomenclature. Taurasi is the region's greatest red wine and rich and smooth it is! A cousin of Basilicata's Aglianico del Vulture, it derives from the same grapes. It must spend one year in wood and its four-year-old *riservas* are most impressive.

Lacrima Christi comes to us both red and white. It is grown on the slopes of Vesuvius. The white is amber tinted, superlatively delicate and slightly aromatic – an extremely good wine with the superb fish of the district. The red wine from the eastern and southern slopes of Mount Vesuvius is brilliant red and smooth to the taste. There is an ordinary Vesuvius wine made on the south-east slopes with rather less alcohol content. It is purplish in colour, but extremely pleasing.

The wine of Capri is straw-coloured, and very pleasant, but Capri is so beautiful that it would be difficult to find a bad wine.

Apulia (Puglia) and Basilicata

San Severo white is a pale yellow wine that can be quite strong, with a dry, velvety taste. Red and *rosato* wines are also made.

Martina Franca and Locorotondo, from the hills of the Martina Franca, are slightly greenish-straw-coloured and dry in flavour. Both producing areas also make good table wines which are the basis for both the local vermouth and, when sold to the big makers, that made in vast quantities in Turin.

Castel del Monte can be either deep ruby red, rosé or white, and the rosé, which is rather fruity but dry and smooth, is especially noted.

Aglianico del Vulture, as yet Basilicata's only DOC wine, is one of Italy's most distinguished wines and is garnet red in colour with a full round taste. It is a remarkably good wine from a poor region of Italy.

A not uncommon sight in Italy. Oxen are used in more rural areas to pull a plough in the vineyards.

Left: Pruning the high-trained vines of the Veneto.

Italian vintages (south)

1965	Good to excellent. Avoid Sardinia.
1966	Good to excellent in south, more varied elsewhere.
1967	Good to excellent.
1968	Excellent; many exceptional.
1969	Mostly good. Some excellent, including Puglia. Avoid Calabria.
1970	Good to excellent.
1971	Similar to 1970, but Sardinia disappointing.
1972	Good to excellent in southern part of zone. Campania and northern section mediocre. Avoid Basilicata.
1973	Mainly excellent.
1974	Excellent in Abruzzi. Otherwise good, although poor in Lazio.
1975	Good to excellent, although Sardinia moderate.
1976	Puglia excellent, otherwise mainly mediocre to good. Poor in Campania and Calabria.
1977	Campania exceptional; others mainly excellent.
1978	Excellent.
1979	Mainly excellent. Southern part of zone good, including splendid Taurasi.
1980	Good to excellent.
1981	Excellent in south and for Verdicchio; otherwise good.
1982	Although quality is very high, desiccation has cut crops by up to 50%, resulting in reduced availability.
1983	Average to good.
1984	Very good in Sicily, average or less elsewhere.
1985	Good to excellent.
1986	A good vintage.
1987	Moderate to good.

Some recommended wines from southern Italy and the islands are briefly described below. Most Italian wines are reasonably priced and the star coding is used here as an indication of the quality of the wine: (★★★★) exceptional; (★★★) very good; (★★) good. Stars refer only to wines and growers specified.

Campania
Region in the south-west with few DOCs but those it has have star-status. Otherwise, reds are mainly big and strong, and whites lighter and drier than they used to be.
Fiano di Avellino ★★ Fine dry white with distinctive aroma and tangy elegant finish.
GROWER: Mastroberardino.
Taurasi ★★★★ Anyone dismissive of southern Italy's wines has never tasted this complex, sumptuous dry red with its silky presence and lasting finish.
GROWER: Mastroberardino.

Apulia
The high heel of the Italian boot produces some surprisingly elegant wines amid the traditional volume output. Reds are good and full with whites more difficult to make distinctive, although several DOCs are just that.
Il Falcone ★★ Sumptuously-styled dry red.
GROWER: Rivera.
Favonio Pinot Bianco ★★ Very good acidity/fruit balance from surprising location for this dry white from Alsace grape.
GROWER: Attilio Simonini.
Five Rosés ★★ Lay down a rosé? You could with this one – satisfyingly substantial with a splendid finish.
GROWER: Leone de Castris.

Basilicata
With only one DOC, this southern region does indeed have a most noble wine to help put the area on the wine map.
Aglianico del Vulture ★★★ Pronounced 'Vool-toor-ay'; a very big, complex dry red with resonant, extended finish.
GROWERS: Fratelli d'Angelo, Paternoster.

Calabria
The toe of the Italian boot where producers are now responding to market calls for less ultra-assertive wines.
Cirò ★★ Smooth dry red with depth and resonance.
GROWERS: Caparra and Siciliani, Antonio Librandi.
Greco di Bianco ★★★ Very fine golden dessert wine.
GROWER: Ceratti.

Sicily
Corvo and Marsala are the two names immediately associated with Sicily, and indeed the former's better batches of red (for they *do* vary) can be splendid. Much new planting and continuing experimentation throughout the island have rendered many new-look wines attractive to our modern tastes.
Corvo ★★★ Often full and well-balanced dry red.
GROWER: Duca di Salaparuta.
Moscato Passito di Pantelleria ★★★★ Clean and aromatic sweet white dessert wine. Try it served *very* cold.
GROWER: Ag. Ass. Pantelleria.
Rapitalà ★★★ Straight dry white, fine and with good acidity.
GROWER: Conte de la Gatinais.
Regaleali Rosso del Conte ★★★ Elegant dry red with long finish.
GROWER: Conte Tasca Almerita.

Sardina
The sun on the island is never a problem, but often the rainfall is insufficient to swell the grapes. Traditions of heavy, sweet and fortified wines have yielded to modern stylistic aims, although often with traditional methods. Many of the wines are worth investigating and the range of types is fascinating.
Cannonau ★★★ Dry red. Becomes round and splendid at five years' ageing.
GROWERS: C. S. Dolianova, C. S. Jerzu, Sella and Mosca.
Torbato di Alghero ★★★ Dry white with pleasing substance and presence of fruit.
GROWERS: Sella and Mosca.

Calabria
Travelling south through Italy, the simple table wines tend to become more and more harsh, but there are always some good wines made on the foothills of the mountains. Among them are: Savuto, from the province of Cosenza, a dry, velvety rich, red wine, sometimes with as much as 13° alcohol; Cirò, named after the coastal town; and Melissa from near the fabulous Cirò Massif, the Switzerland of Calabria. Melissa can be found dry or sweet; usually dry.

Greco di Gerace, or di Bianco, is from the province of Reggio Calabria and right in the toe of Italy. It has a fantastic alcoholic content of 17° and is bright amber yellow. The delicate bouquet is said to be redolent of orange blossom. It is an excellent dessert wine.

Sicily
Marsala, I suppose, is the best-known wine of Sicily. It is in fact fortified like port and Madeira, and has very many of their virtues. Some is made on the *solera* system and lasts to a very great age and, I think, has more affinity with Madeira than port. Certainly, Marsalas last thirty, forty or fifty years. Raleigh Trevelyan's book *Princes of the Volcanoes* (Macmillan, 1972) is well worth reading on the origins of the Woodhouse dynasty, which developed this wine.

The wines of Etna are very good indeed. The slopes of the volcanoes are wonderfully fertile, which seems to be the only justification for living on that very chancy mountain, as anybody who has travelled round it will know. Nevertheless, this is the most thickly populated area in Sicily, the main reason being the richness of the soil. The Etna wines are made white or red and are generous, fruity and good. Rosé types are also produced.

Malvasia delle Lipari is made from Malvasia grapes on the Aeolian Islands and also those of Salina and Stromboli. Golden-yellow in colour, it is a rather sweet dessert wine.

Moscato di Pantelleria, made from Muscat grapes on the isle of Pantelleria, is also bright amber and rather sweet, but an excellent wine nevertheless.

Mamertino from the Messina province of Sicily is golden and dry with a characteristic strong bouquet. There is also a sweet quality made as a dessert wine.

Faro, made in the hilly region above the Straits of Messina, is dry, bright red, rich and agreeable.

Eloro is made both red and white, the red being slightly stronger. Both are very good and not sweet. Mention must also be made of the Corvo wines made and bottled by the Duca di Salaparuta – wines which have a character of their own and, when drunk at the right time, are delicious.

Moscato di Siracusa (an extremely rare wine) and Moscato di Noto, made from Muscat grapes, are, as may be expected, extremely sweet. They are rich wines with a pleasant bouquet.

Rapitalà, technically a Bianco di Alcamo, stands out in a somewhat neutral DOC group with its attractive positive character and shows how successful gifted experimentation within the regulations can be. Regaleali wines are, in effect, branded *vini da tavola*, but are consistently interesting and well made south-east of Palermo. Settesoli red and white, also *vini da tavola*, are starting to appear in London wine-bars.

Sicilian wines have the reputation of being unexpectedly heady, and indeed they are. It is as well to look out after the first bottle.

Sardinia

The Vernaccia di Oristano DOC from the lower Tirso Valley is a very strong wine indeed with up to 18° of alcohol. It is a bright amber colour with a strong flavour and claims to be one of the noblest white wines in the world. It is certainly an exceedingly interesting one. Noble it may be, strong it certainly is, but great I doubt.

Nuragus di Cagliari is heady, like most of these island wines, but dry and clean, with up to 15° of alcohol. Nasco di Cagliari, golden yellow in colour, is rather sweet with a dry finish. Monica de Sardegna, made from the Monica grape, is purplish, mellow and very sweet. Girò di Cagliari has very much the same characteristic as the Monica but is made from the Girò grape. Oliena, the favourite wine of the poet d'Annunzio, is a rich red wine with lovely bouquet and rather an odd after-taste. It is made from the Cannonau grape, which is widespread on the island. In fact, Cannonau di Sardegna is the best-known wine of Sardinia. It comes in several forms and Sardinians consider it their greatest wine. Whether DOC or not, many of these reds are extremely good, full-bodied, velvet-smooth wines and I would commend them to anyone prepared to track them down. The best dry white on the island is Torbato di Alghero, a *vino da tavola* produced in the north-west. Vermentino di Gallura is straw-coloured, dry and heady.

Spumante

Spumante simply means 'sparkling' and the famous sweet moscato wine from Asti in Piedmont has achieved such remarkable worldwide success that it has completely overshadowed the fact that Italy also produces much DRY sparkling wine. Most of it is made by the normal commercial Charmat method as in France, Germany and elsewhere, i.e. within an enclosed vat where the carbonic acid gas from the fermenting must is not permitted to escape and hence dissolves into the wine.

There is, however, a coterie of producers who make wine by the *méthode champenoise*, called *metodo classico* in Italy, and it includes most of the famous names like Cinzano, Martini and Rossi, Antinori, Gancia, etc. Italian wine made this way is good value since it costs a good deal less than Champagne while having some of its elegance. *Méthode champenoise* wine, however, is expensive *per se* because the sparkle is created in each individual bottle, making it very labour-intensive.

Spumante versions are made of certain well-known still wines, such as Frascati, Soave and Verdicchio, but perhaps the sparkling wines that most deserve seeking out are those produced in northern Italy in the regions of Friuli, Piedmont, Trentino and Veneto. The grapes of Champagne itself – Pinot Nero and Pinot Bianco – are often used for both Charmat and *classico* types although the soils are obviously not the same as those of the Champagne area. Chardonnay and Pinot Grigio are also used in varying proportions.

The following is a list of selected labels which can be relied upon (dry styles only):

Charmat (or tank) method Riccadonna's President Reserve, Collavini's Il Grigio, Gancia's Pinot di Pinot, Cinzano's Principe di Piemonte.

Classico method Fontanafredda's Contessa Rosa Nature, Martini & Rossi's Brut di Montelera, Castello di Bevilacqua's Brut Quarto Vecchio, Carpene'-Malvolti's Brut, Antinori's Marchese Antinori Nature, Cinzano's Cinzano Brut, Contratto's Reserve for England, Calissano's Realbrut.

Remuage at Falcini, makers of Asti Spumante, Italy's best sparkling wine.

SPAIN

Above: Zapatos de pisar, *the cowhide boots studded with flat tacks, formerly used for treading the sherry grapes.*

Opposite: The tree-fringed River Ebro near Briones in the Rioja Alta.

Vines are grown and wines are made in most districts of Spain except along the wet Atlantic coast in the north. I can claim some considerable personal experience of Spanish wine because nearly twenty years ago I travelled over the whole country researching my book *Sherry and the Wines of Spain* (Michael Joseph, 1966), now long out of print since it is very much out of date.

The most important and prestigious of Spanish wines is sherry. From its heyday in the late eighteenth and early nineteenth centuries, it has remained the market leader in foreign sales. Wines have been made in Spain from time immemorial, and it is probable that Spanish wine was imported into England long before the Middle Ages and possibly even in Roman times. Certainly in the Middle Ages

sherry was drunk under the name of Sack. Remember Falstaff's constant demands for that sweet but evidently delicious liquid, now commemorated by a very marketable product called Dry Sack. This comes ritually covered with sackcloth (though the real derivation of the name is from the Spanish *sacar*, to export), which, if it does not improve the wine, adds to the appearance.

Sherry

Sherry is a blend and never the wine of a single vineyard or year. The wealth of Jerez lies in the great *bodegas*, which house the butts of sherry used for blending, collectively called *soleras*. The soils in this dry and arid district, where rain may not fall for many months, are typically snowy white, a mixture of chalk, clay and sand, though some are darker in colour because of the presence of iron oxide. Their great virtue is that they dry without caking, slowly releasing the trapped moisture to the vines, whose roots may grow down as deep as 3 to 4 metres (10 to 13 feet).

Before being pressed, the grapes were formerly left in the sun for a shorter or longer period to concentrate the sugar, but this method is not now much used except for fruit intended for the sweet dessert wines. When I was last in Jerez in 1956 or 1957, I saw the grapes being trodden in the vineyards by men wearing *zapatos de pisar*, cowhide boots studded with flat tacks to avoid bruising them. The first fermentation then took place *in situ* in oak butts; but, again, methods have changed. The grapes are nowadays left on the vine until fully ripe and then taken in plastic baskets to the *bodegas*. Here they are lightly crushed and then passed to horizontal presses of German design, where an inflatable bag squeezes them against the sides of a stainless steel cylinder. Yet more modern continuous presses apply increasing pressure, the must that first separates being more likely to become a delicate *fino* and that obtained by firmer pressure a fuller-bodied *oloroso*. A few of the more traditional *bodegas* still ferment the wine in wooden butts, but it is more usual to use large stainless steel tanks or vessels of cement and to transfer the must to butts for maturation once the first tumultuous fermentation is over.

At the *bodega* the new wine is sorted out into the class of sherry for which it is most suitable. For

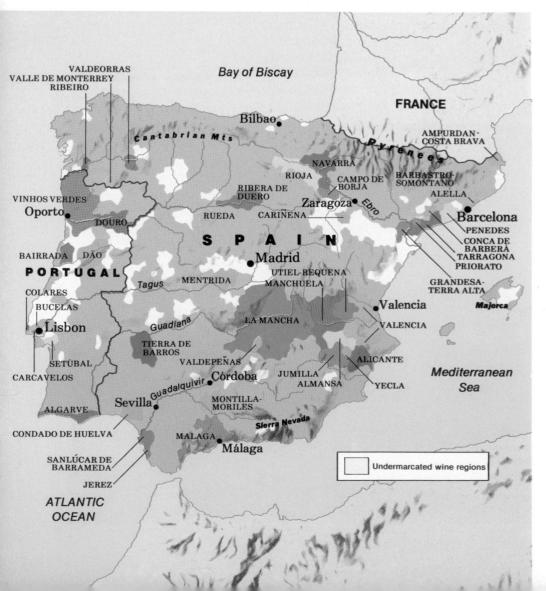

Above: Manzanilla *is made only at Sanlúcar de Barrameda.*

instance, the wine made from the Palomino grape, grown in the white *albariza* soils to the north and west of Jerez, is most suitable for *finos*; while that from the Moscatel and Pedro Ximénez (PX), flourishing in darker and richer soils, is used for blending to produce sweet sherries.

Sherry needs to be of consistent taste and quality, and this is achieved in the vast, cathedral-like *bodegas* by means of the *solera*, an arrangement of hundreds of 490-litre (108-gallon) butts of sherry containing wine of the same type but different ages stacked in tiers. Wine is taken for blending and shipment from the mature butts, which are then refreshed from the younger. Generally, the youngest butts are on top of a four-tier *solera* with the oldest at the bottom – though the complete *solera* may well comprise more tiers or 'scales' housed in a separate building – and the wine of one butt is never entirely the original; all have been refreshed. According to the quality, refreshing takes place more or less frequently. I knew of one *solera*, containing old and rare wine used for blending, of only three butts. From the lowest, started in 1770, the equivalent of twenty-four bottles, or four per cent, was taken every two years, and it was

refreshed from a butt laid down in 1819, which was in turn refreshed from the finest and oldest *amontillado* available. I hope it still exists.

The brands that you and I know, ask for and expect to get – the Tio Pepe of Gonzalez Byass, the Bristol Milk of Avery's or the Bristol Cream of Harveys – are not straight *solera* sherries, but are still further blended. This is an extremely skilful process and something that is very remarkable to see. To assess the development of the wine the *capataz* of the *bodega* dips his *venencia*, a thimble-like cup on the end of a long cane, into the middle of the barrel through the bung-hole. He swiftly brings out a sample and pours it instantly and at arm's length into a glass (the cane is about 1 metre, or 3 feet, long).

Fino sherries develop their delicate flavour beneath a *flor*, or film of yeasts, which grows spontaneously on the surface of the wine in the loosely stoppered butts, so protecting it from oxidation. They are very sparingly fortified before passing to the *solera*, and those for export are further fortified with grape spirit before shipment. *Olorosos*, on the other hand, grow little or no *flor*, and what there is, is killed at an early stage by more drastic fortifica-

Right: Butts in a sherry bodega. *The horizontal tiers or 'scales', containing wine of different age, collectively form the* solera.

Below: Carboys containing sherry with a thick layer of the flor *or layer of yeasts under which the* fino *wines develop. A little of this concentrate is added to the butts of young wine to initiate its growth.*

Spanish wine law

Spanish wines fall into three main categories: the aperitif and dessert wines from Andalusia; the fine table wines from the temperate regions of the north; and everyday drinking wine produced in vast quantity in the central area.

Overall control of the wine industry lies with a central agency of the Ministry of Agriculture, the *Instituto de Denominaciones de Origen* (INDO), and *all* Spanish wines must conform to the procedures and standards laid down in the lengthy *Estatuto de la Viña, del Vino y de los Alcoholes*. Beyond this, INDO deputes authority to *Consejos Reguladores* responsible for setting and maintaining standards in 32 demarcated regions. All wine made in accordance with the regulations of a *Consejo Regulador* is labelled with a *Denominación de Origen* (DO) corresponding to the French *Appellation Contrôlée* (AC), but standards are not uniform and the overall quality of the wine varies considerably from one demarcated region to another.

Terms used on wine labels
Blanco White
Bodega A winery
Clarete Light red table wine
Cosecha/Vendimia Vintage, e.g. Cosecha 1976
Dulce Sweet
Embotellado Bottled
Reserva, Gran Reserva Wine of good vintage matured for long periods in cask and bottle
Rosado Rosé
Seco Dry
Tinto Full-bodied red wine
Viña Vineyard
Vino Wine
Vino de mesa Table wine
Vino espumoso Sparkling wine
Vino generoso Fortified aperitif or dessert wine
Vino verde Young *pétillant* wine
4° año etc. Bottled during the fourth year after the harvest etc.

tion, so that maturation is purely physico-chemical.

Sherry varies greatly in price according to the quality of the grapes and age of the wines used for blending and, indeed, its sweetness. It can be blended to sell at all prices, and dessert sherries have a fair quantity of a sweetening agent, often a sugary must made from the Pedro Ximénez grape. Good sherry is not cheap but, in view of the care and time taken in making it, it is excellent value.

The principal styles of sherry are:

Fino Pale in colour, of 15° to 18°, and the lightest, driest and most delicate of sherries. It does not keep at its best once the bottle has been opened and should be served chilled.

Pale Cream is a light dessert sherry made by sweetening a *fino* with PX or Moscatel musts.

Manzanilla A pale, crisp and extremely dry *fino* from the town of Sanlúcar de Barrameda, west of Jerez, with a typically salty tang. I have a tender memory of a delicious all-fish dinner at a restaurant literally on the sands of Sanlúcar on a summer's evening. The wine? Manzanilla.

Amontillado Amber-coloured, more fully bodied, with a dry, nutty flavour and of 16.5° to 18° strength. It may be drunk as an aperitif or with soup and light dishes.

Oloroso Dark in colour, of 17.5° to 23° strength, and the softest, fullest bodied and most fragrant of sherries. In its natural form, as in sherries such as Rio Viejo, it is completely dry and is drunk (at room temperature) as an aperitif.

Dessert and Cream sherries Mahogany-coloured varieties made by sweetening an *oloroso* with PX or Moscatel musts. The traditional dark dessert *olorosos* will keep for many years, eventually developing a dryish finish because of slow consumption of the sugar.

Montilla-Moriles

Montilla, to the south of Córdoba, makes excellent sherry-like wines, but they differ from those of Jerez in being made from the Pedro Ximénez grape, picked young and fermented to completion, and in being fermented in earthenware jars, or *tinajas*. Thereafter the wines are aged in the oak butts of a *solera*.

The styles are the same as for sherry, but because of legal action on the part of the sherry shippers, Montilla is sold in the UK as 'fine dry', 'medium dry' and 'cream'. Until recently I had in my cellar a last bottle of 1875 Montilla, bought from a country-house sale and authenticated as of that date, which was still bone dry and very drinkable. In the past, a great deal of Montilla was shipped to Jerez, blended and sold as sherry. The practice was outlawed in 1944, when the region was demarcated. Montilla remains an excellent – and very reasonably priced – wine in its own right.

Left: The sherry harvest in the vineyards of Gonzalez Byass. The Palomino grapes are nowadays gathered into plastic containers to avoid bruising and premature fermentation and transported to the vinification plant at the bodega within minutes of being picked.

Below: The 'sunning' of grapes for sweet sherries in the vineyards of Gonzalez Byass near Jerez. This concentrates the sugar in the must, and the amount of heat which they receive may be regulated by means of the plastic covers.

The wines listed below represent a limited and personal choice; except when otherwise noted they are from demarcated regions. The majority of Spanish wines are very reasonably priced. Four-star wines (★★★★) are exceptional; three-star wines (★★★) are very good; two-star wines (★★) are good and one-star wines (★) are inexpensive.

Sherry ★★★ – ★★★★

There are four main styles of sherry: the light, dry and delicate *finos* and *fina* Manzanillas; the fuller-bodied and nutty *amontillados*; the dry *olorosos*, dark, fragrant and high in alcohol; and the dessert and cream sherries drunk after a meal.

Barbadillo SA. Makers of some of the best Manzanillas.
Garvey SA. San Patricio *fino*, Tio Guillermo *amontillado*, Ochavico dry *oloroso*.
Gonzalez Byass & Co Ltd. Tio Pepe *fino*, La Concha *amontillado* and a range of splendid old dessert and cream sherries.
La Riva SA. Its Tres Palmas *fino* is one of the best.
Pedro Domecq SA. La Ina *fino*, the excellent dry Rio Viejo *oloroso*, Double Century and Celebration Cream.
Harvey & Sons Ltd, John. Famous for its Bristol Cream.
Sandeman Hnos. y Cía. Apitiv *fino*, Dry Don *amontillado*, Armada Cream.

Montilla-Moriles ★★ – ★★★

The region makes aperitif and dessert wines, very reasonably priced and generally similar in style to sherry.

Alvear SA. Fino Festival, Fino C.B., dry Oloroso Pelayo Seco and a range of dessert wines.
Gracia Hermanos SA. Kiki Pale Dry, Montiole Medium Dry, Ben Hur Rich Cream.
Monte Cristo SA. Monte Cristo Dry, Medium, Pale Cream, Cream.

Málaga

Málaga is famous for its rich, sweet dessert wine; it also makes *amontillados* for drinking as an aperitif and lighter dessert wines reminiscent of tawny port.

Barceló SA. ★★ Traditional sweet Málagas.
Scholtz Hermanos SA. ★★★ Makers of a good dry Seco Añejo 10-year-old and the famous Solera Scholtz 1885.

Rioja

These best-known of Spanish table wines are predominantly fruity reds with a pronounced oaky nose and flavour.

Berberana SA. ★ – ★★★ Red Carta de Plata, Carta de Oro and *reservas*; dry white.
Bilbainas SA. ★★ – ★★★ Red Viña Zaco, Viña Pomal and Vendimia Especial *reservas*; dry white Viña Paceta.
Campo Viejo SA. ★★ – ★★★ Inexpensive young red San Asensio and big, fruity red *reservas*.
CVNE. ★★ – ★★★ Red Cune, Imperial and Viña Real *reservas*; popular white Monopole with restrained oak.
Domecq Domain ★★ – ★★★ Sound reds and fruity whites.
La Rioja Alta SA. ★★ – ★★★★ Young red Viña Alberdi and soft, fruity Viña Ardanza, Viña Arana and Reserva 904.
R. López de Heredia SA. ★★ – ★★★★ Wines in the traditional oaky style: red Cubillo, Tondonia and Bosconia; classic old oaky white wines.
Marqués de Murrieta SA. ★★ – ★★★★ Famous for its red wines, including the old and prestigious Castillo de Ygay.
Marqués de Riscal SA. ★★ – ★★★★ Another aristocrat, maker of light and somewhat claret-like red wines.
Marqués de Cáceres SA. ★★ – ★★★ Its red wines are less oaky than most and its fresh young white is outstanding.
Olarra SA. ★★ – ★★★ Largest of the modern *bodegas*, making sound red wines and a fresh young white.

Navarra

Abutting the Rioja, the region makes sturdy red wines; the best, from near Pamplona, are comparable with Riojas.

Señorío de Sarría ★★ – ★★★ Young red Viña Ecoyen and mature Viña del Perdón and Gran Vino del Señorío.
Vinícola Navarra ★★ Best is the full-bodied Castillo de Tiebas.

Málaga

Málaga was at one time extremely popular as a sweet dessert wine, but it has largely gone out of favour and it is difficult to find a vintage Málaga on a wine list today.

The wines are made from PX and Moscatel grapes grown in the hills to the north and west of the city. They are subsequently aged in a *solera* and often sweetened with a boiled-down must, but Málagas, such as the gloriously fruity and complex Solera Scholtz 1885, are bitter-sweet rather than sweet and somewhat resemble good tawny ports.

I am glad to say that I still have memories of a Málaga which was pre-1850 from the same country-house sale as my Montilla. I had five bottles and they were all very good indeed. Málaga is sometimes used in Spain as Communion wine, and I once bought in a Restell auction a lot containing 'six bottles, believed to be Communion wine'. It was, because on one remaining tattered label was the legend: 'Guaranteed pure by the R. Rev. the Lord Bishop of Málaga'!

Rioja

The wines of the Rioja have a great deal in common with the finer French wines and are mostly of the claret type, although made from different grapes and to suit most palates. When the French vineyards were devastated by oidium and phylloxera in the latter decades of the nineteenth century, the French *vignerons* came to Spain, bought vineyards, improved the viniculture and made good wine to add to their very depleted stocks in Bordeaux. This tradition, including the custom of ageing the wines for long years in 225-litre (49½-gallon) oak casks, has been kept up, and when later the French, having cured their own ills, left Spain and let the phylloxera in, the know-how remained. I think that the Rioja with its three sub-regions of Rioja Alta and Rioja Alavesa (producing the best wines), and the hotter Rioja Baja to the east, is one of the most beautiful wine districts in the world and travellers to Spain should take the trouble to visit Haro and Logroño and taste some of the delicious wines made in and near those towns.

Like other leading wine districts in Spain, the Rioja is demarcated and controlled by a government body, the Consejo Regulador. On the back of every reputable Rioja bottle you will find a little label stating that the wine is one of four classes. Class 1 certifies that the wine comes from the Rioja: a guarantee of origin. Class 2 is *vino de crianza*. This wine has spent a minimum of one year in oak casks and some time in bottle and may not be sold until its third year. Class 3 is the *reserva*. This wine has been selected from a good harvest and has then been matured for a minimum of two years in cask and one in bottle. Last and best of all is the *gran reserva*,

Rioja vintages	
1975	average
1976	good
1977	very poor
1978	excellent
1979	fair
1980	very good
1981	good
1982	very good
1983	good
1984	average
1985	very good
1986	good

Left: The grape harvest in the vineyards of the Marqués de Riscal in the Rioja: loading the fruit into a plastic-covered trailer for transport to the bodega.

Below: Cabernet Sauvignon vines in the vineyards of the Marqués de Riscal.

selected from an exceptional harvest and then matured for a minimum of three years in cask and two in bottle. Additionally, the *gran reservas* must be aged for a total of seven years before leaving the *bodega*. The system is comparatively new, so that if you have an old wine, it may not bear a label of this sort.

The *reservas* and *gran reservas* come to the table in rather beautiful wired bottles, which do not, of course, improve the taste of the wine, but look very well. Under new EEC regulations, Rioja wines shipped abroad must be marked with the year of vintage, though I have always found that Riojas vary less in this regard than French wines. That of the famous Marqués de Riscal has generally been marked with the year of its birth. Only recently I opened a bottle of the 1925, which proved excellent; and certainly the label corresponded with the date stamped on the cork.

The fifty or so *bodegas* of the Rioja produce many excellent wines and few that are less than good. Among the best are those of the three Marqueses: the Marqués de Riscal, the Marqués de Murrieta and the more youthful Marqués de Cáceres. You may confidently buy wines from any of the firms listed on the opposite page and, at about half the price of comparable wines from Bordeaux or Burgundy, they are excellent value. My favourite Rioja wine and the one which I use most at home is the Majestad Rosada (rosé) 1971 from AGE, but I am told that there have been changes in the making of

the wines since the *bodega* was taken over by the American firm of Schenley and the Banco Español de Crédito. Another favourite is the always reliable Viña Ardanza from Bodegas La Rioja Alta, fruity and velvety with long finish and widely distributed in the UK.

Catalonia

Of the many first-rate wines from Catalonia the best are from the Penedès, where the principal centre for making table wines is Vilafranca del Penedès. The most famous firm is that of Bodegas Torres, where, over the last two generations, Miguel Torres Carbó and his remarkable and talented family have made formidable contributions both to viticulture and vinification and to the export of Spanish wines. They grow some half of the grapes in their own extensive vineyards, and one of their achievements has been the successful acclimatisation of noble foreign varieties, including the white Chardonnay, Gewürztraminer and Riesling, and the black Cabernet Sauvignon and Pinot Noir. Torres was also a pioneer in introducing stainless steel fermentation tanks and in the cold fermentation of white wines, so as to preserve the freshness and fruit. Their wines, most reasonably priced, include the dry white Viña Sol in various styles, the semi-sweet Esmeralda, made from Gewürztraminer and Muscat d'Alsace, and the now famous Gran Coronas Black Label, made from Cabernet Sauvignon

Above: Hand-corking of an old reserva *in the cellars of the Marqués de Riscal.*

The wines listed below represent a limited and personal choice; except when otherwise noted they are from demarcated regions. The majority of Spanish wines are very reasonably priced. Four-star wines (★★★★) are exceptional; three-star (★★★) are very good; two-star wines (★★) are good and one-star wines (★) are inexpensive.

Catalonia

The best of the wines, some of them rivalling the Riojas, are from the Penedès, west of Barcelona, particularly noted for its well-balanced whites. Alella, north of Barcelona, also makes good white wines; those from the hilly Priorato are almost black in colour and high in alcohol and extract.

Alella Vinícola, Co-operative ★★ White Marfil blanco and Marfil seco; red Marfil tinto.

Bach, Masia ★★ — ★★★ Fruity red Penedès wines and the oaky and delicious dessert Extrísimo Bach.

De Muller SA. ★★ — ★★★ Most famous of the firms in Tarragona; luscious dessert wines in the style of *oloroso* sherry.

Marqués de Monistrol ★★ — ★★★ Young, slightly *pétillant* Vin Natur *blanc de blancs* and fruity red wines.

Scala Dei, Cellars de ★★ Makers of a superior red Priorato.

Torres, Viñedos ★★ — ★★★★ Producers of the best Penedès wines, including the range of dry white Viña Sol, semi-sweet Viña Esmeralda, and the red Tres Torres, Viña Magadala and famous Gran Coronas Black Label.

Old Castile

Centring on the Duero Valley, the region produces fruity red wines east of Valladolid and fresh whites and light red wines to its west.

Agrícola Castellana, Co-operative ★★ Traditional sherry-like Rueda and fresh young white Verdejo Pálido.

Ribera de Duero, Co-operative ★★ Fruity reds, including the mature Protos.

Vinos Blancos de Castilla SA. ★★ Dry white Marqués de Riscal.

Vega Sicilia SA. ★★ — ★★★★ The *bodega* makes some of the best red wine from Spain, sold as Vega Sicilia with ten years in cask, and the younger Valbuena.

Galicia

This wet and northerly region produces *pétillant* wines in the style of the Vinhos Verdes from neighbouring Portugal.

Ribeiro, Co-operative ★ — ★★ Red, white and rosé Pazo.

Albariño de Fefiñanes ★★★ The most famous wine from the area, made with the white Albariño grape.

La Mancha

The largest wine-producing area in the country, making sound, but earthy wines, mostly white, for everyday drinking. The best is, however, the red Valdepeñas.

Morenito SA. ★★ Reliable *bodega* in Valdepeñas: Fino Tres Pistolas, Fino Morenito, Reserva 72, etc.

Levante

A large-scale producer of full-bodied Mediterranean-type wines.

La Purisima, Co-operative ★ — ★★ Largest producer in the DO Yecla: red and white Viña Montana.

San Isidro, Co-operative ★ — ★★ Another huge co-operative in the DO Jumilla, making sturdy red wines.

Sparkling wines

Most of the best Spanish sparkling wine – clean, fruity and made by the Champagne method – is from the Penedès in Catalonia.

Codorníu SA. ★★ — ★★★ The colossus of the sparkling wine industry, best known for its dry Non Plus Ultra.

Freixenet SA. ★★ — ★★★ Makers of the popular dry Cordon Negro and superior Brut Nature.

Gonzalez y Dubosc ★★ Non-vintage Jean Perico is good value.

Perelada, Castillo de ★★ — ★★★ Apart from inexpensive *cuve close* sparklers, the best of its wines, made near the Pyrenees, is the Gran Claustro.

Segura Viudas ★★ — ★★★ Reserva Heredad is first-rate.

and Cabernet Franc and winner of so many international awards. Other leading Penedès firms are Masia Bach, Bosch-Guell, René Barbier, the Marqués de Monistrol and the Conde de Caralt.

Tarragona is a name once well known in Britain, because a cheap, fortified *clásico* (also known as Red Biddy or 'poor man's port') was formerly sold for a few pence by public houses in large dock glasses and was considered to be rather violent in its effects. The *clásicos* of a firm such as de Muller (also noted for its altar wines) are in a different league; made by the *solera* system they much resemble fine old dessert *olorosos*. However, Tarragona is mainly concerned with the blending and bulk export of inexpensive table wines for sale in large bottles and also with the manufacture of vermouths. It is of interest that the brothers of La Grande Chartreuse set up a distillery in Tarragona for making their famous liqueur after their expulsion from France in 1903. This is still in operation, the only difference between the French and Tarragona-made Chartreuse being that the Spanish is very slightly drier – but vastly less expensive!

I have touched briefly on some of the other Catalan wines in the wine lists (see left), of which one of the most individual is Priorato, much of which, because of its strength and body, is used for blending. There are, however, more sophisticated Prioratos from de Muller and the Cellars de Scala Dei, still potent wines of some 14.5°, but eminently drinkable with their deep blackberry flavour.

Wine in bulk

The largest source of wine for everyday drinking is the great central plateau of La Mancha, much of the wine being made in its four hundred and fifty co-operatives. This is the country of Don Quixote, of the windmills and of whitewashed villages and *bodegas*. Its best known wine town, possessing no less than eighty *bodegas*, is Valdepeñas (from *Val de Peñas*, meaning the 'valley of stones'). Indeed, its name is sometimes used to describe the wines from the region generally, although, in fact, unlike the other demarcated regions in the area, it produces more red wine than white. This is made in timeless fashion in large earthenware vessels descended from the Roman *amphorae*, from which it is usually sold young in the year following the harvest.

When I was last there, the wine was very honest, very good, light, clean with quite a lot of alcohol, but earthy. I suppose it would be wrong to call Valdepeñas the Beaujolais of Spain, but not very wrong. I think it could become just as fashionable and is certainly much cheaper.

One of the best of its *bodegas* is Morenito, which ages some of its wine in cask, but it is somewhat fruitless to look for names and labels, since much of the best of it is sold young in *jarras* (or earthenware

Penedès vintages			
White		**Red**	
1975	very good	1975	good
1976	excellent	1976	good
1977	very good	1977	good
1978	very good	1978	excellent
1979	good	1979	average
1980	very good	1980	very good
1981	excellent	1981	very good
1982	very good	1982	very good
1983	good	1983	good
1984	very good	1984	good
1985	very good	1985	very good
1986	good	1986	good
1987	very good	1987	very good

jugs). In the little wine shops around the Plaza del Sol in Madrid, one could once buy a glass of good Valdepeñas wine and three or four grilled *gambas*, or large shrimps, for three or four pesetas.

I will conclude this section on Spanish table wines with an apology, because space precludes my mentioning many other wines which I have drunk in my time and thoroughly enjoyed. Some, at least, are briefly described in wine lists in this chapter. Time was when Spanish wines were only available from specialist wine importers and merchants, but wines like Rueda, León and Yecla are becoming increasingly familiar on the shelves of off-licences and supermarkets. Many are unremarkable except for their basic qualities of honesty and cheapness. All I can suggest is that when you see a wine that you don't know with a Spanish label, try it, and if you like it, buy more. It certainly won't break the bank.

Above: The vineyards of the Señorio de Sarría in the uplands of Navarra, south of Pamplona. The vines are grown low, as in the Rioja, and the varieties are the same: Tempranillo, Garnacho, Graciano and Mazuelo.

Left: The distillery in Tarragona, where Chartreuse has been made since 1903 following the expulsion for a period of the monks from France. Production is now shared with the sister establishment at Voiron in Provence.

Above: An old wine press, dating from the early eighteenth century and one of a number preserved at Bodegas Torres in Vilafranca del Penedès in Catalonia.

Right: Cavas Freixenet in San Sadurní de Noya, one of the largest of the Spanish firms producing sparkling wines by the Champagne method. San Sadurní in the Penedès is the centre of the industry, and the wineries are known as cavas *rather than* bodegas *because of their deep underground cellars.*

The sparkling wines of Spain

First of all, I should mention the Spanish Champagne case fought in the English courts in 1960. The Spanish had been making sparkling wine by the *méthode champenoise* since 1872, but the French Champagne Association, alarmed by its popularity, argued that it should not be called Champagne. The Spaniards maintained, quite justifiably, that some of their sparkling wine is as good as Champagne, and this may well be true of the lesser French growths. After a long and bitterly fought action, the court decided in favour of the French, so that, in the EEC at least, Spanish sparkling wine may not be called Champagne. However, I notice that a recent advertisement for Spanish sparkling wine ends: 'any resemblance to Champagne is purely intentional'. Well, you can't be blunter than that!

Your first encounter with Spanish sparklers may well be at the beautiful fourteenth-century castle of Perelada (which also boasts a casino and a fine wine museum), just across the eastern end of the Pyrenees. Besides some good whites and rosés, Perelada makes an excellent Gran Claustro by the *méthode champenoise*, while its sister ship the Cavas del Ampurdán is one of the largest producers of a drinkable *cuve close* sparkler made in pressurised tanks. The wines are available abroad, but certainly it is preferable to drink them on the spot.

The largest producer is the firm of Codorníu in the Penedès, whose 18 kilometres (11 miles) of underground cellars in five tiers are reputedly the largest in the world. It is close-run by Freixenet, also located in San Sadurní de Noya; between them they produce some seventy per cent of all the sparkling wine made in the region, but there is a host of other firms, some very sizeable. I have been to Codorníu and, *pace* the French, much enjoyed its large range of wines, of which the best is the Non Plus Ultra. Other well-known firms making these sparkling, or *cava*, wines are: Castellblanch, Segura Viudas, Conde de Caralt, Marqués de Monistrol, René Barbier, Mascaró and Gonzalez y Dubosc, makers of the popular Jean Perico.

To sum up, Spanish sparkling wines are well made, clean and refreshing with a fine and long-lasting bubble, but one should not expect them to be comparable with those from Rheims, made as they are with the local Xarel-lo, Macabeo and Parellada grapes rather than Chardonnay. You should try these wines and come to your own conclusions.

Left: Glass carboys, or bombonas, at Bodegas Torres in Vilafranca del Penedès. Loosely stoppered and open to the fresh air and sun, they are used for making sherry-like rancio wines.

Below: Copper stills at Bodegas Torres in Vilafranca del Penedès used for making the superior Miguel Torres Black Label brandy by the Charentais method, involving double distillation and the retention of only the middle fraction or brouilli.

Brandy

Vast quantities of brandy, often, to the discomfort of the French, known as *coñac*, are produced in Spain, where it is a great deal more popular than sherry and cheaper than the better table wines. The brandy-making centre of Spain is Jerez de la Frontera, but the sherry grapes are far too valuable to be distilled into brandy; and the great bulk of the big-selling brands is made from sixty-five per cent grape spirit, or *holandas*, produced in continuous stills up and down the country from grapes surplus to use in wine making. This spirit is sent in tankers to Jerez, where it is broken down with water and subsequently aged in *solera* in the manner of sherry.

Brandies of this type are quite good, and I enjoy the odd glass of Fundador, Soberano or Veterano, though they tend to be over-sweet and caramelised, lacking the finesse or ultimate quality of Cognac and Armagnac.

There are, however, other much more select brandies made by double distillation in small pot stills by the Charentais method employed in Cognac. Some of these, like the expensive Lepanto from Gonzalez Byass or Marqués de Domecq, are delicate and first rate. Catalonia, too, produces some excellent brandy by the Charentais method, less oaky than that from Jerez, since it is aged in individual casks like those from Cognac. It is, in fact, very difficult to distinguish it from good Cognac or Armagnac. Among the best are those from Mascaró and the Miguel Torres Black Label.

PORTUGAL

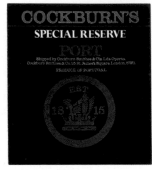

Above: Cockburns are one of the oldest port shippers.

Right: Pipes of port maturing in one of the eighteenth-century lodges in Vila Nova de Gaia. Port was formerly shipped in cask, but it is now bottled in the lodge or despatched in containers.

Below: One of the few surviving barcos rabellos, formerly used for ferrying the new port from the Upper Douro to the lodges, moored by the quays of Vila Nova de Gaia, with Oporto across the river.

The name 'port' has long been applied to the rich, sweet, after-dinner wine, but, though the best known, it is by no means the only wine to be produced in Portugal. There are many, indeed dozens, of very good table wines, some from pre-phylloxera vines virtually unknown elsewhere. Since port is so well known, we will, however, deal with it as a separate subject and then with the other wines of Portugal.

Port

Port is a wine that owes its existence to political expediency. England has been the traditional ally and trading partner of Portugal since 1373, when an agreement was signed pledging friendship between the two countries. From the beginning, wine was always a principal trading commodity, but the Portuguese wines of the period were thin and acidulous and, not surprisingly, made little headway against the round red wines of Gascony. In the late seventeenth century the traders turned their attention to the Douro valley. Its wines turned out to be full-bodied and exceptionally full of sugar, but the problem was that the flavour bubbled away fast and furiously in the heat of the Douro autumn, and at this juncture the wine makers hit on the expedient of

Right: Picking the grapes at Aveleda in the Vinho Verde area of northern Portugal. The vines are trained high to keep them clear of the ground in a region which is wet for much of the year.

Below: The Douro Valley near Pinhão, showing the steeply terraced vineyards where the port grapes are grown, two of the quintas *where they are vinified and the railway at water level. Many of the vineyards were abandoned after the phylloxera epidemic of the nineteenth century, and, like those across the river, are now planted with olives.*

checking the final stages of fermentation by adding brandy, so leaving the wine smoother and sweeter. This, in essence, is the way that port has been made ever since. Approaching hostilities with France and the signature of the famous Methuen Treaty of 1703, establishing preferential tariffs for Portuguese wines, paved the way for the enormous expansion of the port trade during the eighteenth and nineteenth centuries.

In the days of our great forefathers, port bottles held about a pint – that is to say, about two-thirds of the amount of the present bottle, hence the reputed three-, four-, five- and even six-bottle men of the eighteenth century. I am not sure whether port was as heavy and strong as it is now, but during the Napoleonic Wars it was largely drunk as a substitute for claret. I imagine that it was not so strong, because it was not regularly fortified in those days.

All port, whatever its style, is made from grapes grown in terraced vineyards in the upper reaches of the Douro river. The wine is vinified at the *quintas*, or farms, of the thousands of small proprietors or, increasingly, at the large and modern establishments of the large port firms. At the right moment the boisterous fermentation is checked by running

Left: Vineyards in the Alentejo near Reguengos de Monsaraz.

off the wine into vats or casks, where the correct amount of brandy is added. This pure grape brandy is made from Portuguese wine and gives to the port its tremendous staying and lasting power. After resting for some months, the new wine is transported to the lodges of the great port shippers in Vila Nova de Gaia opposite Oporto, where it is matured according to type and quality by the methods to be described later. In days past the wine was shipped down the river in the picturesque, square-sailed *barcos rabelos*, but nowadays almost all of it goes by road tanker.

A word must be said about the great port houses, whose headquarters and rambling old red-tiled lodges for maturing the wine are on the bank of the Douro facing Oporto proper. When the Methuen Treaty was signed, a great many members of the British wine trade, often Scotsmen, went to Portugal and founded branches of their companies. These houses still exist today, and indeed continue to flourish in spite of the decline in the demand for port. The lodges face, on the north bank, the greatest wine club in the world, the Factory House, which was established by the British merchants in the eighteenth century and which has been a shrine for port lovers all over the world ever since. Here you will find the visitors' book signed by the Duke of Wellington's officers during the Peninsular War and, in the cellars, some wine like that drunk by Wellington at the time, although I doubt whether it would be given to you and me.

Let me now describe the main styles of port,

officially classified by the controlling body, the Instituto do Vinho do Porto, such as vintage port, late bottled vintage, vintage character, wood port (including tawny and the popular ruby) and white port.

Vintage port

First of all, and most famous, there is vintage port. This is port of a given very exceptional year blended from wine made from grapes of that year and of such supreme quality that the shipper will declare the vintage and ship the wine under the year in which it was made and under his own name.

Once the new wine has been blended at the lodge, perhaps with the wine from other *quintas* of the same year, it is left in casks (or pipes as they are called) containing about 650 bottles. It is bottled about two years later, so that wine lists contain terms such as Cockburn's 1963 bottled 1965 or Sandeman's 1955 bottled 1957.

There has, however, been a fundamental change in the production of vintage port over the last few years. Up to World War II, vintage port was almost always shipped in wood and bottled abroad at the most suitable time by a shipper with centuries of skill behind him. During the war, it was no longer possible to ship port to England – except towards its end, when the commonest types came over in barrels. Consequently the port houses bottled their own vintages in Oporto, later shipping them as '45s and so on. I have drunk a fair amount of Oporto-bottled war-time port; it was pleasant enough, and in fact I still have a couple of bottles and look forward to them. More recently the Portuguese government, in its zeal to maintain standards, has decreed that no vintage port may be shipped unless it is bottled in Portugal. There are therefore no more English-bottled vintage ports. Many, and I am one, think that this is unnecessary and a very great pity. It is a snub to the great expertise and traditional skills of the famous foreign port houses.

Wine merchants sell vintage port in pipes, or multiples or sub-divisions of pipes, to their wealthier or less rich friends, as the case may be. The bottles are then transferred to the cellars of the lucky buyers. Beyond this, it is sold in dozens or half-dozens or the odd bottle or two to ordinary people like, perhaps, you or me.

Thereafter, the wine lies in bin for many years. Vintage port used not to be labelled, and we have all seen bottles with merely a dash of whitewash at the bottom to show which way up they should lie. Since the bins in port cellars are usually dark, the mark shows up in the faint light of a candle. There the port lies, always in the same position, and a crust will form and lie along the bottom of the wine in the bottles. Crust is a living organism, an almost microscopic life form, which has its being, lives and dies and sinks to the bottom, rather like coral in the sea. At some time or another, vintage port ceases to throw off crust, and at that time it may be said to be dying, but it takes a very long time to die. Because of the crust, vintage port is always decanted.

Most vintage ports, if they are properly made and shipped by a great house, will last for fifty years, but today they are rarely left for that long and it is advisable to sample a port more than thirty years old before buying it. The great years of the last century are venerable, and that is why they stand out as milestones in the history of wine – for instance, the comet year of 1811 and the marvellous 1847, which is still being drunk today if it can be found. The trouble with port is that it does rot the cork, and that is why care must be taken to recork old ports at intervals.

Vintages are declared according to the judgement of individual firms and in consultation with Instituto do Vinho do Oporto. In 1911, for example, only two firms, Martinez and Sandemans, felt that they could ship a vintage wine. This was because their vineyards happened to be in a district of the Douro where rain fell, and they knew that it would materially alter the quality of the crop, whereas in other parts of the Douro where rain did not fall the crop was not sufficiently good to declare a vintage. This quite often happens, but the fact that Cockburn, Graham, Warre or Fonseca (or, indeed, any of the good names) declare a vintage is sufficient guarantee for you and me.

Very little remains of pre-war vintages, and certainly practically none which can be bought. Every

now and then a lot will come up at Christie's of London of, say, 1927 port, probably the greatest vintage of the century so far and still at its delicious peak, but it will cost a great deal. The best port years of this century, apart from 1927, which was undoubtedly the best, were: 1900, when all the shippers except Dow and Graham shipped; 1904, which was splendid and of which I have many pleasant recollections; 1908, which, until the 1927 ports came into their full power, I always considered the finest I had ever drunk; 1911 was shipped only by Martinez and Sandeman for the reasons explained and was very good indeed; the 1912s are excellent, and then we have to go to 1917, which was a quality rather than a quantity year and shipped by a number of houses; 1920 was a good year, or good enough at least for most of the houses to ship a vintage; 1922 was good, and also 1924. As I have said, 1927 was outstanding; and he is a very lucky man who is given it after dinner. Thereafter, 1935 was good, and also 1942 and 1945. The main vintages of more recent years are 1955, 1960, 1963, 1967, 1970 and now 1975 and 1977, 1983 and 1985.

Nowadays few people can afford to lay down a pipe of port or to lay down very much at all. It gets no cheaper and this is one of the reasons why it has gone out of favour, because to appreciate port to the full you need to drink it fairly regularly. If you do not, because of its special alcoholic quality it is prone to give you a hangover next morning; and this, too, I think, has contributed to its decline in popularity. Nevertheless, port drinking shows signs of coming back, and a very good thing too. It has been well said that drinking port after dinner brings out the best in everybody – good conversation, good humour, wit and benevolence.

Above right: Vineyards near Vila Real, north of the port region. The grapes are used for sparkling rosés or still red table wines.

Right: Large mahogany vats, or balseiros, *used for maturing port in the lodges of Vila Nova de Gaia.*

Opposite: Bottle store in one of the lodges of Vila Nova de Gaia, with vintage port undergoing its lengthy maturation.

There are other styles of port made from wine of the same year, but not of the supreme quality of a declared vintage. **Late bottled vintage port** is so called because it is wine of a single year kept longer in wood before bottling – usually for about five years. **Port with the year of harvest** stated is wine of a single undeclared vintage matured in wood for at least seven years.

The remaining styles of wine differ radically from the above in being a blend of wines of different age.

Vintage character port is port of a similar style to vintage port, but is a blend of fine years and is matured in cask, not in bottle. It much resembles **crusted port**. No longer recognized by the Instituto, this was a cask-aged blend of vintages of good wines.

Port with an indication of age is labelled, not with the vintage, but as ten years old, twenty years old, thirty years old or over forty years old. It must be sold in bottle and, in addition to the indication of age, the label may also state the year of bottling.

Above: The Quinta da Insua in the Dão, a headquarters of Wellington during the Peninsular War, possesses a tiny winery and vineyards planted with Cabernet Sauvignon.

Opposite: Old port vineyards with high retaining walls (on the left of the bullock track) and new plantations (on the right) in the valley of the River Torto, a tributary of the Douro.

different class from cheap imitations made by blending red and white ports. Once bottled, tawny ports do not throw a crust or improve with age.

All of the above types are made basically from black grapes; there are also **white ports**, made by separating the skins from the must at an early stage. Traditional white ports are sweet or very sweet, but the shippers have more recently introduced a drier type for drinking as an aperitif. Still less dry than a *fino* sherry, it should be drunk chilled and is much improved by a twist of lemon peel.

Serving port

A solemn warning: at the dinner table port must always be served clockwise, from right to left. Never pass the port to your right or across the table unless you make the circuit first. For the Devil himself lurks at your right shoulder and if you should forget, he will pass his hand over the port and then goodness knows what will happen to you, your family and your dependents. So be warned!

The Port Wine Shippers Association numbers forty-two members. Among the most famous names are:

Cockburn Smithes; Croft; Delaforce; Dow; Ferreira; Feuerheed; Fonseca; Gonzalez Byass; Gould Campbell; Graham; Mackenzie; Martinez Gassiot; Offley Forrester; Quinta do Noval; Rebello Valente (the vintage mark for Robertson Brothers); Sandeman; Smith Woodhouse; Taylor, Fladgate & Yeatman; Tuke Holdsworth.

The natural wines of Portugal

The natural wines of Portugal – that is to say unfortified table or beverage wines – have become increasingly available abroad, especially the branded and widely advertised rosés. Foremost among these is the enormously popular Mateus Rosé, sold in a flagon rather like the German *Bocksbeutel*, with a beautiful label depicting the Mateus Palace near the winery. A lovely rosé colour, it has a subdued sparkle or *pétillance* and is slightly sweet; like the German Liebfraumilch, some think it is a good wine to order for a mixed dinner. It is not, however, for the sophisticated wine lover.

The following are the principal wine-producing districts of Portugal, together with the types of wine they produce, though not all are available abroad. They are honestly made and some have remarkable keeping qualities and marked individuality of their own, and can well hold their own with all but the more select French wines. Like the Spanish, they are excellent value for money.

Vinhos verdes

Vinhos verdes or 'green wines' are made in the north of Portugal from the fruit of high-growing vines and are dry, *pétillant* wines, very pale in

Wood port is defined as a blend of wines from different vintages matured in cask until ready for drinking. In the form of the popular **ruby** it is the staple of the shippers, and most club ports are of this sort. The young rubies, aged for only two or three years and relatively inexpensive, are clear in colour with an attractive full-bodied freshness. Other more expensive types are darker in colour, given much longer in wood and somewhat resemble the vintage character wines.

The aristocrat of wood ports is **tawny**, matured for long periods in cask. This results in paler, less full-bodied and very aromatic wines, preferred by some connoisseurs, who find the vintage and vintage character ports too rich and heavy. Fine old tawnies, such as Delaforce's ten-year-old His Eminence's Choice or Ferreira's twenty-year-old Duque de Bragança, are expensive wines, but in a colour and are drunk 'green' or young. Fresh, clean and very moderately priced, they are at their best with light food or before a meal. Bone dry red wines of the same type are made in even larger quantity in Portugal, but their consumption is mainly local.

Dão

Best known of still Portuguese wines, Dão is made in a mountain-bound enclave of central Portugal. The typical wines are dry, full-bodied reds, more in the style of Burgundy than claret, and improving greatly with bottle age. The region also produces some dry, fruity white wines.

Wines of the Centre

The Portuguese demarcation system, now undergoing radical revision, has always laid great stress on the classical wines from four tiny regions near Lisbon. First popularised in Britain by the officers of Wellington's army, they are available only in minuscule amounts.

Red Colares is grown in the dune sands of the coast near Sintra and is made from the grapes of one of the very few pre-phylloxera vines remaining in Europe, the Ramisco. A superb wine when properly matured, it is extremely astringent when young and approaches its magnificent best only after some twenty years in bottle.

Carcavelos, on the outskirts of Lisbon, produces only some 90 hectolitres (1,980 gallons) of wine in an average year. Topaz-coloured and of some 19° strength, the wines vary from medium-dry to sweet and are either drunk chilled as an aperitif or with a dessert. I can vouch for its lasting properties, having only recently drunk my last bottle of a small bin of 1845 – an incredible age for a white wine. Every bottle was drinkable, a little tired perhaps, but no more so than I shall be at half the age!

The white wines of Bucelas, just north of Lisbon, are made from the Arinto grape, sometimes supposed to be descended from the Riesling. The younger wines shipped abroad are light, dry and delicately perfumed, and go well with fish. The Portuguese prefer older, oakier wines with a very dry finish, at times lemony and at others reminiscent of bitter almonds.

Moscatel de Setúbal, made in the Arrábida Peninsula, south of Lisbon and the Tagus, is among the world's great dessert Moscatels. Those made by the leading producer, J. M. da Fonseca, and sold as six-year-old or twenty-five-year-old, have an extraordinary taste of fresh grapes. This results from steeping grape skins in the wine after fermentation; it is then fortified and matured for long years in oak.

Bairrada

The wines from the Bairrada, a newly demarcated region lying in the coastal area between Oporto and

Top: Decorative tiled mural of the typical blue and yellow azulejos *at the railway station in Pinhão in the heart of the port-growing region.*

Above: Harvest time in one of the port vineyards of the Upper Douro. Because of the steep terrain, the grapes are first picked into baskets and then carried to the waiting ox-carts or tractor-driven trailers.

Right: The eighteenth-century Manueline-style Palace of Mateus in Vila Real, adjoining the SOGRAPE *winery and featured on the labels of Mateus Rosé.*

Coimbra, are typically red and made from the Baga grape. Full-bodied and astringent when young, they repay long ageing in bottle. Some of the old vintage wines, especially those made in small quantity at the Palace Hotel in Buçaco, are very fine. The Bairrada also makes large amounts of rosé wines, as well as good sparkling wine by the *méthode champenoise*. These sparkling wines are mainly from the Maria Gomes grape. They are clean and fruity, but are somewhat heavier than the sparklers from Rheims and the Penedès.

Upper Douro
The Upper Douro makes even larger amounts of red table wine than port, among the best being the Vila Real *claretes* from the makers of Mateus Rosé and Evel from the Real Companhía Vinícola do Norte de Portugal. In a class of its own is the red Barca Velha made by the port house of Ferreira in limited quantity. Like the Spanish Vega Sicilia, which it resembles in its deep, fruity nose and flavour, it is available only at the best hotels and restaurants.

Wines of the South
The best wines from south of Lisbon are the reds from the firm of J. M. da Fonseca made at Azeitão in the Arrábida Peninsula near Setúbal. They include the consistent and most drinkable Periquita from the grape of the same name and Camarate, a lighter wine which contains a proportion of Cabernet Sauvignon. Over to the east near the Spanish frontier, Borba, Redondo and Reguengos de Monsaraz in the Alentejo produce sturdy red wines, high in alcohol, with a deep blackberry flavour.

Wines in bulk
Most of the everyday wine drunk in Lisbon, both red and white, is produced around Torres Vedras and in the Ribatejo rather north of the capital. They are sound but somewhat 'earthy'. Apart from some old *garrafeiras*, or vintage wines, the best is the popular Serradayres. The name means 'mountain of air' and the wine originally hailed from Borba, but is now blended by Carvalho, Ribeiro and Ferreira near Lisbon. Lighter in style than Dão, it is often served at the Factory House in Oporto.

Madeira

The other great Portuguese aperitif and dessert wine takes its name from Madeira, an island about the size of the Isle of Wight some 800 kilometres (500 miles) out in the Atlantic off the coast of Morocco. It was discovered by the Portuguese navigators João Gonçalves Zarco and Tristão Vaz Teixera in 1419. At the time the island was covered with forests, which were burnt down by the early colonists, who set about the construction of the terraces on which the grapes are grown today. Since the calamities of oidium and phylloxera, from which the trade has never fully recovered, the vines have been grafted on to American stocks.

Madeira is a wine with a romantic and extremely well-documented history, beginning with the harbouring of Prince Rupert's fleet by the Portuguese. After the ensuing war with the Commonwealth, one of the conditions of the peace signed in 1654 was that British merchants should be given special privileges, and by 1708 they had established a 'factory' in Madeira. The mid-eighteenth century saw the arrival of merchants like John Leacock and Francis

One of the small terraced vineyards in Madeira. The vines grow in the volcanic soils of the mountainsides. The grapes were formerly trodden on the spot, but are now transported to the adegas of the large firms in Funchal and crushed mechanically.

Newton, who founded two of the famous firms of today, while John Blandy, who served as quartermaster with the occupying forces during the Peninsular War, remained to found another. By the end of the eighteenth century, Madeira was more popular in England than port, and the Apsley Papers describe how 'military manners prescribed officially a monthly ration of fifteen bottles of Madeira as the bare limit of necessity'.

All Madeira is fortified, but, unlike port, very little vintage wine is now produced. It is often made like sherry by the *solera* system – with the important difference that it is heated in *estufas* or stoves to 113°–122°F (45°–50°C) for three or four months. The practice dates from the days when it was shipped through the tropics in sailing vessels and was found to be greatly improved by the heat and shaking of the voyage. Unlike the lighter sherries, Madeira of all wines improves with really prolonged maturation in bottle, and it is quite possible to get the great Madeira *soleras* of 1789, 1795, 1846 and so on, which are all excellent.

Like port, it can be drunk as a dessert wine or, in its dry styles such as Sercial, instead of sherry before a meal. One is always hearing about a glass of Madeira and a biscuit with one's bank manager at eleven in the morning, but I personally never had such an enlightened bank manager, or if I did I never knew it, for I did not come under the category of customers to whom bank managers give glasses of Madeira. Be that as it may, a glass of Bual Madeira with a dry biscuit either at mid-morning or in the afternoon is a very happy institution, and I can recommend it.

It is, indeed, a wine much to be praised. Delicious whether dry or sweet, it is agreeable to the palate and never harsh and has a flavour all its own; it is also very comforting to the stomach, or at least to mine. Although there has been some abuse of varietal names, the different styles are named, in ascending order of sweetness, after the grapes from which they are made: Sercial, Verdelho, Bual and Malmsey. The Malmsey (or Malvasia) grape was brought to the island from Cyprus early in its history and makes rich and luscious dessert wines. One also encounters other types, such as the picturesquely named Rainwater, a light, fresh wine.

Among the principal shippers, some household names, are: Barbeito, shippers of one of the driest Madeiras, the Island Dry; Blandy, one of the oldest and most famous firms, best known for its Duke of Clarence Malmsey; Cossart Gorden, famous for some of the finest *solera* and vintage wines; Henriques and Henriques, makers of the aperitif Ribeiro Seco; Leacock, an old firm famous for its Penny Black Malmsey; and Rutherford and Miles, exporters of possibly the best known of Madeira wines, Old Trinity House.

CENTRAL EUROPE

Above: The undulating vineyards of Luxembourg.

Opposite: The vintage at Yvorne in Chablais, a wine canton of Switzerland.

There are many good and refreshing, if not great, wines grown within the continent of Europe apart from in France, Germany and Italy. I will start with a wine that is not often sold abroad but comes from a country well worth a visit.

Luxembourg

The grapes from which Luxembourg wines are made are grown from vines on the low hills along the upper Moselle and they have a good deal of affinity with the German Moselle wines. There is no tradition of making great wines, as in Germany, but substantial quantities of very good wine are made, the best of them from the Riesling grape. The vineyards start where the German vineyards end, at Wasserbillig on the frontier, and go on through Grevenmacher, Wormeldange, Remich and Wellenstein. Quite wisely, the Luxembourgians drink their own wine and do not bother to import or export very much.

As far as I know all the wine is white. They make a wine that is found hardly anywhere else and this is the Luxembourg *perlé*, which is a semi-sparkling or *pétillant* wine of considerable liveliness and charm. One can now buy it in the UK. I invariably order it as an aperitif if it is available. It is not that it is as good as Champagne (which is the perfect aperitif), it most certainly is not, but it is quite cheap, very clean and altogether excellent.

Switzerland

The wines of Switzerland are essentially for the Swiss as there are hardly enough produced for their own consumption. Since Switzerland is an extremely lovely country, it is worth drinking a few Swiss wines on a visit there, or on your way through Switzerland to sunny Italy. I would particularly recommend the wines of the Valais, that long, fruitful valley between the Lake of Geneva and Brig, *en route* for the Simplon Tunnel. All along this valley very good wine is made and it is well worth stopping for a little *dégustation* in the morning or, indeed, at any time. The best red wine of the Valais is known as Dôle. To qualify for this name the wine must be made of both the Pinot Noir and Gamay grapes. There is an inferior kind of Dôle called Goron. The best of the white wines is Fendant. If you are in no hurry and can take your trip from Lausanne in a leisurely manner, call in at Martigny or maybe Sion or any little off-beat place amid this most marvellous scenery and eat well, wine well and sleep well. It is, as Michelin says, well worth the detour.

In Switzerland they do not go in much for dates and, in point of fact, it does not matter much because the wines are skilfully made and they do not last that long, particularly the whites. Probably the most famous Swiss wines come from Neuchâtel, and these wines can indeed be found in one or two good restaurants in London, notably those where the managing director is Swiss, and at the Swiss Centre in Leicester Square. They are extremely good wines with something of an affinity with the Hermitage along the higher Rhône, but they are not made to keep or travel and must be drunk within three or four years and, unless imported in bottle, they will not be nearly so good as in their own country.

Both red and white wines are made in most of the

The ripening grapes in this Swiss vineyard are protected from the ravages of greedy birds by brightly coloured nets.

Swiss cantons, and in general they tend to resemble the style of wines made in the countries adjoining. In the German-speaking cantons, for example, the reds have a good deal in common with the South German red wines, while those made in the Ticino, where Italian is spoken, resemble the dry reds of Piedmont. The best of all Swiss wines, however, undoubtedly come from Neuchâtel and the Valais, and wines produced in the other areas do not really compare with them.

Austria

Austrian wines are at their best when drunk in Austria, and especially in Vienna. Many of them never reach the bottle, being consumed fresh, green and still prickling from fermentation straight from the cask in the many *heurigen*, cellars-cum-wine gardens, which ring the suburbs of the capital beneath the Vienna woods. It is then that they are at

The Ried Klaus vineyard on the banks of the Danube in Austria.

their most delicious, *gemütlichkeit* apart.

The Austrian wine laws are much stricter than they used to be, and the days when an Austrian label was little more than a transit visa are long since departed. Production is now strictly controlled under four main regions of which the most important are Lower Austria and the Burgenland. All of the regions are divided into sub-districts, of which probably the most famous is the Wachau, a spectacular gorge through which the Danube flows past steeply terraced vineyards on its way downstream to Vienna. The best wines of the Wachau are dry, steely white wines made from Rhine Riesling and Grüner Veltliner, while Burgenland, on the flatlands bordering the Hungarian Great Plain, specialises in sweet dessert wines on the German pattern, described by the German terms *Spätlese, Auslese* and so on up the scale. Excellent red wines are also made in Austria, particularly in Vöslau, just south of Vienna: they tend to have a slight, distinctive bitterness of finish, which many well appreciate.

Adjoining Vöslau is Baden, whose best-known wine is the heady white Gumpoldskirchener.

Austrian white wines are often regarded as interchangeable with German wines, but almost the only similarity derives from the fact that most of the German grape varieties are grown in Austria. The wines they produce tend to reflect the drier Austrian palate: the most typical of all Austrian whites are made from their own Grüner Veltliner, and these tend to be bone dry and even slightly austere.

All the Austrian vineyards lie in the east of the country, where the Alps give way to rolling agricultural country and eventually to the plains of Central Europe. Vienna lies at the very heart of Austrian viticulture. Apart from Paris, whose tiny vineyard on Montmartre is little more than a curiosity, the city must qualify as one of the only world capitals to boast vineyards within its city limits, and providing not the least of its many attractions.

Yugoslavia

There is quite an important wine-making tradition in Yugoslavia, which embraces the old kingdoms of Serbia and Montenegro. Wine is made all along the Adriatic, from the Italian border down to Albania, and there are extensive vineyards internally.

Yugoslavia is now the tenth largest wine-producing country in the world making 6,297,000 hectolitres (about 138,000,000 gallons) of wine a year. I have found the Yugoslav wines universally good. Certainly the export white wines are not only cheap but of some distinction. These wines are generally exported in bulk and bottled abroad, and for what they cost are extremely good value, comparing favourably with the wines of any other country at that price.

The foreign exchange situation in this Communist

country probably operates in our favour with regard to the price, and we ought to take advantage of it because the wine is clean and mostly dry, well, dryish. The Riesling (or, rather, the 'Laski' Riesling, a cousin of the classic 'Rhine' Riesling) is the principal grape in general cultivation, but there are a number of different varieties of grape grown which have various degrees of sweetness. Other grapes used for Yugoslav wines include many of the classic European varieties, such as Sauvignon and Traminer for the whites, Cabernet Sauvignon, Pinot Noir and Merlot for the reds, but they appear to have their own national character. In Yugoslavia itself I have found the wine everywhere very drinkable and since there are no great wines, only good, they taste very good in their native land.

The exported wine most often found is Lutomer Laski Riesling. This is a fragrant, slightly sweet white wine best drunk with fish but which, as in the case of Liebfraumilch and Mateus Rosé, can really be drunk with almost anything. It is a wine of some character.

At Carlowitz (now Sremski Karlovci) in Serbia, which sits on a bend of the Danube some 80 kilometres (50 miles) north of Belgrade, they used to make a rich golden wine which became extremely popular in court circles in the middle of the last century. I have in my possession a pair of decanters capable of holding three bottles each, which were sandblasted with the inscription, 'Finest Carlowitz by Royal Appointment to Her Majesty Queen Victoria'. When I acquired the decanters they were, alas, empty and I have never tasted that wine, but it must have been good to achieve such distinction.

Hungary

There is a good deal of white wine made in Hungary and at one time it was extremely popular in the UK. I suppose that, most of all, Hungary is famous for Tokay, which has always been a byword for richness, fatness and good living. The best Tokay is the Imperial (I suppose from the Royal cellars) and even above that, and perhaps because of it, is the world-famous Tokay Essence or Eszencia. Edmund Penning-Rowsell, during a visit to Hungary, was given half a litre of this fantastic wine, which is still made but rarely sold. Through his courtesy I have been privileged to drink a glass. It is a superlative wine, not so sweet as one would pehaps imagine, but of tremendous concentration and character. At a recent sale at Christie's a half-litre bottle of this wine (admittedly 1888) fetched £130.

Tokay is made in a strictly limited area and the wine varies from dry to very, very sweet indeed. The predominant grape variety is Furmint. In some ways the styles available conform to the German pattern of wine making, from the ordinary wine made from ordinary grapes to the great *Trocken-*

beerenauslese wines which are made from hand-picked overripe grapes, wrinkled and fat with sugar and covered in *pourriture noble*. In the great days of Imperial Tokay, they went even further than this: the grapes were left so long that they were sometimes gathered in the snow in late November; then heaped in the vat so that the pressure of the grapes above broke the skins of those at the bottom. The viscous liquid which emerged was carefully collected and made into the fabulous Eszencia. It is reputed that from many acres of grapes of the finest quality very few bottles would be made, and it had a high reputation for keeping millionaires alive, being a pleasant substitute for oxygen. According to Morton Shand, the wine does not have a high alcoholic content, merely 7° or 8°, but it is reputed to have a fantastic delicate sweetness and takes years and years to mature, including four to eight years in

Walled vineyards in Yugoslavia, near the town of Primosten in Dalmatia. This part of the country produces a considerable variety of different wines.

Above: Vintage time in the vineyards producing Tokay, Hungary's famous sweet dessert wine.

Below: A typical view of vineyards near Lake Balaton, where some of Hungary's good-quality white wines are made.

gonci (casks) embedded in rock. It has a reputation (perhaps with some reason) of having aphrodisiac qualities. Morton Shand quotes a Dr Robert Druitt MRCP, sometime medical adviser of health for the Parish of St George's, Hanover Square, who in a lecture, said of Tokay: 'Nor need I mince matters and refrain from saying that "when childless families despair", when January is wedded to May, and when old men wish to be young again, then Tokay is in request.' It was, I am told, a favourite drink of the Court of King George IV.

Ordinary Tokay, if it can be so called, is described according to the number of *puttonyos* (small wooden measures) of *aszú* paste put into each cask. This paste is made from overripe grapes affected by *pourriture noble*. Thus you will see on the label 'Tokay, Aszú, three puttonyos', which means that it is a medium kind of wine and not over-sweet. The maximum is the 'six puttonyos' which is a very thick, sweet wine, but three, four or five is more usual.

Mention should also be made of two others – I suppose one could call them the minor Tokays – the Tokay Furmint, which is also a wine of the Furmint grape and is rich, and full-bodied, and the Szamorodni or Tokay Szamorodni, which is the wine with no *aszú* paste added and is therefore a quite dry, altogether excellent wine.

Good wines are made on the north shore of Lake Balaton which has now become one of the principal Iron Curtain tourist resorts. The wines are not in themselves very special but are good and are known under such labels as Balatoni Riesling or Balatoni Furmint. They are not commonly met with outside Hungary.

Red wines are made, but not to the same extent as white, but there is an almost black wine called Bikavér, which means 'bull's blood', that is made in the Egri district. This is a sound big wine and it can be bought in the UK and is deservedly well known.

Czechoslovakia

Few, if any, Czechoslovak wines are exported and I am again indebted to Edmund Penning-Rowsell, who has recently returned from Czechoslovakia, for the information that the wine yield exceeds that

of Switzerland and that Czechoslovak domestic demand far exceeds supply. Consequently it is extremely unlikely that we shall see any of it here for some years to come, but if you go to Prague or take a tour of that delightful country, you can expect to drink both red and white wines, and they are soundly made, honest wines. The white wines are in my opinion better than the red, the most commonly found being Vlassky Ryzling.

Romania and Bulgaria

I have never travelled in these two countries, but the wines of both of them are becoming more readily available. Even so I am chiefly indebted for my knowledge to the few books available and especially to Hugh Johnson's invaluable *World Atlas of Wine* (Mitchell Beazley, 1971) to which I can refer the reader if his curiosity causes him (and I hope it does) to require further knowledge. According to Johnson, the principal wine of Romania, historically at least, is Cotnari and he says 'Cotnari is a natural white dessert wine like Tokay only with rather more in delicacy and less in density. There is no doubt in tasting it that one is tasting something of an unusual quality and character.' On this recommendation I should certainly make special efforts to look at this wine but I do not particularly want to go to Romania to do so.

The grapes used for Romanian wines are Furmint again, as in Hungary, Riesling, Cabernet, Muscat and Pinot Noir, and the wine is exported largely to other Iron Curtain countries and to Germany. A surprisingly large amount of the world's wine is made in Romania. In 1980 as much as 7,593,000 hectolitres (about 167,000,000 gallons) were made, mostly white. The vineyards extend through most of the Romanian provinces, with good white wines being made in Transylvania to the west, reds on the eastern slopes of the Carpathians, and dessert wines along the coast of the Black Sea. The Tîrnave river is one of the best regions for white wines, and Dealul Mare for reds.

Bulgarian wine labels used to be printed in Cyrillic characters which, as far as I am concerned, rendered them indecipherable. Nowadays they are more export conscious. The wines are of a high standard, particularly the Cabernets and Rieslings, which are the best of their type from Eastern Europe.

The Soviet Union

Russian wines may be bought outside the USSR, if you can find them. I have only drunk these wines during a visit to Russia, that is to say, Moscow and Leningrad, and I took every opportunity of looking at them. They are, by and large, sound enough but tending to sweetness, which I believe is to the taste of the Soviet people.

The export wines are usually sound, low-priced, rather fruity wines with their own peculiar flavour, the appreciation of which might be termed an acquired taste. The sweet wines can be over-sweet. They may be made from either Muscatel grapes, or perhaps the Spanish Pedro Ximénez grape, from which the very, very sweet sherries are made. Some of the red *ordinaires* are good enough: they generally come either from the Crimea or from the former Romanian province of Moldavia. So-called Russian Champagne is made in considerable quantities in the Crimea and also farther south in the Russian and Georgian republics. It is, again, over-sweet and it would take me a century or two to acquire any taste for it. The only affinity with the true Champagne, as far as I can see, is that they both have bubbles and I suppose you could say that they sparkle. But Champagne: no! and a dozen times no!

The only advice I can give the reader is to make sure that you visit Leningrad (especially) and Moscow, for the sake of those two cities and all the wonders that they contain.

The vast plains of Moldavia that border the Russian frontier account for a considerable amount of Romania's large wine production.

EASTERN AND SOUTHERN MEDITERRANEAN

Above: A detail from a mosaic on the floor of the third century villa at Paphos in Cyprus. Dionysus was the Greek god of wine.

Opposite: The tiny terraced vineyards of the Greek island of Samos, famous above all for its Muscat. Cypress and olive trees mingle with the vines.

Greece

Greek wine has been made for longer than recorded history can tell. Since the days of pre-classical Greece, the wine cup has been a decorative motif on the shards of pottery, of which there are so many lovely specimens in existence. The wine cups and *kraters* of classical Greece were highly decorated and H. Warner Allen in his *History of Wine* (Cassell, 1961) gives an excellent account of wine drinking and some of the 'parlour games' they played with the wine and wine cup in ancient Greece.

Modern Greek wines are becoming quite well known abroad. These are generally strong, heady, beverage wines sometimes tinctured with resin, which have a certain appeal for people who like a distinctive, tasty drink. This resinous wine is not to everyone's taste, and certainly it does not go well with any kind of delicate food. The truth is that Greek wine is made (as it should be) to suit the climate and the food of the country, and the rather oily cuisine of Greece is very suited to the heady resinous wines. Personally, I have no great objection to it in Greece, in fact, I rather like it.

The addition of one to three per cent of resin to the young wine has gone on from time immemorial and it is said that this admixture helps to preserve the wine and renders it more wholesome – a sentiment rather than a fact, I fear. Fortunately, however, modern Greek practice tends to produce wines with and without resin.

In my opinion the majority of Greek wines are without any great character. But there are exceptions and among them I would mention the following:

The Rotonda of Boutari is a dry, red wine; rather fine like a red Graves from a minor château.

Château Carras, *tête de cuvée rouge*, château bottled at the domaine of Port Carras in Sithonia, is a deep rich colour with a good character, not unlike good quality Côtes du Rhône.

Calliga's Robola of Cephalonia is a white wine of little character but quite receivable. It is dressed in sackcloth and is sealed on the label with a lovely wax seal for which no doubt one pays extra.

Cava Calliga is a dry red wine, rather like a *bourgeois* Graves, full-flavoured, quite palatable and not expensive.

Look also for the red wines of Nemea on the Peloponnese, and Naoussa from Macedonia in the north: these are both among the country's best.

Demestica red is the drinkable Beaujolais of Greece. The white is perhaps the Liebfraumilch of Greece, but a great deal heavier and without much character. I find Samos Muscat rather too sweet, though it is reputed to be the finest Muscat in the world. It is a heavy wine of up to 15° of alcohol, more aromatic but not dissimilar to Barsac. Not too much attention should be given to the date on the neck label of the wines from Greek islands and Greece itself. The climate does not change from one year to

The dramatic terraced vineyards of the Troodos mountains in western Cyprus. As well as vines, almond trees flourish in the poor soil.

another and nor does the soil. Modern vinification has, in any case, tended to correct the inadequacies of nature.

In the old days, by which I mean before tourism more or less took over the Greek restaurant, Retsina was always served as a matter of course and still is in off-the-mainroads tiny *tavernas*. If you ever visit Greece (and I hope you will) you have a great treat in store: visit a *taverna*, enter through the kitchen, choose a dish or dishes from one of the dozen or so cooking on the stove, and sit down to the food with a carafe of ice-cold Greek wine. Long may you survive!

Transport in Cyprus is still primitive; the mule brought the grapes from vineyard to village and a lorry will deliver them to the co-operative to which most growers belong.

Cyprus

Cyprus grows vines and makes wines both red and white. They have a considerable affinity with Greek wines. Cyprus may well be the origin of that butt of Malmsey wine so beloved of historians, in which the infamous Duke of Clarence was supposed to have been drowned in 1478. Malmsey, a name derived from the Malvoisie grape, is usually associated with Madeira and the Canaries where it is made today, but legend has it that the first cuttings came there from Cyprus. Nowadays I do not know if any Malvasia comes out of Cyprus, but there is another, quite famous, sweet wine which has a character of its own: Commandaria, sometimes called Commandaria St John. I have drunk nineteenth-century Commandaria wines and they have some affinity with the luscious Bristol Cream kind of sherry, even though they are made from grape varieties native to Cyprus.

Among the dry or semi-sweet wines there are one or two worthy of your opinion and I would include Domaine d'Ahera, a dry red, and Aphrodite, which is medium-dry and white. Othello is a full, red, dry wine and should be drunk like Burgundy or claret with red meat. However, the principal wine production of Cyprus is 'sherry' in one or other of its many forms and some of these can be comparable to the real thing.

The wine industry in Cyprus is very largely in the hands of three main operators or co-operatives: SODAP, Keo and Etko-Haggipavlu. The wine-growing area of Cyprus covers about eight per cent of the surface of the island and cultivation and harvesting are carried out by about 10,000 Cypriot families, but the production of the wine is controlled by the above companies, who have installed the most sophisticated methods of vinification.

Turkey

The odd thing about the wines of Turkey is that I cannot find any reference to them in the older books of my gastronomic library. Although Turkey holds fifth place among the grape-growing countries of the world it holds one of the lowest places among the wine-producing countries, because most of the grapes are either sold as raisins, currants or sultanas, or for table grapes, or for making grape syrup. According to André Simon, it was not always so and, at the beginning of the century, Turkey produced as much as 68,000,000 litres (15,000,000 gallons) of wine a year, eighty per cent for export; I know not to where or for what purpose.

Every kind of wine is made, but more white than red, and some of it is quite heady with an alcohol content of up to 13.5°. Considerable effort is being made to improve the quality of the wines, a few of which are available abroad. Tekirdag is one such white wine, or rather a golden wine, not unlike a good Entre-Deux-Mers and up to the standard of other wines sold at the same price. The quaintly named Buzbag is probably the best of the reds exported from Turkey; deep red, robust and full-bodied.

I have drunk Turkish wines without much effort in Istanbul, and I can at least say that I enjoyed them for what they were and say that they go well with Turkish food.

Israel

In the ninth chapter of Genesis, Noah, the first 'vigneron', is recorded as having planted a vineyard. However, wine making in Israel on the modern pattern is only a hundred years old. Two important and quite different outside influences can be seen at work. The first began with the foundation, under the patronage of Baron Edmond de Rothschild, of the two large co-operative wineries of Richon-le-Zion and Zichron-Jacob, which together account for the major share of Israeli wine production today. The grape varieties, also French, include Carignan, Grenache, Alicante (reds) and Sémillon, Clairette and Muscat d'Alexandre (whites), which until recently produced all the more notable Israeli wines.

The second, twentieth century, influence has grown out of the special relationship which modern Israel has enjoyed with the USA. To this influence can be ascribed the new breed of 'varietal' wines produced from single classic grape varieties, such

as the Cabernet Sauvignon and Sauvignon Blanc.

Israel's vineyards lie in three main zones. The coastal plains, south from Mount Carmel to Tel Aviv and neighbouring uplands inland towards Jerusalem, form the first and most extensive area, followed by the northern shores of Lake Tiberius and the semi-desert vineyards around Beersheba in the south.

Israeli wines are marketed in the USA and the UK by the Carmel Wine Company, all export wines being certified as kosher. Apart from the new 'varietal' wines, the more traditional types fall into two basic categories: sweet dessert types, including some excellent muscatels, and conventional table wines. Some of the labels most often seen include Carmel Hock and Château de la Montagne among the whites; Adom Atic is a popular red, Carmel Topaz, Partom and Almog are dessert types and The President's Sparkling Wine is also worth trying.

Selling wine in Istanbul; presumably licensing laws are non-existent.

A vineyard in Israel, south of Jerusalem. There are three main vineyard zones in Israel, including areas of semi-desert in the south.

Above: Viticulture in the Lebanon is very primitive. This vineyard on the plain of Bekaá is still ploughed by a donkey, as it has been for centuries.

Below: The vineyards of the plain of Bekaá. Miraculously they have survived the current hostilities.

The Lebanon

These red wines are beginning to be available abroad and by courtesy of Paul Levy, who gave me some bottles of a wine called Château Musar, château bottled and imported to the UK under the name of the proprietor, Gaston Hochar (his son, Serge, is now the wine maker), I can vouch for their quality and interest. I was given a bottle of 1964 and another one of 1977 and I must say that the 1964 was surprisingly good. I say surprisingly good because I did not expect really good wine from this very hot country. Mr Hochar is certainly making an excellent wine of its class which I much enjoyed.

Egypt

Modern Egyptian wines, which can only be bought in Egypt, are made in the delta near Alexandria, and rumour says that they are made from raisins rather than grapes which, from the taste, is quite possible. They are dull with nothing much to commend them, least of all the price, which is high, but they have lovely names – Clos de Cléopâtre and Cru des Pyramides and, appropriately, Omar Khayyam among them. They are not much to our taste, but in a Moslem country wines are not very popular and viticulture lacks encouragement. Mohammed was against it and he says in the Koran: 'There is a devil in every berry of the grape.' Historically, Egyptian records of wine and wine making are the earliest extant and from the first dynasty, about 3000 BC onwards, there is constant reference in tomb carvings and paintings to the place of wine in Egyptian life. As I have already mentioned in my Introduction, an interesting fact not generally known is that the most definite proof of the number of years which the young King Tutankhamen reigned was from the seals of the wine jars buried with him with his fabulous treasure in the unplundered tomb, found in 1922. Tutankhamen died in or about the year 1350 BC and the wine jars bear the royal seal, stating that the wine was made in the royal vineyards in the delta in the ninth year of his reign. Since wine in the East is always drunk very shortly after it is made, it can be reasonably assumed that the wine in the King's tomb was that of the last vintage, and thus we know how long this young king reigned. The jars were sealed, but alas no wine remained, only a desiccated powder. There is an apocryphal story of archaeologists finding in a royal tomb which had

been plundered of its treasure, like most of the others, two *amphorae*, or wine jars, lying in the corner. These had been opened and the wine drunk by the robbers (most of the tombs were plundered in deep antiquity). Upon one of the *amphorae* the robber had scratched: 'This one contains the best wine.'

What the wine was like in those days we cannot know, but Islam has certainly done nothing for the modern Egyptian wine industry.

North-west Africa

Quantity rather than quality used to be the rule in the three wine-producing countries of North-west Africa, respectively Algeria, Tunisia and Morocco. Their traditional speciality was the production of robust, alcoholic wines for blending with the thin reds of Southern France. However, with the withdrawal of the French colonial power and the disappearance of a ready market, more attention is now being given to improving quality. The best wines of these regions are red, generally dark, soft and smooth, and there are also some pleasant dry rosés. All are best drunk young. The whites, being especially prone to oxidation, should be avoided.

Algeria is by far the most important of the three countries, both in the quality of its wines and in the scale of production. The largest vineyards lie in the province of Oran, followed by Alger and Constantine. Quality is determined not so much by the location of the vineyard as by its altitude, the best wines coming from the northern slopes of the Atlas. Names to look for are Coteaux de Mascara, Haut-Dahra, Tlemcen, Monts du Tessalah, Medea and Côtes du Zaccar. Vast vineyards lie nearer to the coast, but these produce wines of a more basic standard.

Wine production in Tunisia is controlled by the State, in the shape of the UCCVT (Union des Caves Coopératives du Vin de Tunisie). The vineyards lie in the north of the country, in a crescent stretching from Bizerte, inland from Carthage and Tunis, to Sousse and Hammamet. The best of the wines are red. Two worth trying are Coteaux de Carthage and Haut Mornag. Another speciality is the dry Muscat of Cap Bon.

The Moroccan wine industry is modern and forward-looking, with some thriving private companies at its head. The best wines come from vineyards on the slopes of the Middle Atlas around Meknès and Fès. Guerrouane and Beni M'Tir, two supple, powerful reds are particularly recommended. Other, more prolific vineyards line the coast from Rabat in the north to south of Casablanca. The best of their production are a breed of pale dry rosés, marketed as *gris* like their counterparts from the French Midi, which are enjoyable drunk young, fresh and well chilled.

Vineyards in Egypt at Oase Feiran. The vines are pruned almost like small trees. The rugged hills of Sinai rise up in the background.

Malta

Vines have been grown and wine made in Malta since the time of the Romans, but until recently the production has only been sufficient for domestic consumption. A few years ago I visited Malta for a few days and was able to study the wines at first hand; I had the advantage of being taken round the wineries by an official of the Maltese Ministry of Agriculture.

This tiny island, with its even smaller sister island of Gozo, is rocky, stony and sandy, and if poorness of soil is a qualification for making good wine Malta certainly ought to make it, and so it does. The wines have a strong affinity with the Italian wines and quite a lot of the expertise that is used in the making, blending and storage of the wines comes from northern Italy. Grapes are grown in very small holdings on both islands, and they are sold to wineries established in three or four places, but mostly in the suburbs of Valletta. Great progress is being made in the improvement of the wine under governmental encouragement. Until recently, wines were made to be consumed in the year after vintage – that is, quite new. They varied in quality from very rough to moderately good, but there are now some excellent wines produced and Malta is beginning to export. In most cases, Maltese wines are used to assist other countries to close the gap between their domestic supply and demand. This is a pity, because Maltese wine in its export quality is stable, extremely clean, palatable, rather light and a very good beverage wine. No fine wines are produced, let alone great, but perhaps this will come, because the soil is right, and certainly there is plenty of sun to ripen the grapes. It remains to be seen whether the wine will keep for very long.

ENGLAND

Pilton Manor is one of the most established English vineyards, which can be recommended.

It is important to make a distinction between English and British wines. English wines are those made in England from the freshly gathered grapes of the vineyards in which they are grown. British wines are generally wines made in England from imported grapes and grape juices and certainly not fresh-gathered fruit. One can buy British wines in the form of 'sherries', 'ports' and table wines, but generally I think they are over-sweet and over-strong. English wines are quite another matter.

Historically, vines came over here with the Romans, who found that communications were not all that good between Gaul and Britain and sometimes the legions were left without their wine, causing an understandable drop in morale. So they planted vines and made wine. The Saxon and Anglo-Saxon preference for beer caused the Roman vineyards to be neglected and, in fact, there is no doubt that they went out of production. But then came St Augustine with his monks and with him the necessity for wine for Communion. From that time most monasteries (and there were very many of them) grew their own grapes and made their wine until perhaps the thirteenth or fourteenth centuries and indeed up to the time of the Dissolution of the Monasteries, when supplies had become reliable. Consequently, there was a hiatus in vine growing of half a millennium or so until after World War II.

Sir Guy Salisbury-Jones planted his vineyards in Hambledon and made a very drinkable white wine,

Right: The vintage at Hambledon with the village of Mill Down in the distance. The leaves have already changed colour and the grapes are protected by nets against the birds.

Figures indicate number of vineyards in county

FRANCE

The vines of Wootton in Somerset, which were first planted in 1971.

which is still known as Hambledon and still sells very well to visitors, although it is not easily available in shops. In my cellar book I see that I bought a case of Hambledon 1959 as long ago as 1961 and I still have a bottle in my cellar, now 24 years old. I kept it largely for curiosity but I shall have to open it soon if it is going to be drinkable, though the wine when last tasted was in good order. From Sir Guy Salisbury-Jones's efforts to establish English wines has grown the whole industry. There are now about two hundred vineyards making wine in England. Most of the vineyards are in the south, a few are in the Midlands and the most northerly is Renishaw in Derbyshire. Some of the wine produced in England is good, nearly all of it is drinkable, and vineyard owners are still learning.

There is no reason why England cannot make good wine. Most of the vineyards are on much the same latitude as the great wines of Germany and have much the same weather conditions from year to year. Time and experience will tell, but in the meantime most of the wines that I have drunk are of good average quality if expensive in comparison with what one can buy nowadays from Germany and other vine-growing areas on the Continent. It is likely that in time the English vineyards will become, if not famous, certainly noteworthy.

My advice on English wine is to take the trouble to find out when you are touring on holiday where these two hundred vineyards are and whether they are visitable (one cannot expect just to walk into every vineyard without notice). There are many who welcome visitors. A Source of Wine map is available giving the location of the vineyards, and an enlarged version in colour is obtainable from the English Vineyards Association at Drusillas, Alfriston, Sussex, for only £2.

Most of the English vineyards grow German varieties of grapes because of the similarity in the climatic conditions. However, I have found in the course of my researches that English wines have a character in common: that of a definite taste of the grape. The wines tend to be a little on the sweet side, although there are some dry ones, and the bigger vineyards make a selection of wines from the very dry to the quite sweet.

Probably the largest wine-growing area in England is on the Isle of Wight at Adgestone, where an excellent selection of wines is made, all of which can be rated as being not only reliable but very good. Apart from Adgestone's advantage of being the most southerly vineyard, the owners say that reflected sun from the sea also helps to ripen the grapes, and this may well be true. The grapes grown are the Müller-Thurgau, the Reichensteiner and the Seyval Blanc.

Hambledon wine is made from Pinot Meunier, Chardonnay and Pinot Noir grapes and they also grow Seyval. Visiting the vineyard is by appointment only and a small fee includes tasting, colour slides, and general information.

Lamberhurst Priory in Kent, on the Sussex border, which can be visited at any time, produces some worthwhile English wines, mostly from the Müller-Thurgau grapes. It is not the cheapest wine by any means but those that I have tasted have been quite good with the true English character. They are available in either dry or medium-dry styles.

While in Kent, the Tenterden Vineyards of Spots Farm, Smallhythe, are very well worth a visit. Again the principal wines are Müller-Thurgau, which can be very dry or medium-sweet. They also make an excellent Seyval Blanc which is medium-dry and considered to be an ideal aperitif wine.

Some of the best English wines I have drunk come from D. Carr-Taylor's vineyards at Westfield, near Hastings in Sussex. They make white wines from Gutenborner grapes of the medium-dry variety. Those made in 1980 were very good indeed.

Fairfields Fruit Farm at Newent, Gloucestershire, make very good English wine under the brand name of Three Choirs. The wines are fresh, *pétillant* and crisp and very pleasant to drink, largely made from a cross between the Müller-Thurgau and the Reichensteiner grapes.

With two hundred vineyards to visit it is not possible to mention more than very few and equally impossible to taste everything. But to repeat my previous advice, buy your Source of Wine map from the Vineyards Association and travel through southern England.

One last word of warning: the one or two red English wines are not very good, rather like the red German wines from Baden as compared to the white wines of the Rhine, Moselle and so on. But the English red wines are rarely to be found.

Below: Vintage time at Adgestone on the Isle of Wight, one of England's most successful vineyards.

Bottom: The vineyards of Flexerne at Fletching Common in East Sussex being sprayed against pests and rot.

AUSTRALIA AND NEW ZEALAND

Opposite: Vineyards as far as the eye can see in Mildura, an important wine region of Victoria.

When Captain Arthur Phillip took the first fleet to Australia in 1788, he included in his inventory of equipment, plants and seeds for the first settlers and a few varieties of vines from France and Germany. Within three years he saw that the soil and climate were suitable for the vine and reported accordingly. But it was left to James Busby, a Scottish immigrant, to provide the impetus for the growth of the industry. After an earlier unsuccessful attempt by William Macarthur to import a wide selection of European grape varieties, Busby returned to England and assembled over four hundred vines from sources across the length and breadth of Europe which he brought back in 1832. A nursery was established at the site of the present Botanical Gardens in Sydney, and soon commercial vineyards were flourishing in the Camden and Hunter Valley areas.

Throughout the remainder of the nineteenth century the Australian wine industry flourished. Victoria soon overtook New South Wales as the colony's most important wine-producing state. In 1886 Hubert de Castella, the Swiss-born *vigneron* who did so much to promote the wine industry at that time, published a book on Victoria called *John Bull's Vineyard*. But all four states – Victoria, New South Wales, South Australia and Western Australia – were producing table and fortified wines of at times astonishing quality. Results from the great international trade exhibitions, which were so much a part of the Victorian free-trade era, put that proposition beyond doubt.

With the advent of the twentieth century the Australian industry entered a dark age, which was to last for more than fifty years. The noble grape varieties – Cabernet Sauvignon, Pinot Noir, Merlot, Chardonnay and the like – which had played an important part in the development of the industry, disappeared and the wine map shrank into itself. All attention turned to high-yielding varieties grown in warm to hot areas, usually with the aid of irrigation, suitable for making cheap fortified wine for the domestic and export markets. It is a little-known fact that in 1928 more Australian wine (almost all fortified) was imported into the United Kingdom than from any other country.

The memory of those times – of Emu Wine and of cheap port and sherry – linger on, and Australia has a long way to go before it can rehabilitate itself in the eyes of the world as a serious producer, albeit on a modest scale, of fine-quality table wines. And I am afraid it must be said that in some ways the industry is its own worst enemy in that endeavour.

While it has had labelling requirements in force for twenty years which were far more advanced than those of California or South Africa, the plethora of brand names, bin numbers, regions, styles, varieties and other methods used to identify particular wines leaves the outsider shaking his head in wry bewilderment. For an Englishman – or I suppose even more for a Frenchman – the most obnoxious practice is the use of terms such as Champagne, Chablis, Burgundy, Hock and the like. The most confusing are the Bin Numbers – 'Bin 3456' and so on – which may or may not change from one year to the next, and which may or may not contain some hidden code decipherable only by those in the know. Mercifully, both practices are slowly falling into disrepute, although it would be too much to hope that they will disappear altogether.

Appellation control might cure some of these ills, but only three isolated districts – Margaret River/ Mount Barker in the Great Southern region of

Above: A world of contrasts – wines aged in barrel.

Above right: The Mitchellstown vineyard of Victoria in its autumn colours.

Below right: Fermentation tanks have careful systems of temperature control, essential in a hot climate.

Victoria

No other state has matched the rate of change and expansion in Victoria over the past decade. At the end of the 1960s wine was produced in only four areas: the North-east (around Wangaratta), the North-west (Mildura/Robinvale/Swan Hill), Great Western and the Goulburn Valley.

Now many of the areas devastated by phylloxera and out of production for eighty years are burgeoning once again. The Yarra Valley, Geelong, Mornington Peninsula and Sunbury – all on the outskirts of Melbourne – are providing some of the most eagerly sought after (and I might say most expensive) wines in Australia. Farther afield, Bendigo has eleven wineries, headed by Stuart Anderon's impeccable Balgownie wines; while Drumborg, Gippsland, Ballarat and the so-called Pyrenees district (Avoca/Moonambel) are all producing first-class wines.

It is impossible to list all the wineries in these new areas; there are upwards of one hundred in all. But they are producing wines of a radically different style to the erstwhile epicentre of Victorian production, the North-east. Here luscious fortified dessert wines of a style and quality equalled nowhere else in the world are produced by companies such as Baileys, Campbells and Morris. In the new areas the accent is on elegant Cabernets, intense

but refined Chardonnays, and on Pinot Noirs that actually taste of Pinot. Nor should I omit the sparkling wines made at Great Western by Seppelt. Over the years Seppelts have gone to great lengths to make wine of a style equivalent to that of Champagne – regrettably they call it just that – employing French-trained wine makers and using the *méthode champenoise* for their top wines. In recent years they have commenced using Pinot Noir and Chardonnay, which may well assist their endeavours.

South Australia

South Australia is Australia's leading state, producing almost sixty per cent of all Australian wine, and twice as much as New South Wales. Its principal regions are the Riverland (corresponding to the Murrumbidgee Irrigation Area of New South Wales and the North-west of Victoria), the Barossa Valley, the Clare Valley, Southern Vales and Coonawarra/Padthaway. There are also vineyards at Langhorne Creek in the Adelaide Metropolitan area and on the Adelaide Plains.

The heart of the industry lies in the Barossa Valley. Even though the Riverland is quantitatively the most important area, much of the fruit grown there is crushed and processed in the Barossa. It is a prolific producer of Rhine Riesling – with the best wines coming from hills surrounding the Barossa

and adjoining Eden valleys – and of full-bodied Shiraz and Cabernet Sauvignon reds. As with most Australian areas, it is very common to blend Shiraz and Cabernet together. The Rhine Rieslings of Orlando and Leo Buring and the marvellously textured oak-matured reds of Penfolds can be outstanding. Some other Barossa wines tend to be pedestrian. The major wineries are:

Hardy's Siegersdorf; Kaiser Stuhl (now part of the Penfolds Group); Krondorf; Leo Buring (owned by Lindeman); Masterson; Orlando; Penfold's; Saltram; Seppelt's; Wolf Blass and Yalumba.

The Clare Valley lies due north of the Barossa and makes intensely flavoured and coloured reds and some equally distinctive whites. Stanley Leasingham's winery is the most important, while Tim Knappstein's Enterprise winery consistently produces some of the region's best wines.

The Southern Vales, to the south of the city, encompass all of the Reynella and McLaren Vale wineries. It has been the scene of feverish activity over the past ten or fifteen years (in contradistinction to the Barossa). There are now almost forty wineries operating, ranging in size from tiny to very large. The largest are:

Hardy's McLaren Vale; Chateau Reynella (recently acquired by Hardys) and Wynn's Seaview.

The Barossa Valley of Southern Australia, one of the best areas for white wines, especially with its German origins.

Above: Riesling grapes being crushed.

Above: Red grapes fermenting furiously.

All styles of wine are made here; the district's reputation for heavy, ferruginous reds is slowly changing under the impact of modern wine-making techniques and the progressive introduction of premium varieties such as Chardonnay, Pinot Noir and Cabernet Sauvignon.

In my view, Coonawarra ranks as Australia's finest wine region. Its *terra rosa* soil, cool climate and high water table combine to produce red wines of considerable finesse and which have affinity with those of Bordeaux. More recently some high-quality botrytised Rhine Rieslings and interesting Chardonnays have added a further dimension to the region. Nearby Padthaway (confusingly also called Keppoch) shares a similar, although not identical, soil structure and climate, and is producing large quantities of white wines. The principal wineries are:

The Bowen Estate; Brand's Laira; Hungerford Hill; Katnook; Lindeman's Rouge Homme; Mildara; Redmans and Wynn's Coonawarra Estate.

Seppelts and Hardys have extensive vineyards at Padthaway (together with Lindemans and Wynns) but no wineries in the region.

Western Australia

Just as in Victoria, the wine map in Western Australia is changing by the minute. Whereas fifteen years ago wine making was restricted to the Swan Valley, there are now five areas: the Swan Valley/Bindoon region; the Lower Great Southern Area (often called Mount Barker); Margaret River, and the South-west Coastal Plain.

These days, Margaret River, with eighteen wineries and five additional vineyards (two of which are major developments), is one of the most talked-about regions in Australia. No doubt the initial involvement of California's Robert Mondavi in Leeuwin Estate (he no longer has any interest in it) helped public awareness and also contributed to technical know-how. Some of Australia's best red and white wines are coming from the region; astonishing, given that the first vineyards were not planted until 1967 and that most of the wine makers are local doctors fleeing the pressure of their waiting rooms.

The Lower Great Southern is an immense area; the round trip within its boundaries is close to 400 kilometres (250 miles). During that time you will find seventeen vineyards and wineries, mostly small and not infrequently primitive. Viticulturally it has immense potential, with a climate cooler than much of France. From a wine making point of view, its performance has been decidedly inconsistent, but most keen judges believe it will be a force in the future.

The Swan Valley remains the crucible of the state's industry. If the Barossa Valley owes its wine heritage to Germany, the Swan owes its to Yugoslavia. Many of the thirty or so wineries are owned and run by the descendants of Yugoslavs who came to Australia after the First World War. Notwithstanding the ferociously hot climate, some pleasant wines are made by the following wineries:

Evans and Tate; Houghton; Olive Farm; Sandalford and Vignacourt.

Tasmania and Queensland

Queensland produces wines in the Granite Belt near Toowoomba and farther north at Roma. They are much loved by Queenslanders, but seldom seen outside that state – which, I suspect, is a desirable situation from all points of view.

Tasmania is an altogether different situation. The industry there is in its infancy, but we shall hear much more of names such as Pipers' Brook and Heemskerk in years to come. Pinot Noir looks especially promising in this ultra-cool climate, not dissimilar to that of Rheims.

The wines of New Zealand

I first visited New Zealand in 1967 for three or four days and then only, I think, the South Island, but in 1974 my wife and I called there for four or five days on a round-the-world trip. In the first instance I was squired around Christchurch and elsewhere by the local chapters of the International Wine and Food Society of which I was then the Chairman, and I met Frank Thorpy, the doyen of New Zealand wine writers to whom I am indebted for a great deal of information and help.

Frank Thorpy, in his two books *Wines in New Zealand* (Collins, 1971) and *The New Zealand Wine Guide* (Books for Pleasure, 1976), ascribes the honour of planting the first grapes in New Zealand to Samuel Marsden, an Anglican Missionary and Chief Chaplain for the Government of New South Wales. Samuel Marsden made seven visits to New Zealand between 1814 and 1837 and brought with him vines and seeds which were planted, grew and gave encouragement to the local farmers. He was

Above: Watering the young vines at Wynn's in Coonawarra. Unlike most parts of Europe, irrigation is an essential factor in Australian viticulture.

Left: Vineyards near Merrivale in Southern Australia. They are part of the Southern Vales, a general name for several pockets of vineyards south of Adelaide.

followed by James Busby, one of the Fathers of Australian viticulture who left Australia to become the first resident British agent in New Zealand under the New South Wales Government. Busby planted a vineyard and from these vines grew the now quite considerable New Zealand wine industry.

The vineyards of New Zealand are scattered over both North and South Islands, with the greater proportion in the North, but the biggest single planting is near Blenheim, in the South Island.

From rather humble beginnings during the second half of the last century, wine making in New Zealand is now a multi-million dollar business. The earlier diet of rather gluggy sherries and ports, with some very ordinary whites and reds (made from inferior hybrid grapes) suffering from noticeable faults is now a thing of the past.

The greatest improvement over the last twenty years has been in grapes – where it all starts – in wine making, machinery, technical advancements and in more devoted attitudes and application to the skills of a centuries-old craft, the basic

Corban's winery in the Gisborne area on New Zealand's North Island. As befits a new industry, the equipment is ultra-modern.

fundamentals of which have remained virtually unchanged.

There are nearly 600 commercial vineyards, over 9.0 million vines producing in excess of 50,000 tonnes of grapes occupying a net area of 4,753 hectares, 90 per cent of which are *vitis vinifera*, with 97 per cent of this total producing wine.

The main grape-growing region in New Zealand is the Gisborne, Poverty Bay area, which contains the greatest concentration of contract growers and also has the main wineries of Montana, Corbans and Penfolds, three of the largest companies in New Zealand. Just south, and on the same eastern coast-line of the North Island, is the area of Hawkes Bay, which embraces the twin cities of Napier and Hastings. Several wineries are situated in Hawkes Bay, including Vidal's in Hastings and McWilliam's in Napier. Greenmeadows is the picturesque Mission Vineyards established by the Catholic order of St Mary in 1851, the oldest wine-making establishment in New Zealand.

The vineyards of Montana, Corbans and Penfolds, in the Marlborough region, assisted by a clutch of contract growers, form the third largest grape-growing area in New Zealand, and it is these fertile plains in and around the Wairau Valley near Blenheim that have experienced the greatest increase in plantings over the last ten years. The region is fast developing as a premium grape-growing area with the major varieties being Müller-Thurgau, Chardonnay, Sauvignon Blanc, Rhine Riesling, Chenin Blanc, Gewürztraminer, Cabernet Sauvignon and Pinot Noir.

The most recent figures released by the Department of Agriculture and Fisheries clearly indicate that sweeping changes have been made with vine selection, and New Zealand is now growing more of the type that produces the better wines in other regions of the world that have similar climate and soil conditions. The most widely planted grape is Müller-Thurgau, the grape which also occupies first place in German viticulture. By net area, Müller-Thurgau has over thirty-eight per cent of the national area.

The Müller-Thurgau grape is made into a plethora of styles from bone-dry to freeze-concentrated, a technique which produces wines with a high degree of residual sweetness. By far the greater proportion of Müller-Thurgau wines are stop-fermented (showing degrees of residual sugar), or back-blended (the addition of small quantities of unfermented grape juice, or sweet reserve, to the wine after fermentation), resulting in unique, fruity wines that highlight the characteristic flavours of the grape in a style that is indigenous to New Zealand. These wines can be confusing to the novice as they are labelled either Müller-Thurgau, or Riesling Sylvaner, but they are made from the same grape. Information contained on labels is fairly descriptive, but it pays to check the small print.

The range of premium varietal white wines in New Zealand includes Chardonnay, Chenin Blanc, Rhine Riesling, Gewürztraminer, Sauvignon Blanc, Pinot Gris, Golden Chasselas and Sémillon.

The most widely planted red grape is the classical Cabernet Sauvignon, with the total acreage overtaking all the prolific bearing hybrids. A proportion of the Cabernet acreage is in young vines, and once these are producing and Cabernet Sauvignon becomes more plentiful (1984), the red wine outlook in New Zealand will be revolutionised.

Other red varieties include Pinotage (a grape from South Africa, purported to be a cross between Pinot Noir and Cinsaut), which is produced as a straight varietal and also in blends with Cabernet. The very best Pinotage wines have been likened to being somewhere between the styles of Burgundy and Rhône. Pinot Noir has started to develop as a straight varietal showing considerable promise and Pinot Meunier has been around for a while. The range of premium varietal wines, both white and red, are virtually all in the NZ$5.00 to $8.00 bracket with the only exceptions being one or two wood-aged Chardonnays – wines that are fast developing an international reputation.

Here are my tasting notes:

McWilliam's Cresta Dore 1979 – this is a good, crisp fresh, dry wine.

Marlborough Riesling from Montana Wines, 1979 – a sound wine, not too sweet, but crisp.

Cook's 1980 Chardonnay Bin 93 – 12.1° of alcohol and in a 75 cl bottle, bottled on the estate; a thoroughly good wine.

Among the red wines there was Nobilos Huapai Valley Cabernet Sauvignon 'classic Claret' 1978. It has 10.5° of alcohol and is not much like a claret but is light and dry and a very good drink indeed.

Going back to the white wines, I have just looked at Matawhero Gewürztraminer 1978 which is delicious with a strong hint of the grape. It is a wine for all seasons and most foods.

You will enjoy New Zealand if you ever go there and you will also enjoy very much some of the good wines they are now producing.

The vineyards and winery of Cooks, a progressive new winery on North Island, known especially for its Cabernets and Rieslings.

SOUTH AFRICA

Nederburg are famous for their annual auction; Edelkeur is the answer to Trockenbeerenauslese.

Pinotage is a peculiarly South African combination of Pinot Noir and Cinsaut.

In comparison with the wine-growing regions of Europe, the South African wine industry is relatively young, having been producing wine for just over three hundred years. All the wine is produced in the Cape and the area is not large, the vineyards radiating within the area 161 kilometres (100 miles) from Cape Town.

The first vines were planted in 1655 by Jan Van Riebeeck, sent out by the Dutch East India Company to establish an outpost to revictual the Company's ships on the long sea voyage to the Far East. The first wine was made four years later in February 1659.

Van Riebeeck's successor, Governor Simon van der Stel, took a keen interest in viticulture, planting 100,000 vines and establishing in 1865 his renowned Constantia Cellar, where the famous wine Constantia was produced. Much sought after, it was served at the tables of all the crowned heads of Europe and Napoleon, when imprisoned on the Island of St Helena, asked for claret, Champagne and Constantia.

The Estate exists today, known as Groot Constantia, and produces fine red wines. Sadly the exact method of producing the wine Constantia has been completely lost. It resembles a white fortified wine made from Muscat grapes. When the contents of Ashburnham Place in Sussex, which included the contents of the cellar, were auctioned I was fortunate enough to purchase some of their pint bottles of Constantia. Over the bin in which they had been stored was a traditional white porcelain label marked 'Cape 1830' together with the name of the supplier, 'Mr Frisby'. Mr Frisby was obviously an excellent taster as after more than one hundred and fifty years the wine was in fine condition.

South Africa is perhaps best known for its sherries and port-type wines. Today the quality of South African sherry is indisputably high and in most cases better quality than its Spanish counterparts. The KWV wine growers' co-operative, founded in 1918 at a time of disastrously low prices, is the major producer. Their Onzerust, Renasans, Mymering and Cavendish ranges are excellent. Fine sherries are also produced and marketed by the Drostdy Cellars at Tulbagh. As for port-type wines, the days of 'Empire Ruby' are long gone and although no vintage port in the accepted sense is

Opposite: Large oak vats, carved in the German tradition, for maturing wine in the cellars of the KWV or Wine Growers' Co-operative.

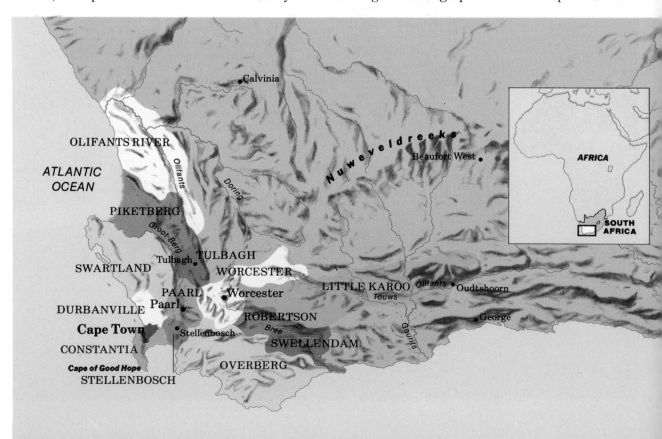

produced, there are some fine wines available that have been aged in wood. A range of vintage wines from the KWV under the Cavendish label, 1949 and 1956 vintages, together with an Estate port from Allesverloren – Old Ruby 1974, 1975 and 1976 vintages – are the best.

Over the last decade, the progress in light or table wines has been little short of miraculous. The Cape has some of the finest vinification equipment and technology in the world.

In 1972 a law delimiting sixteen Wine Areas of Origin came into operation. This Act also provided for the registering of individual estates. There are five major regions, which are further sub-divided into districts. The Coastal Region contains the districts of Constantia, Durbanville, Paarl, Piketberg, Stellenbosch and Swartland, and the Boberg Region takes in part of the districts of Paarl and Tulbagh. The large region of the Breede River contains Robertson, Swellendam and Worcester. The two lesser known regions are the Olifantsriver and the Little Karoo, or Klein Karoo, with its district of Overberg.

The largest proportion of the light wine sold in South Africa and exported is marketed under cultivar or varietal names; these are the vine varieties from which they are produced. For white wines the main cultivars are Chenin Blanc, also called Steen, Cape Riesling (not to be confused with Alsace or Rhine Riesling as the wine is completely different), Sémillon and Colombard. New varieties include Gewürztraminer, Weisser Riesling (Rhine), Chardonnay and Sauvignon. (A lot of wine is sold as

Above: The vineyards of Stellenbosch that produce some of the Cape's finest estate wines.

Opposite above: The attractive Goede Hoop estate in Stellenbosch in the heart of the South African wine industry.

Opposite: Groot Constantia, an historic estate near Cape Town. It is now government owned with an excellent reputation for red wines.

Stein, which denotes a style of excellent medium-dry, and although mainly produced from Chenin Blanc should not be confused with Steen.) For red wines the best known are Cabernet Sauvignon, Shiraz (Syrah), Cinsaut (sometimes known locally as Hermitage) and Pinotage (a cross between the Pinot Noir of Burgundy and the Cinsaut grown in the southern Rhône, the wine tasting exactly like a blend of good Burgundy and southern Rhône). Pinotage was until recently unique to the Cape, but New Zealand is also now producing wine from this variety. The most unusual wine is that made from a port grape called Tinta Barocca, an amazingly full-bodied rich and powerful wine. Newer varieties include Pinot Noir, Merlot and Cabernet Franc.

The white wines range from bone dry to luscious noble late harvest, which are very similar to the *Trockenbeerenauslese* wines of Germany. The red wines tend to be full-bodied, soft and round without any of the unpleasant acidity sometimes found in European wines. Over the last five years the wine makers have concentrated on producing better-balanced wines. Most have an alcohol content of eleven and a half per cent to twelve per cent as opposed to the wines of the 1950s and 1960s, which were high in alcohol, heavy and flabby.

Since 1972, forty-seven estates have been registered and it is from these estates that the Cape's finest wines are now being produced. Their wine makers are the entrepreneurs and innovators who are planting and producing from the new varieties an ever-increasing range of exciting wines. Many, such as Meerlust, only bottled their first wine under their estate label in 1975, so one has not had a real chance to see how they improve in bottle, but all the signs are encouraging. For red wines the best estates are Allesverloren, Alto, Backsberg, Meerlust, Meerendal, Spier, Uitkyk and Zandvliet. The best white wines are from De Wetshof, Koopmanskloof, Le Bonheur, Theuniskraal, Boschendal, Simonsig and Twee Jongegezellen.

Sparkling wine is produced mainly by the *cuve close* method. The wine is clean, fresh and very acceptable, but this is an area where there is room for improvement.

As for spirits, two locally produced products are consumed in large quantities, cane spirit and brandy. Cane spirit is a white spirit distilled from molasses and tastes similar to a cross between vodka and Bacardi. Three million cases of locally produced brandy are consumed annually. It is a blend of a minimum thirty per cent pot still (French Cognac is one hundred per cent pot still) and the balance is produced in a continuous still as for French Grape Brandy. The best known are KWV 10 year Old and Oude Meester VSOB.

Fortunately, there is now no need to visit the Cape, often said to be the most beautiful wine land in the world, to sample their fine wines, sherries and brandies. The five major wine companies all export. Look out for the Fleur du Cap, Grunberger and Drostdy ranges, KWV, Nederberg, Bellingham and Bertrams wines. Under these names are sold all the well-known cultivars. The wines are fairly widely available, but if you have problems in obtaining them your local wine supplier should be able to help.

NORTH AMERICA

by Robert J. Misch

Cabernet Sauvignon from Almadén, one of California's oldest wineries.

What do you make of a nation that ranks sixth in the world in production of wine, and thirtieth in consumption? Oh! well, Luxembourg, they say, is the first in consumption. (Actually, people from a lot of bordering countries trek into Luxembourg to buy wine to take home across a half-dozen borders.)

The US consumption of table wines is rising at an average rate of seven to ten per cent a year, which is not too bad. (France's consumption actually fell a bit last year.) The USA is drinking about 450 million gallons per annum these days, and the pundits, seers and prophets foresee 900 million to a billion gallons by 1990.

Of the current US consumption, about seventy-one per cent comes from California, eleven per cent from other states, and eighteen per cent is imported. These days, about seventy-nine per cent is 'table wine'; dessert, fruit and speciality wines make up the other twenty-one per cent. Twenty years ago, it was just the reverse.

The wine industry of today

Opposite: A dramatic aerial view of the hillside vineyards of the Chappellet winery and the Napa Valley.

Below: Inside the Chappellet winery. The unusual design is in the shape of a pyramid.

I have noted, recently, the use of the term 'world class' to suggest excellence in everything from high school gymnasts to coffee cake. Well, now the USA may well lay claim to such nomenclature for a number of its wines. California has an ever-increasing number of wines that may be considered world class, and the East is not too far behind. As a matter of fact, it is just possible that too much emphasis on producing super-bottles and winning

The Robert Mondavi winery, built in the elegant style of architecture of the early Spanish missions in California.

Tending the vines on one of Paul Masson's vast estates.

competitions may adversely affect the industry as a whole.

Wine is simply a pleasant beverage that goes nicely with most food. It is not from on high. It is not the Treaty of Vienna. It is the *nouveau* drinker and the recent amateur at the bungs who makes most of the fuss about labels, vintages, estates, etc., etc. Not that I am opposed to wine knowledge, know-how and professionalism, but it is sometimes my feeling that too much punditry tends to put off too many people. They say, 'If I have to know all that to buy a bottle of wine at the store, or order one at the restaurant, I think I will stay with a whisky or a pint!'

Every bottle does not have to be Pétrus or Musigny, Mondavi '71 or Heitz 'Martha's Vineyard'. A decent bottle of affordable wine, from a known practitioner, at a modest price, multiplied by the thousands – and hopefully millions – will do more for the wine maker, dealer and buyer than that once-in-a-while lord of the realm.

The United States – people and government – will have to stop looking upon wine as The Sin Industry. This thinking culminated in 1920 with the advent of Prohibition, which lasted through the years until December 1933. But the Puritan tradition goes deep. Fifty state laws control fifty ways of getting a bottle. In one state, only the state store may sell wine at retail. In another state, only licensed dealers may purvey wine; in this one, you buy a bottle along with your soft drinks and sandwiches at a supermarket; in still another, you can buy aspirin, Johnny Walker and Gallo's Burgundy at the same counter.

Probably the climactic nonsense is provided by the BATF. This is the Bureau that controls all aspects of the alcoholic beverage market from the national point of view. BATF stands for 'Bureau of Alcohol, Tobacco and Firearms'. In other words, a glass of Château d'Yquem or Château Haut-Brion equates with nicotine and/or a revolver in the eyes of the powers that be.

France does not claim four stars for all its wines – five to six per cent may be AC aristocrats. It is the excellent run of *vins ordinaires* that makes France great. It might be wise for California to concentrate a bit more on good 'plonk' instead of expending so much energy on competitive blind tastings, matching this Cabernet against a famous French château-bottled wine, and that Pinot Noir against some

A few recommended wines

'What is there to drink at my price in 1988? This is what most people want to know.

The recommendations that follow may give you some new ideas for exploration in the field of North American wine. Remember two things: first, seek out a good, reliable dealer; second, keep in mind that prices can and do vary and change rapidly. Three-star wines (★★★) will cost £10 or more; one-star wines (★) will cost £5 or less.

White

Sauvignon Blanc
Chateau St Jean Fumé Blanc 1985
Dry Creek Vineyards Fumé Blanc 1985
Fetzer 1983
Carmenet 1984
Grgich Hills Fumé Blanc 1980 and 1981
Berenger Fumé Blanc 1985
Clos du Bois 1985
Chateau Ste Michelle Fumé Blanc 1980 (Washington State)
Robert Mondavi Fumé Blanc 1984
Chenin Blanc
Robert Mondavi 1984
Dry Creek 1984
Fetzer 1983
Pine Ridge 1985
North Coast Cellars – no vintage
Chardonnay
Paul Masson 1984
Grgich Hills 1979 and 1978 ★★★
Chateau St Jean 1985
Robert Mondavi 1984
Beringer 1984
Clos du Bois 1984 ★
Edna Valley 1984
Trefethen 1983

Firestone 1983
Mark West 1980
Pine Ridge Oak Knoll Cuvée 1984
Sonoma-Cutrer 1983 ★★★
Simi 1983
Stags' Leap 1984 ★★★
Cuvaison 1985
Iron Horse 1984
Wente 1984
Acacia Carneros 1985
Bethel Heights Vineyard 1984
Fetzer Barrel Select 1984
Riesling
Firestone 1984
North Coast Cellars – non vintage
Trefethen 1980
Stags' Leap 1985
Mark West 'late harvest' 1983
Firestone 'late harvest' 1982
Chateau St Jean 'late harvest' 1983
Joseph Phelps 'late harvest' 1983
Gewürztraminer
Chateau St Jean 1985
Firestone 1984
Simi 1984
Clos du Bois 1983

Red

Zinfandel
Wente 1983
Heitz Wine Cellars 1981
Ridge Vineyards Geyserville 1983
Fetzer 1982
Fetzer Lake County 1984
Pedroncelli 1984
Konokti 1982
Château Monteleno 1979
Merlot
Firestone 1983
Clos du Bois 1983
Clos du Val 1984
Stags' Leap 1983
Louis Martini 1984
Gundlach-Bundschau 1983
Pinot Noir
Rutherford Hill 1982
Chalone 1982 ★★★
Trefethen 1983
Calera Jensen Vineyard 1983 ★★★
Mondavi 1983
Acacia 1984
Chateau Bouchaine 1982

Firestone 1982
Clos du Val 1983
Petite Sirah – Not to be confused with the Syrah grown extensively in the Rhône region.
Stags' Leap Wine Cellars 1982
Monterey 1982
Monterey Peninsula 1983
Gamay
Wente Gamay Beaujolais 1981
Cresta Blanca N.V.
Cabernet Sauvignon
Trefethen 1982
Chateau Montelena 1978
Robert Mondavi 1982
Heitz Martha's Vineyard 1979 ★★★
Stags' Leap 1982
Clos du Bois 1983
Joseph Phelps 1981
Firestone 1982
Arbor Crest 1984
Cakebread Cellars 1982

other local grape. After all, only a very small segment of the US wine pyramid sells in the higher price bracket and one of the great strengths of American wine producers is their delightful, fruity everyday 'jug' wine.

Vineyard workers at Chalone, a hilltop winery in the central coastal area, with a reputation for Pinot Noir and Chardonnay.

The wine drinkers

Who actually drinks wine in the USA? This is an interesting question, when you remember America 'gave birth to the blues' of Prohibition!

If you estimate the population of the whole country to be 220 million people, eighty million are children, or at least below drinking age. Forty million are either confirmed dries, have allergies, don't like the taste of wine, or have religious scruples. Of the remaining 100 million, only six million are hard-core regulars, drinking 114 litres (25 gallons) per annum or more; ninety-four million are 'sometimers'. It is that six per cent of real drinkers who must be catered to and, at the same time, a

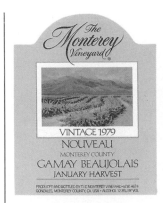

A Beaujolais Nouveau label, Californian style.

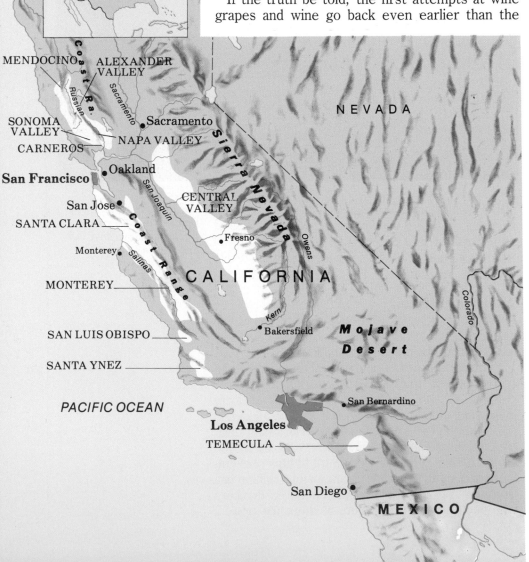

portion of the ninety-four per cent must be shuffled into the 114-litre (25-gallon) bracket. It can be done, if America and the wine trade remember a few things. The USA is *not* a Latin country born to wine, drinking wine with mother's milk, and using wine simply as food. It is more akin to Britain (without the long years of expertise of the middle- and upper-class British).

Historically speaking

California Most people credit the Hungarian Agostin Haraszthy with having been the father of the California wine industry. While it is true that at the instigation of the State of California he brought thousands of cuttings of the European grapes to the New World, actually some *viniferas* were there long before that and the first wine in California, made by the Franciscan padres between the end of the 1700s and the beginning of the 1800s, was from the Criollas grape, a member of the *vinifera* species – albeit not a very good one! No, Count Haraszthy was not the father exactly (nor was he even a Count), but he did contribute greatly, thanks to his cuttings (for which he was never paid his due by the State of California).

If the truth be told, the first attempts at wine grapes and wine go back even earlier than the eighteenth century. The French Huguenots are supposed to have experimented with wine from native Scuppernongs in the 1562-64 period; William Penn dabbled in wine in 1683, and Lord Baltimore tried wine making in Maryland as long ago as 1662 – without success, I might add. Nicholas Longworth, in Ohio, made his now famous sparkling Catawba way back in 1823, which inspired the poet Longfellow, in 1854, to pen his immortal tribute to its taste as 'dulcet, delicious and dreamy'.

The first commercial wine grower of whom we have records, about 1834, is Jean Louis Vignes (appropriately enough). The succeeding decades of the 1880s were a long series of boom and bust – grapes selling at $2 a ton, and wine at 50¢ a gallon or less. The great earthquake was in 1906; Prohibition and its aftermath continued from 1920 to 1933.

New York The first vineyard in New York State dates from 1818. It was on Lake Erie in the Chautauqua grape belt. However, the accolade of 'first' is generally given to the Rev. William Bostwick, an Episcopal minister of Hammondsport, for wine he produced there in 1829.

A word about New York wines, which applies to most of the Eastern states:

Wine was first made from native American grapes; grapes of the *labrusca* genus. They were growing wild, from Canada to Florida – the Concords, Catawbas, Delawares, etc. – when Columbus reached the New World. In 1953, the first *vinifera* grapes (the grape family of Europe and California) were grown in New York by an emigré German, Dr. Konstantin Frank, who was in the employ of the Gold Seal Winery of the Finger Lakes area. Dr. Frank had learned about vines and wine making in the rugged clime of the Ukraine, and felt that New York winters were no harsher than that and therefore could support *vinifera* growth. He was right, as the burgeoning *vinifera* acreage shows, but every once in a while Mother Nature drops her gloves and shows her claws. This happened in the winter of 1980, when temperatures plummeted at Christmas. To this day, this is known as the 'Christmas Massacre'. Fortunately, the growers and the vines were resilient enough to survive. So, *viniferas* are still much in the running.

Finally, we come to the third category of wine grapes, perhaps destined to become the most important in the East – the French-American hybrids. (The French, especially M. Seibel, had a great deal to do with this development.) These are strains of hybridised grapes, produced by the crossing of French wine varieties with hardy American stock. The results are the cold-resistant Maréchal Foch, de Chaunac, Seyval Blanc, Vidal Blanc, Ravat, etc. They make new wines of real merit and often excellence.

Above: The 1982 'crush' or vintage at Cascade Mountain.

Top: The vintage at Chateau St. Jean in Sonoma Valley. This winery has a reputation for fine white wines. The pronunciation of Jean is English rather than French.

Left: Aerial view of a winery in northern California. As usual the vineyards are immaculately kept.

The new developments

Such a discussion requires a breakdown between new developments with wine itself, and new developments in the making of it. Let us talk about the wine scene first.

The most amazing change has been in the composition of the wine picture. Barely twenty years ago, the United States consumed about eighty per cent red wine and twenty per cent white. In two decades the picture has just about reversed, and America is drinking eighty per cent white wine. Why this switch? My guess – and I think it is a pretty good one – is that America is a 'cold-drink' country: chilled ginger ale, chilled beer . . . chilled Chardonnay. Personally, I rather deplore the extent of this 'white front'. Of course, people should drink what they want, but it seems a shame to lose the complexity of the reds, the pleasure of the soft tannins,

in the simplistic, 'A glass of white wine, please.'

I have a thought – and I am promoting it as best I can. Chill reds! I don't say chill Château Lafite. But I do say that there are plenty of lesser, lighter reds that would actually benefit from a bit of 'coolth'. It covers a multitude of shortcomings in a wine, for another thing. Besides, the time-honoured saying was, 'Reds – serve at room temperature'. Fine, but in those days, rooms were not kept at 26°C/80°F as so many are today.

In the same fifteen or twenty years the composition of wine consumption has changed from twenty per cent table wine and eighty per cent dessert or sweet specialities to exactly the reverse. The vermouths and ports and 'Sauternes' and branded specialities – not forgetting the fruit nectars and Uncle George's home-made Concord – have given way to table wines. By definition, these are 'natural'

Top: Ripe Cabernet Sauvignon grapes in the vineyards of Sterling.

Above: Replacing stakes in the vineyards of Chateau St. Jean.

Right: The 1982 vintage. The grapes are handpicked, in small boxes, with every care taken that they arrive at the winery undamaged.

wines, fermented, racked, filtered, aged and bottled. Nothing added. Sugaring, or *chaptalization*, is today seldom practised – indeed, it is not even necessary.

Sparkling wines are very much in vogue – both imports and home-grown. Sparklers made by the true *méthode champenoise* are few indeed. Most American bubblies come out of the tanks of the Charmat process. The secondary fermentation is induced in pressurised tanks. Some is 'transfer process'; i.e., the secondary fermentation is produced in the bottle, but then, instead of the laborious riddling and disgorging, the bottles are emptied into pressurised tanks, the spent yeast cells and impurities are removed and the clear wine is rebottled. By US law, *méthode champenoise* wines may carry on the label, 'Fermented in THIS Bottle'; 'transfer' wines may use 'Fermented in THE Bottle'; and tank-fermented wines carry the legend, 'Bulk' or 'Charmat'.

I may add that the nomenclature 'Champagne' is perfectly legal in the USA, if preceded by the correct geographic word in equal size and strength; such as California Champagne, New York Champagne or American Champagne. Truth be told, a dozen or so other European wine-type names, in addition to Champagne, are legal, if qualified by the place of geographic origin; for example, Burgundy, Claret, Chablis, Chianti, Málaga, Madeira, Moselle, Port, Rhine, Hock, Sauternes, Sherry, Tokay.

This name gambit *is* a touchy subject. The American's excuses for his arrogation of such names are: We have long used the names; If we can say Venetian blinds, English muffins, Swedish meat balls, Swiss cheese, why not California sherry? It helps popularise the various wines to the Americans, who hence drink more of it. It is a fair point and you may agree or you may not.

One other thing about 'name'. Until the American vintner decided to classify his best wines under varietal names – Riesling, Chardonnay, etc. – wines were usually blended and named Château Lafite or Montrachet, Chianti or Rioja. Now, even Europe is issuing varietal Chardonnay, Pinot Noirs and the like. Coincidentally, as these words are written, the regulations governing nomenclature for varietal

wines have undergone a radical change.

Formerly, the requirement was that fifty-one per cent of the name grape be used in the wine. As of 1st January 1983, the requirement was seventy-five per cent. Additionally, the wines must also carry an appellation of origin as to where the grapes were grown – Sonoma, Monterey, etc. – and seventy-five per cent of the grapes must have come from that region. If the region should be a 'viticulturally approved' area (such as Napa or Carneros), then eighty-five per cent of the grapes must come from that area.

Historians say that wine was once called simply French red or German white or Italian pink. The first 'name' wine is said to have been 'Commandaria' from Cyprus, named by the Knights Templar, who found the wine in Cyprus during the Crusades, liked it and named it. It is still available under that name.

California vintages

Grape	1975	1976	1977	1978	1979	1980	1981	1982	1983	1984	1985	1986
Cabernet Sauvignon	Good	Good	Good	Good	Good	Good	Good	Excellent	Excellent	Good	Excellent	Good
Chardonnay	Good	Good	Good	Good	Good	Excellent	Good	Good	Good	Good	Excellent	Excellent
Zinfandel	Good	Good	Good	Good	Good	Good	Good	Good	Good	Good	Very good	Good
Pinot Noir	Average	Below Average	Good	Good	Good	Good	Good	Good	Good	Good	Very good	Excellent

The vineyards of California

To you who have already toured the vinelands of California – lucky you. To others, the following may give you a little idea of what is in store.

The first thing that will strike you, I think, is the beauty of the place. Mountains, seascapes, rivers, sweet cities, charming hamlets. Automobile is the way to travel. (I cannot possibly do justice to all the vineyards that are multiplying across the state. Forgive me, I know many wineries have been left out or given short shrift.)

Napa

Cross the Golden Gate Bridge and head north on Highway 29. Do not worry about where to stay or where to eat – there are plenty of places for both that will suit your dollars, francs, lira, or pence.

Without any sense of geography, in Napa do try to take in some of these wineries (some are open to visitors; some require a telephone call in advance. All will be friendly.) Call the Wine Institute in San Francisco for information.

Christian Brothers. The largest winery in Napa, run by a religious teaching order founded in France in the 17th century. Excellent (and modestly priced) Cabernet Sauvignons, Chardonnays, fresh and fruity Chenin Blancs, Gamays, Zinfandels – and the much-touted Chateau la Salle dessert wine. And, incidentally, Christian Brothers is also America's number one brandy producer.

Robert Mondavi is Mr California Wine. His efforts and experiments have benefitted the California wine industry as well as himself and his peers. His Cabernet Sauvignons, while pricy, are stunning. His Fumé Blancs created a new world for Sauvignons. His Chardonnays – experimentally aged in every oak on the face of the earth – have contributed greatly to the increasing excellence of this wine.

Trefethen. A medium size producer of a spectacular Chardonnay. Pricy but Eshkol, their private blends, are splendid value.

Acacia. Relatively new, but producing sensational wines. One of the finest Pinot Noirs in California.

Beaulieu. The wines, especially the Cabernet Sauvignons, are world-famous, for which the great Tschelitscheff, wine maker extraordinaire, can take the credit. Today it is owned by the Heublein Corporation. BV Reserve Cabernets are sensational, and collector's items.

Mayacamas. The Taylors had the temerity to start it, and five hundred investors bought stock. Great wines, featuring Cabernet, Chardonnay, Chenin Blanc and Zinfandel Rosé.

Inglenook. A Heublein property. Nice Cabernets and the secondary line, called Navalle, is true value.

Franciscan. This property is a creation of the Franciscan fathers, who produce excellent wines at reasonable prices. Four hundred and sixty-nine acres – no midget, this. Excellent Cabernets, Chardonnays and Rieslings.

Heitz. A legend in his time. His Martha's Vineyard Cabernet Sauvignon is probably the most distinguished and famous Cabernet in California.

Sutter Home. A sizeable affair making nice wines at nice prices. Dates back to 1904. Famous for Zinfandels and Muscat Amabile.

Louis Martini. What the Rock means to Gibraltar, Martini means to California. Louis Peter Martini has run a tight ship since 1960, and never produces a poor wine nor an overpriced one. His Cabernet Sauvignon is first class.

Beringer. This is the oldest winery in Napa, going back to 1876. Myron Nightingale, another great among wine makers, is the moving light. Nescafé is the present proprietor. Beringer produces 300,000 cases, these days, of fine Cabernet, Chardonnay, Chenin Blanc and Riesling.

Chas. Krug (CK). These are the original Mondavi estates, going back to 1860. Run by Robert Mondavi's brother, Peter, and well run. Fine jug wines under the CK Mondavi label.

Freemark Abbey. One of the greats. The wines have always been medal-winners. Top Chardonnays and a noted late-harvest Riesling called Edelwein.

Schramsberg. The first, and perhaps still the best, of the bubblies made by the true *méthode champenoise* by the Jack Davies.

Served by Presidents!

Cakebread. Don't laugh. Just say it and get some of California's finest wines. They make only about 10,000 cases of super Cabernet and Chardonnay.

Grgich. You don't say it, you sneeze it. Mike Grgich is one of Napa's greatest wine makers, and is the name on some of its greatest wines. Chardonnays and Zinfandels are world-class.

Sterling. A showplace, reached in the hills by funicular, no less. Beautiful for scenery and for wine. Seagrams is the current owner. Their line has been trimmed to Merlot, Cabernet, Chardonnay and Sauvignon.

Chateau Montelena. In all California, you cannot ask for better wines. Only about 20,000 cases a year. Their Chardonnay is rightly renowned.

Cuvaison. Another 20,000-case producer – of Cabernet, Zinfandel and Chardonnay.

Hanns Kornell. A top-drawer, old-line maker of bubblies (also some still wines). His Sehr Trocken is famous; a truly dry sparkler. His Muscat of Alexandria is a fine dessert.

Stony Hill. The white wines of this property are modelled on Corton Charlemagne, which should give you some idea of their superb quality. Quite small (3,000 cases). You will have to get on the mailing list to obtain any wine!

Quail Ridge. Tiny, but excellent; around 2,000 cases Chardonnay and Cabernet.

Clos du Val. Especially fine for reds – Merlot, Cabernet and blends of same. Their Zinfandel is heroic.

Joseph Phelps. A quality house producing 40,000 cases. Superb late-harvest Gewürztraminer and Rieslings, and splendid private red blend, Insignia.

Conn Creek. Established in 1974, and already a super Cabernet.

Domaine Chandon. Established in 1973. A sparkling wine house owned by Moët & Chandon of Champagne.

Chappellet. Excellent Cabernet, a dry Chenin Blanc, and a slightly sweet Riesling.

Stag's Leap Winery. A small winery producing an excellent Petite Sirah.

Stag's Leap Wine Cellars. Medium size, superb Cabernet and Chardonnay.

(Do not confuse them – everyone does.)

Burgess. Established in 1972. Tom Burgess is truly a master of wine. He states he wants 'unique' wines, and proves it with superb Zinfandels, Chenin Blancs and Cabernets.

Durney. Only 10,000 cases, mostly Cabernet Sauvignon, but *what* Cabernet Sauvignon. Superb!

Jekel. Founded in 1978 and quite small. Riesling and Chardonnay excellent.

Spring Mt. 20,000 cases, including stalwart reds and intense Chardonnays.

Monticello Cellars. Excellent Gewürztraminer, Chardonnay and Sauvignon Blanc.

And there are many other fine wineries in Napa.

Sonoma

Along with Napa, this is California's top county. Only a few mountains separate them.

Chateau Souverain. A big winery. An old name but the present Souverain dates back to 1973. Recently taken over by Nestlé.

Iron Horse. Forrest Tancer, wine maker, and a beautiful lady proprietor show they can make great wines. The Chardonnay is particularly splendid.

Buena Vista. Agostin Haraszthy's original vineyard in his adopted land, founded in 1856. Subsequently owned by Frank Bartholomew of United Press, and now in German hands. Sizeable – in the 100,000-case range. Good Cabernets and Zinfandels.

Sebastiani. August Sebastiani was a character with a capital 'C', he raised rare birds, wore only custom-made overalls and made a lot of good wine. His son, Don, still does – nearly four million cases of it. His Proprietor's Reserve Vintage wines are collector's items. Also produces fine jugs.

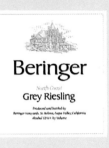

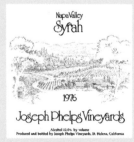

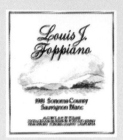

Above right: The flowering gardens of Christian Brothers; largest of the Napa wineries.

Sonoma continued.

Chateau St. Jean. One of the most innovative (and successfully so) of all Californian vineyards. Dick Arrowwood, super wine maker, can take the credit. St. Jean is especially famous for 'late-harvest', luscious whites, and splendid Chardonnays.

Rodney Strong Vineyards. Rod Strong started at fertile Tiburon and moved on to splendid Sonoma. He is now producing Piper-Sonoma, a Champagne-method bubbly, with the co-operation of technicians from Piper Heidsieck. Three types: Brut, Blanc de Noir, and Tête du Cuvée.

Hanzell. Small, but James Zellerbach, the paper king, modelled it after Burgundy's great Clos de Vougeot reds. Rare wines, especially Chardonnay and Pinot Noir.

Gundlach-Bundschu. If you can pronounce it, you will get superb wines from one of California's oldest wineries; it dates to pre-Prohibition. Family-owned. Fine Cabernets, Chardonnays and Zinfandels.

Korbel. 1886 saw its founders come from Bohemia. Now owned by the Heck brothers, its bubblies are among the country's very best. Over 600,000 cases of Champagne-method wines and 500,000 cases of brandy.

Windsor. Rod Strong performed his magic and Peter Friedman put it in bottles with a 'Bottled expressly for . . .' personalised label. Now part of Rodney Strong Vineyards.

Foppiano. One of the bigger wineries but also a good one. It has been in operation since 1896. A 200,000-case operation, once known only for jugs but now moving into good varietals.

Simi. A name to conjure with. Zelma Long, California's number-one lady vintner, first made these great wines and now Schieffelin markets them. Zelma has moved on to her own vineyard but her magic remains.

Pedroncelli. Dating from 1904 as a bulk wine House but, since 1955, this winery has risen from bulk to premium!

Geyser Peak. Owned by the Trione family. It is the wine that made Geyserville famous! Today, a 200,000-case operation – mostly Gewürztraminer, Pinot Noir, and Sauvignon Blanc.

Clos du Bois. Established in 1976, one of the true greats of Sonoma. Superb Alexander Valley Cabernets, Gewürztraminers and Rieslings.

Davis Bynum. Produces 20,000 cases of varied wines. Reds especially good.

Italian Swiss. A vast winery complex founded in 1887, representing many labels. Recently re-acquired by Allied Grape Growers.

Jordan. Established in 1976. Mostly Cabernets – big, fleshy fellows, but lately somewhat toned down. Some Chardonnays.

Dry Creek. A 20,000-case operation offering fine Chenin Blancs, Fumé Blancs, and Chardonnays.

Hop Kiln. Small, but their Petite Sirah and Zinfandels highly regarded by the wine circle.

Lytton Springs. Not much of it, out of a 5,000-case total, but the big Zinfandel is championship class.

Mendocino

Parducci. The Tuscan family out-sat Prohibition to operate this big winery, which now produces three million bottles a year. Splendid Chenin Blanc, varietals and jugs.

Cresta Blanca. One of California's great names. Not large but not small – 13,500 gallons. The first 'Yquem style' outside of Bordeaux. Besides varietals, excellent sherries and ports, and Cresta Blanca is one of California's largest and best brandy makers.

Fetzer. In operation since 1957; a good name to remember for first-rate wines at a reasonable price, especially varietal reds, Petite Syrahs and Zinfandels.

Lake

Guenoc. New as a wine contender, yet Lilly Langtry knew the place. It was hers! Guenoc is already a contender.

Edmeades. Their Rain Wine blend alone is worth the price of admission.

Alameda, Solano

These counties lie east of San Francisco (Livermore is the city).

Concannon. One of the oldest wineries in California, dates back to 1883. Tops in Petite Syrah and originators of splendid Muscat Blanc. Owned by Distillers'.

Wente. One of the real entrepreneurs dating back to the 1880s. A great family making splendid wines at superb prices and never a bad bottle. Chardonnay is splendid, and priced in single digits; Pinot Blanc is fine. For their centenary they launched a sparkling wine – Wente Brut.

Weibel. A fine old name, especially for their sparkling wines and sherries. Its history includes earthquakes and Leland Stanford.

Santa Clara

The county south of San Francisco Bay, stretching from San Mateo to San Luis Obispo.

Paul Masson. One of the legendary names of California, dating from 1896. Wine now made elsewhere. 'Pinnacles Selections' have few superiors in premium Californias. Emerald Dry, Rubion and Souzao Port are household words among Masson specialities.

David Bruce. One of the truly annointed wine makers. Just taste that Zinfandel!

Martin Ray. A famous name since 1946. Only about 1,500 cases but the reputation of the Chardonnay is state-wide.

Almadén. This is a vast operation (eleven million cases), proving that size need not mean mediocrity. It offers popular mountain wines along with premium Charles Lefranc beauties. You always get your money's worth with an Almadén wine.

Mirassou. Founded in 1854 by the oldest wine-making family in America and in the hands of the fifth generation. Splendid Rieslings and, of late, a Champagne-method sparkler.

San Martin. The only winery in northern Santa Clara, the garlic centre of the world. The wines don't show it! Fine Amador Zinfandel and Chenin Blanc.

Chalone. One of the greatest – and smallest. Just 14 hectares (35 acres) of excellence high in the Gavilan Mountains. Pinot Blanc and Pinot Noir – outstanding.

Monterey

Monterey. Monterey Vineyard is wine wizard Dick Peterson's domain, which is operated by Dick under the Monterey name and also under Taylor California Cellars. (It has now been taken over by Seagrams.)

Other Monterey names worth knowing are **Monterey Peninsula** (just to complicate things) and **Jekel** in the micro-climate of Arroyo Seco, which makes the sensational 'late-harvest' Riesling possible.

Ficklin. A bit of a maverick, but a highly successful one, making one prime wine – port. Lately, a few varietals have been added, especially a supreme Emerald Dry.

Giumarra. Another very large establishment (one and a half million cases), covering wine from jug to premium; said to be number-one table-grape shipper in the USA.

Calera. Founded in 1976. A small winery producing a number of different Pinot Noir wines, including some of the best in California.

Riverside (Temecula)

Callaway. Thanks to fissures in the coastal mountain range, cool Pacific air comes in and makes some great wines possible. A late-harvest Chenin Blanc has achieved widespread fame as Sweet Nancy.

Santa Barbara (Santa Ynez Valley)

Firestone. From rubber tyres to some of the best red wines in town. Again, mountain fissures make for a grape-growing climate; Cabernets, Merlots, Rieslings are super.

Lodi

If for no other reason, this Sacramento area is worth your attention for it is the home of 'Davis', the University of California's great wine research centre and seat of viticulture and viniculture – famous worldwide.

San Joaquin

Franzia. A huge winery making over thirty wines. Related, family-wise, to the Gallos.
Petri. Another big winery – a Heublein (United Vintners) property.
Christian Brothers. The brandy is made here (the wine in Napa).

Stanislaus

E & J Gallo. The biggest winery in the world (250 million gallons storage capacity); producer of one-third of all California wine. Its major volume is in such famous labels as Hearty Burgundy, but lately, vintaged, small quantity premiums have been launched.
Papagni. My hat is off to Angelo Papagni for making such fine wines in the hot climate of the Central Valley. The only Alicante Bouschet in California. Also sweet dessert – Moscato d'Angelo.

Fresno, Kern County

There are reputedly twenty-three wineries down here. Antonio Perelli-Minetti is said to be the oldest pre-Prohibition vintner in the state.

The vineyards of the Pacific north-west

This is the most recent excitement in a succession of West Coast excitements – the discovery and exploitation of the Washington-Oregon-Idaho wine areas. These are cool states, splendid for raising most *vinifera* grapes. It took quite a long time, even for seasoned grape men, to realize this; or was it loyalty to California?

Washington

Grape producers in Washington have their problems, as winters can be hard, but on the whole the climate lends itself to the production of the light, elegant wines which have become so popular in recent years. Though the state is one of the major grape producing areas of the US, a large percentage of Washington's juice goes out of state to make grape juice, pop wines and for blending.

The first vines were planted in 1872, but it was not until 1969-1970 that Washington became a wine state to be reckoned with.
Ste. Michelle. This is Washington's number-one winery. It is in the fabled Yakima Valley and produces a large amount of superlative wine. Their Cabernet Sauvignons and Semillon Blancs are equal to, if not superior to, many a California version. They owe their excellence to cool summers and long days. The vineyards are mostly all in cool zones 1 and 2.

Other vineyards to visit: **Hinzerling** (their 'late-harvest' Gewürztraminer is a gold-winner), **Yakima River, Preston, Mont Elise, Vierthaler** and **Leonetti.** (And, as I write this, it is likely that more have opened.)

Oregon

Scientists found Oregon's climate not only conducive to good grape growing, but also to be similar to that of the Côte de Beaune in Burgundy. Some of the Oregon wines I have tasted would seem to underline that.
Hillcrest. This is the creation of Richer Sommer, often called 'The Father of Oregon Wine'. Among others, the dry, smoky Gewürztraminer alone is worth the trek to Oregon.
Tualatin. Bill Fuller, who studied first at Davis and then at the feet of Louis Martini, learned well. His Riesling is splendid, but opt for the dry Muscat for an experience.
Amity, Eyrie (What a Pinot Noir!) **Knudsen-Erath, Oak Knoll** are others, and by all means detour to Dundee in the Williamette Valley to see what is going on at **Sokol-Blosser,** Oregon's largest. If you like Merlot as much as I do, try the Blosser one hundred per cent Merlot.

Idaho

Ste. Chapelle. In Snake River Valley, of all places. The pioneer in this region. The Cabernet Sauvignon and Chenin Blanc are 'world class', and the Riesling is 'out of this world'.

Right: Large oak vats at Almadén. Even a winery as large as this values the contribution of oak to its wines.

Below: Enormous stainless steel tanks at Simi in Sonoma Valley. Despite this ultra-modern view, it is one of California's oldest wineries, dating from 1876.

New ways in the winery

A revolution has taken place in the winery. I do not profess to be a professional wine maker, but some of the advances in wine-making technology are worth mentioning.

Cold fermentation in jacketed tanks, to keep temperatures down in the 5°C/40°F range during the rigours of churning fermentation is the order of the day, especially for white wines. This keeps the wines fresher, crisper, fruitier. Reds are fermented at somewhat higher temperatures.

Smaller cooperage (barrels) is being used more and more in place of huge tanks and casks. Vintners say this gives the 'bouquet of Europe'. Some vintners are now practising 'barrel fermentation'.

A number of vintners are using only 'free-run' (first-press) juice in their wine, but some are electing to introduce second and even third pressings for extra flavour and strength (but not, surely, for finesse!).

Wood-ageing is, of course, the norm, but the world is no longer drinking yellowed whites and those heavy, oaky, sometimes rancid reds. The time in oak, used in ageing most Chardonnays, is being reduced so that people don't get splinters in their tongue! However, many wine makers are taking wood very seriously, and experimenting with various oaks to achieve the best results: Tronçais, Jugoslav, American, Limousin, Nevers, etc. Robert Mondavi has made 'oak' a life study.

So much for machinery – there are two major changes in product. First, would you like brown milk or blue strawberries? A lot of California wine makers must think you would, because so many of them are making white wine from red grapes. Of course, a lot of it has to do with the American trend to white wines. Not satisfied with the White Chardonnays, Colombards, Chenin Blancs, etc., they are now making such items as Rosé de Zinfandel, Cabernet Sauvignon Blanc, Blanc de Pinot Noir, and the like.

Second, the other new development – overdone it seems to me – is the trend towards 'late harvest' this and that. I think Zinfandel and Gewürztraminer, for example, are lovely wines, but when I pour out a glass of 'late harvest' and bite into a sweet over-tone, I am not sure that all is right with the world of wine. However, as someone once said, 'everyone to his taste'.

Climate

Climate is the number-one reason for California's rise to eminence as a wine state. The University of California at Davis puts climate far ahead of soil in importance. Micro-climates and mini-climates are the talk-of-the-town. Such wineries as Calloway could not exist without special situations. The southern California climate is too warm for optimum grape growing, but the cool, local breezes, blowing off the Pacific, make Calloway's area not only tenable but great.

California has been divided into climatic zones based on average daily temperature. They record the number of days during which the temperatures exceed fifty degrees Fahrenheit. These are called 'degree days'. For instance, if the temperature on a certain day reaches 75° Farenheit, that day goes down as 25 (75 minus 50) on the 'degree day' side. Here is how it works, reading from coolest, to hottest:

Zone 1 – 2,500 degree days or less, comparable with the climates of Germany and Beaune.

Zone 2 – 2,501-3,000 degree days, comparable with the climate of Bordeaux.

Zone 3 – 3,001-3,500 degree days, comparable with the climate of Tuscany.

Zone 4 – 3,501-4,000 degree days, comparable with the climate of Spain.

Zone 5 – over 4,000 degree days, comparable with the tropics.

Local conditions within zones create mini- or micro-climates that astound the experts, and produce amazing contradictions.

Recent vintages

Over the past few years, California winemakers have developed their own way of doing things. The strong, heavy wines once associated with the US are less in evidence now and the wines are cooler, more restrained and elegant. The 1983, 1984 and 1985 vintages are showing great character, with these from the Napa valley lighter, yet packed with fruit flavour. In particular, 1985 is a superb vintage.

Exports

A few years ago, to talk about US wines in the export market would have been a bit ludicrous. Not so today. While export figures are not likely to frighten the wine maker in Bordeaux or Beaune, Florence or Mendoza, US wines are getting somewhere. This, mind you, despite special taxes, tariffs and impedimenta of one kind or another.

The vineyards of New York State

To tour the Empire State's winelands takes a bit of doing, because distances are greater and all wine-making areas are not contiguous. The Finger Lakes are far and away the prime growing area, but then there are vineyards to see in Chautauqua County on Lake Erie's shore, the Hudson Valley, and now Long Island.

Finger Lakes

This is, of course, the 'Big League' of wine outside of California. Here, along the shores of Lakes Canandaigua, Keuka, Seneca, Cayuga and a few others, grow the grapes (*Vitis labrusca* and hybrids) and rear the plants of New York's mighty. Here are **Taylor/Great Western, Gold Seal, Widmer** and **Canandaigua** – together they produce three-quarters of all New York wines. But there is also a new host of small, quality wineries.

Taylor/Great Western. Close neighbours and now both owned by Wine Spectrum/Coca Cola. Great Western is New York's number-one bonded winery and the largest outside of California. Under the late Greyton Taylor and son Walter it became the home of New York Champagne. There is also a great line of still wines of all types and varieties, especially Taylor's Lake Country line and Great Western's new Ice Wine, hybrids and *labrusca*.

Gold Seal. Founded in 1865, Gold Seal has managed to grow huge (over one and a half million cases) and stay good. That rare combination can be attributed in large part to Charles Fournier, President Emeritus, once of Veuve Clicquot in his native France. He brought know-how to sparkling wine making. His great tradition and willingness to experiment is carried on at the winery.

Widmer's. Since 1882, the pride of Naples, New York. Thirty-five varieties, but especially famous for its excellent sherries.

Canandaigua. Virginia Dare is a US brand dating to 1835. Wild Irish Rose, though more recent, is also famous.

Glenora. Only 25,000 gallons, but superb French-American hybrids and some Rieslings and Chardonnays.

Bully Hill. Since 1970, when Walter Taylor separated from his family's business, he has been making award-winning estate-bottled generics and varietals, and now a Champagne-method sparkling wine.

Chateau Esperanza. Innovative growing techniques plus old-world wine-making methods make this winery unique.

Heron Hill. In operation since 1977 and a medal-winner.

Wagner. Owned and operated by Bill Wagner, wine maker for fifty years. Superb wines from all three types of grape.

Herman Wiemer. A native of Germany, he set up shop in the Finger Lakes in 1973. He specializes only in *viniferas*: Chardonnay, Riesling and Pinot Noir.

Vinifera Wine Cellars. Owner Dr. Konstantin Frank once made wine in the Soviet Union for a German enclave. Escaping Hitler, he carried his expertise to the New World, specifically to Charles Fournier at Gold Seal. He grew the first *vinifera* grapes for Gold Seal, then set up his own shop. He showed New York that *vinifera* vines are feasible in the harsh climate, and his wines from these grapes are collector's items.

Chautauqua, Lake Erie, Niagara

Johnson Estate, Merritt Estate and **Clinton Vineyards** are respected labels hereabouts. Other producers here are **Niagara Wine Cellars, Robin Fils** and **Woodbury.**

Hudson Valley

Brotherhood, High Tor, Hudson Valley. These are the big wineries of the area, but the 'gem or purest ray serene' is little **Benmarl** at Marlboro, owned and operated by the Mark Millers and their subscribers in the Societé des Vignerons. Wines are mainly from French-American hybrids.

Long Island

Hargrave's. Alec and Louise Hargrave were the entrepreneurs, the land-breakers of Long Island. Out towards Cutchogue they planted a sizeable vineyard of 34 hectares (84 acres) in 1973. It has prospered, and these enterprising young people deserve the fine Chardonnays, Sauvignons, and other wines they are making.

SOUTH AMERICA

Vineyards in the province of Mendoza in the Argentine. At an altitude of 2,000 feet they are amongst the highest vineyards in the world.

I was greatly surprised to discover that vast quantities of wine are produced in South American countries. Argentina is the fourth largest wine-producing country in the western world and although these wines are no longer available in the UK, no doubt they will become popular again. The wines of South America are exported abroad and in the UK they can be obtained from supermarkets and multiples. I have tasted them rarely and then only in their own countries. I am therefore indebted to David Stevens MW for his chapter on the wines of South America, published in André Simon's *Wines of the World* 2nd Edition (Macdonald, 1982, edited by Serena Sutcliffe MW). Mr Stevens has travelled in South America and has made a major contribution to the knowledge of wine in this area.

The vine was first introduced into Mexico by the Jesuit Fathers in 1545 and, as has happened so

often, the reason for them wanting to grow wine was for the purely religious purpose of providing wine for Communion. Certainly the idea caught on and more and more vines were grown. From Mexico the Jesuit Fathers travelled north up the Pacific coast into what is now California and undoubtedly started the wonderful Californian wine industry which has become over the last century so prominent in the vinous affairs of man. Southwards, their influence called for vines to be planted in most countries in South America and in 1551 the Spanish Conquistadors (who never travelled without their Jesuits) planted vines in Cuzco in Peru. Thence the vine travelled over and along the Andes, into Argentina and along the long Pacific coast of Chile. Both countries make good wine, but in Argentina vine growing rapidly increased and in 1979 the country produced 26 million hectolitres of wine.

Grape-picking in Salta, a province in north west Argentina.

Vineyards in the province of Mendoza. The Andes mountains rise sharply from the plain.

Argentina

During the immigration upsurge in the nineteenth century, French, Italian, German and Spanish nationals went to Argentina and to California. With the immigrants came the vines and skills of wine making and thus in the Argentine most of the wine is made from the classical French, Italian or Spanish grapes, like the Cabernet, Malbec, Pinot, Pedro Ximénez. Also introduced were some of the bad habits of calling the wine after the Italian and French wine-making areas. Any affinity that the Argentinian wines have to the classical Italian wines is purely coincidental, although they have many virtues of their own.

The chief wine-growing area of Argentina is the province of Mendoza, followed closely by San Juan, Rio Negro, La Rioja (which has no connection with the Rioja of Spain), Salta, Jujuy and Catamarca.

Argentinian wine is uniformly well made wine and is getting better. It is almost certain to be cheap and honest. It is getting better because with modern methods of filtration and vinification, the wine seems clearer, cleaner, and more palatable, and it does indeed travel well.

Many of the great European firms have wholly owned subsidiaries in Argentina, including Moët et Chandon, for instance, who, I am told, make a very drinkable sparkling wine which they call Champaña.

Chile

I have drunk the wines of Argentina in Argentina, but I have travelled more in Chile, and always enjoyed the wines of that country. I had occasion to drink deeply of them when staying on Easter Island, where the only wines available were Chilean. In 1974, my wife and I stayed there for a week in a small but excellent hotel where lobster was served in the restaurant twice a day, I seem to remember. The wine list was good and we tasted extensively. Only Chilean boats came to that delectable island and then only rarely, so only Chilean wines were imported – which was no great hardship.

Vines are grown along most of the length of the Pacific coast of Chile and both soil and climate are more suitable for viniculture than in any other country in South America. The red wines are better than the white but, in my view, both are very drinkable. Viña Tocornal, made from Pinot Noir grapes, is a good, full, fruity red wine and the Cabernet put out by Concha y Toro is the Chilean equivalent of a good, drinkable claret. There are many others and you will not regret the investment in a bottle or two.

Brazil

The story of Brazilian wine began towards the end of the last century. Italian immigrants settled in the mountains of the southernmost part of Brazil around Caxias do Sul in the Rio Grande do Sul.

Despite a latitude of around 28°, which is nearer the equator than the North African vineyards, and a rainfall twice as high as grapes require, Italian perseverance has started an industry which now produces as much wine as Australia. Apart from Rio Grande do Sul approximately twenty per cent of total production is now centred in the State of São Paulo in the São Roque region.

Brazilian vineyards were at first planted with an American *labrusca*-type grape, Isabella and Herbe-

mont predominating. However, with the increasing sophistication of the consumer, better quality grapes such as Cabernet Franc, Merlot and Pinot are now planted. The Moët-Hennessy group from France have bought into the area and are now making a bottle-fermented, sparkling wine under their label as well as a drinkable still white wine.

The largest company, Vinicola Rio Grandense, merchandises blended popular red and white wine under the name of Château Duvalier. They also make a much better red wine from sixty per cent Merlot grapes called, simply, Merlot. Other good brands are Granja Uniao, Dreher, Santa Rosa, known for its Château Lacase, and Vinicola Garibaldi, which is known for its Precioso Grande Reserva made predominantly from Cabernet Franc in the red wine and Riesling in the white. Brazil also turns out a first-class brandy of the armagnac type produced from hybrid grapes.

To conclude this short chapter, I do suggest that, in the true spirit of vinous curiosity, you try these wines as and when you come across them. You will probably not be disappointed and it may well be that you have an agreeable surprise.

Gathering grapes in São Paulo in northern Brazil; an arm-breaking task with the high-trained vines.

Glossary

by Michael Broadbent MW

Acetic. Vinegary smell, tart on the palate. An irremediable fault.

Acid, acidity. Sound healthy grapes contain natural acidity, which gives the wine its crisp, refreshing quality. Too much acidity will make the tongue curl; a flabby finish results from too little. *See also* Malic acid, Volatile acidity.

Aftertaste. The taste that remains after a particularly fine rich wine has been swallowed; a fragrant internal bouquet.

Alcohol. One of the essential components of wine, giving it body and backbone. No smell or taste as such, but 'peppery' on the nose of a young wine, a feeling of weight in the mouth, and warmth as it is swallowed. Alcohol content of 'light' wines varies from around 11 to 14 per cent by volume depending on the sugar content of the grape, which in turn depends mainly on the ripening sun. Of the European classic wines, Moselles and Châteauneuf-du-Pape represent the extremes, and red Burgundy tends to be higher than red Bordeaux. Alcohol has an effect on the central nervous system, which is why there is an anti-drink lobby. *See also* Chaptalized and Fortified wine.

Aroma. The element of smell that derives from the grape. *See also* Bouquet, Nose and Varietal.

Astringent. A bitter, mouth-puckering effect due to excess tannin and acidity, mainly the former, noticeable in young red wines. Unless very pronounced, it usually wears off as the wine matures.

Austere. Mainly in relation to taste: hard, somewhat severe. Not a fault, possibly undeveloped and certainly indicating a lack of obvious flesh and charm.

Balance. The combination and vital relationship of component parts. *See* Well balanced.

Beads at the rim. This is how I describe the string of little tell-tale bubbles clinging to the meniscus which, in my experience, is often a warning that an old wine is cracking up. Not to be confused with *spritzig* (q.v.).

Beefy. An evocative description: a full-bodied wine with high extract (q.v.), a sort of chewable quality and texture.

Beery. The beery, yeasty end taste of a faulty wine.

Beeswing. A traditional and apt description of the filmy pieces of sediment floating in very old port.

Beetroot. Or boiled beetroot: an analogous description of the root-like, mature Pinot aroma.

Bite. An acid grip in the end taste, more than a zestful tang and tolerable only in a rich, full-bodied wine.

Bitter. Either a fault or due to too much tannin. Normally no fine mature wine should be bitter on the palate, though bitterness is considered a normal and desirable feature of some Italian reds.

Bitter almonds. An almond kernel, acetate smell usually due to bad fining. A fault.

Blackcurrants. An evocative smell and taste associated with Cabernet Sauvignon and Sauvignon Blanc.

Bland. Implies lack of character, too mild.

Body. A physical component: weight of wine, alcohol, extract. Varies according to wine type and vintage. *See* Full bodied.

Bottle-age. Hard to describe but easily recognizable once you know what to look for: the ameliorating, softening effect of a wine aged in bottle, detected on the nose; a mellow sweetness; on white wines a honey smell.

Bouquet. The element of smell that is a result of the wine-making process and subsequent development in cask and bottle, complementary to but not the same as aroma (q.v.). Embraces all the subtle and fragrant elements that combine and arise. The bouquet of a fine mature wine is one of the features most appreciated by the connoisseur. 'Bouquet' can also be used loosely as a synonym for the nose or general smell of a wine.

Breed. An abstract qualitative term. A fine wine of good pedigree should display breed.

Burnt. Descriptive, analogous, like singed (q.v.). Red wines, dessert wines and hot-vintage wines can have a burnt character on the nose.

Capsule. 'Cap' for short. Usually lead, sometimes a wax seal over the cork. *See also Goût de capsule.*

Caramel. Sweet, toffee-like smell. Sometimes indicates an acceptable degree of maderization as in old Sauternes.

Cedar. A cedarwood, cigar-box smell characteristic of many fine clarets.

Chaptalized. A French term for adding sugar to the grape must in years when the natural grape sugar is deficient. Without it these wines would be lacking in alcohol and unstable. Chaptalized wines tend not to keep well, though they can be attractive when young.

Characteristic. A characteristic wine possesses all the strengths or weaknesses normally expected of its grape type, district, style, vintage, age.

Cheesy. Or cheese rind: a descriptive term, not usually derogatory, applied to some clarets. Frankly, I do not know the cause; it might just be a stage of development. Sourness is not implied.

Chocolaty. Also descriptive, applying to the nose. I associate the term mainly with some of the sweeter, heavier, usually blended but not unattractive Burgundies. Usually weighty and chunky on the palate.

Chunky. A term I often use to describe a hefty, somewhat coarse-textured red wine.

Clean. Nose particularly; but also taste. Fresh and free from faults.

Cracking-up. A disintegrating wine, usually over-mature and oxidized.

Crème-brûlée. The rich, burnt toffee and butter smell of very mature Sauternes.

Crisp. Firm, brisk, refreshing, zestful. Indicates good level of acidity, particularly in dry whites.

Depth. Depends on the context: a wine can have depth, i.e., richness of colour; depth of nose – the opposite to superficial, one has to sniff long and hard to detect its latent fruit and character; depth of flavour, richness, complexity.

Developed. Usually qualified, e.g. undeveloped, still immature but implying potential. *See also* Well developed.

Dry. In relation to wine always means not sweet (q.v.): sugar fully fermented out. *See also* Medium dry.

Dumb. Usually used in the context of an immature fine red wine with an undeveloped bouquet. Sometimes the dormant bouquet can be aroused by patiently warming the glass in cupped hands.

Earthy. Evocative and descriptive, nose or taste. Not derogatory in normal contexts. Red Graves can have an earthy taste, so, in a different way, can some Australian and California wines.

Esters. Smells are conveyed by volatile esters and aldehydes to the receptors in the nose, a chemical process. The nervous system then takes over.

Estery. Peardrops, a faulty, chemical smell.

Extract. To do with the body of a wine and frequently loosely used. Soluble solids, excluding sugar, which add to the richness and substance of wine, essentially from ripe grapes, a measure of quality.

Fading. Can apply to colour loss and general decline of bouquet and flavour; the result of age.

Fat. Usually referring to a combination of sweetness, alcohol, high extract, possibly glycerine, and implies a slight lack of counterbalancing acidity.

Finesse. An abstract qualitative term related to refinement, elegance.

Finish. The end taste. A good positive finish is essential in a fine well-balanced wine. A poor finish indicates lack of quality, follow-through and acidity.

Firm. Sound constitution, positive. A desirable quality on the palate.

Fixed acidity. Part of the essential make-up of any wine; its backbone or, perhaps a closer analogy, its nervous system. *See also* Volatile acidity.

Flabby. Soft, feeble, lacking acidity on the palate.

Flat. The next stage after flabby, well beyond bland (q.v.). Total lack of vigour on nose and on palate; lack of acidity; oxidation.

Flowery. Evocative. Can refer to nose: fragrant, fresh aroma; developed bouquet, or taste.

Fluffy. This is a term I sometimes use when I note a loose-knit, distinctly unfirm, 'hollow' wine.

Fortified wine. A wine that has had brandy or neutral spirit added during fermentation, or after the wine has been made, or both. Port, Sherry, Madeira, Marsala and the Muscats of Australia are all fortified.

Forward. A word I frequently use to indicate a wine that is quickly developing, mature for its age.

Fragrant. Self-explanatory and highly attractive. Can be applied to aroma, bouquet, flavour or aftertaste.

Fresh. Displaying or retaining attractive youthful properties on nose and palate.

Fruity. Rarely grapy. More a positive, fleshy quality of nose and flavour derived from sound, ripe grapes.

Full. Must be qualified or used clearly in a particular context: e.g., full coloured (better to say deep coloured), full of flavour. Most often used in relation to weight (q.v.).

Full bodied. A big wine, high alcoholic content and extract: a mouth-filling table wine or a robust young port.

Goût de capsule. A curious 'lead-cap', slightly metallic smell associated with some claret.

Grapy. Self-descriptive. Aroma and taste usually associated with very ripe Rieslings and Muscatel-type grapes.

Green. Unripe, raw, youthful on nose or palate. Strictly speaking, resulting from unripe grapes, but also loosely used to describe an immature, acidic wine.

Green tinged. Self-descriptive colour.

Gristly. Gristle: tough textured.

Gritty. Coarse texture.

Hard. On the palate, severe, probably still tannic. Not a fault in a young wine.

Heavy. Over-endowed with alcohol, more than full bodied; clumsy, lacking finesse.

High toned. This is a tricky one. It is an expression I frequently use for the nose of a particularly marked but light volatile character, often associated with considerable fragrance but can verge on, and is probably associated with, highish volatile acidity (q.v.).

Hollow. A wine that has a first taste, something of a finish but no middle palate.

Honeyed. Self-descriptive. Some young, natural dessert wines, if good, have a distinct smell of honey that deepens with age. Even dry wines, if of good vintages, can develop a mellow, honeyed bouquet as they mature.

Hot-vintage character. The smell or taste of grapes baked in a particularly hot summer sun or from an area with a normally hot climate. Tends to be associated with high alcoholic content: peppery (q.v.).

Iron. A character derived from the soil, noticeable more on palate than nose. Lafite often has it, so has Cheval-Blanc. And in a swingeingly metallic, harsh tannic-acid way I have noted it in one or two young Australian and California wines.

Kernel. Or kernelly. Not nutty; for me an undesirable bitter-walnut smell and taste or, bitter almonds (q.v.).

Lean. Self-descriptive. On the palate, sinewy, firm; often the sign of a 'long-distance runner'.

Legs. The viscous droplets that form and ease down the sides of the glass when the wine is swirled.

Light. Referring to body: low alcohol content. Also light colour (pale is a less ambiguous word), light nose (little bouquet).

Long. Refers to length of flavour. A sign of quality.

Macération carbonique. A modern method of vinification that at best produces appealingly fresh and fruity wines, at worst superficial, flimsy, tinny ones. What worries me is that more districts are abandoning traditional wine-making methods. *Macération carbonique* is an easy way out, but I now think of wines made in this way as 'whole fruit drinks'. The method seems to reduce wine to its lowest common denominator, blurring boundaries, reducing character.

Maderized. Heavy, flat 'brown' smell and taste of an over-mature oxidized wine.

Malic acid. A mouthwatering, raw-cooking-apple smell and tartness on the palate due to unripe grapes.

Mawkish. Hard to define: more unpleasant than insipid. Stale character.

Meaty. Rich 'chunky' nose, almost chewable flavour.

Medium. A term that ought always to be qualified. Medium colour, medium body, etc.

Medium dry. Half dry, some residual sugar, for example a *demi-sec*. Vouvray and very many German wines. Or a slightly sweetened fortified wine.

Medium sweet. Self-explanatory. Usually too sweet to accompany a main course. A light dessert wine.

Mercaptan. An unpleasant rubbery smell of old sulphur, mainly on very old white wines.

Milky. A milk-like smell. Lactic acid. Not a good sign but not necessarily bad or undrinkable.

Moreish. Rather a childish term for something temptingly tasty one wants more of.

Mousy. Refers to both a smell and taste. A sign of a bacteriological disease; also the curious 'droppings' taste of wine made from hail-damaged grapes.

Murky. More than deep coloured: not bright, turbid. Mainly a red wine fault.

Must. Grape juice in the cask or vat before it is converted into wine.

Nose. The overall smell of wine. Also, to nose, nosing.

Nutty. The smell of cob nuts (tawny port), and a particular and pleasant quality I associate with oak and the Chardonnay grape and with some old *amontillado* sherries.

Oak. A smell deriving from maturation in small French oak casks. Adds a certain character and style but can be overdone.

Oily. Can apply to a particularly unctuous smell or a texture. A highly viscous white wine can also have an oily look.

Old. In a wine context an old nose or old taste implies signs of decay beyond normal maturity.

Open knit. Can apply to nose or taste/texture of a fairly fully developed wine. Forthcoming, loose-knit, loose textured.

Overblown. The somewhat unpleasant smell of an overmature or faulty wine.

Oxidized. 'Brown,' old straw smell; flat stale taste of a wine destroyed by the action of air in cask or in bottle through a faulty or shrunken cork.

Pasty. I use this in relation to a particular sort of smell and taste, so I suppose I should try to define it: raw, lactic, slightly rough texture.

Peach-like. Evokes the smell of the fruit, e.g., a ripe Ruwer wine (German).

Peacock's tail. The way the flavour of certain great Burgundies can open up and fan out in the mouth.

Peardrops. An acetone, spirit-glue smell. A fault, usually in white wines.

Peppery. The effect of a high alcoholic content in a young wine, noticeably vintage port. Almost a physical, peppery assault on the nose, accompanied by a hot, peppery texture.

Piquant. A high-toned, over-fragrant fruity nose verging on sharp, usually confirmed by an overacidic end taste. Can still be a refreshing, flavoury drink, but not one to keep.

Plummy. Can apply to both colour and taste. A thick red-purple appearance; fruit, some coarseness on palate, often indicating an in-between state of maturity, or a particular style.

Powerful. Really self-explanatory. Assertive, usually full bodied.

Pricked. Distinctly sharper than piquant. Acetic smell, tart. An irremediable fault.

Prickly. On nose and palate, sharp edged, raw, acidic.

Pungent. Powerful, assertive smell, linked to a high level of volatile acidity, e.g., certain old Madeiras.

Ripe. Highly desirable in any context: ripe grapes (with full complement of natural sugar); ripe smell and taste, both exhibiting the softness and sweetness resulting from ripe grapes.

Robe. A rather elegant French term for the colour of wine. An expression I personally use only in relation to fine red Burgundy.

Round. On the palate, a feature of a complete, well-balanced, mature wine. No hard edges.

Severe. Self-descriptive. Hard, unyielding wine.

Sharp. Acidity on the nose and palate somewhere between piquant and pricked (q.v.). Usually indicating a fault.

Silky. Refers only to texture, the feel of a ripe Pomerol, for example.

Sinewy. Lean, muscular on the palate. Usually a wine of some potential.

Singed. An analogous term that I use to describe the smell of some red wines of hot vintages.

Smoky. Both evocative and descriptive: the smell of burnt oak chips, of wood smoke. For me a pleasant type of smell that I associate with the bouquet of good Burgundy and certain other wines.

Spanish root. A smell that reminds me of this root, a sort of liquorice. Certain ports have it.

Spicy. Self-descriptive, recognizable on nose and palate. A good Gewürztraminer is an example.

Spritzig. Or *spritz* for short. A German term. First detectable visually as tiny specks of air in the wine and then as a crisp prickle of youthful acidity and carbon dioxide in the mouth.

Stalky. Nose and taste. Not necessarily a fault, but undesirable; common, not an attribute of fine wines. Probably due to unripe grapes or prolonged contact with stalks during fermentation.

Stewed. An unimpressive, fudged-up, compounded

sort of aroma lacking clear-cut fruit. Often from blended, sugared wines. Quality generally lacking.

Stringy. A texture: on the thin and scrawny side, lacking equability.

Sulphury. The prickle on the nose, rather like a whiff of a burnt match or coke oven, announcing the presence of sulphur dioxide, a common white wine preservative. Not a fault. Often wears off in the glass but should not be too intrusive.

Supple. Texture, balance: pleasant combination of vigour and harmony. Highly desirable in a properly developing red wine.

Sweet. A wine with a high sugar content, natural or added. A property of all dessert wines. Wine can smell sweet, but sweetness is primarily detected on the tongue. The sweetness of Sauternes and German *Beerenauslesen* is the result of fermenting overripe grapes containing a particularly high natural sugar content. Port is made by the addition of brandy, which stops the fermentation, leaving the desired degree of unconverted sugar; sweet sherry is made by adding sweetening wine.

Tang, tangy. Rich, high-toned, zestful bouquet and end taste, particularly in old Madeira, Tokay and some other old fortified wines.

Tannin. An essential preservative extracted from the skins of red grapes during fermentation. It dries the mouth.

Tart. Sharp, nose catching, tongue curling. Americans occasionally use this as a synonym for the natural acidity in wine, but in English wine circles it has an unattractive, even faulty connotation. A tart wine may be drinkable but is less than pleasing.

Tête de cuvée. No hard and fast definition, varies according to district, but definitely implies 'the pick of the bunch', from the best cask or casks in a grower's cellar.

Thin. Deficient, watery, lacking body. Usually used in a derogatory sense. Not a synonym for light.

Tinny. Metallic, acidic at the back of the palate. A fault, but often tolerable.

Toffee-nosed. A literal description: sweet toffee, caramel-like smell. Possibly the first evidence of approaching maderization, but attractive. Nothing to do with being a wine snob.

Tuilé. A colour: tile red. To my eyes the colour of sun-weathered tiles in Provence, not newly made red tiles.

Unripe. A condition of wine arising from the use of unripe grapes containing malic acid, which gives the wine a smell of cooking apples and a raw, somewhat tart, end taste. A word sometimes loosely used as a synonym for immature.

Vanilla. A descriptive word for a smell generally associated with certain cask-aged wines.

Varietal. A distinctive aroma and taste deriving from a specific grape variety.

Velvety. A textural description: silky, smooth, a certain opulence on the palate.

Vin de garde. A wine that needs keeping, ageing.

Vinifying, vinification. The processes of wine making: preparing and fermenting grapes.

Vinosity. An abstract term indicating an intrinsic richness of quality stemming from fine ripe fruit, balanced, supple.

Vinous. Having a pleasant enough, positive winey smell and taste but lacking a recognizable varietal (q.v.) character.

Volatile acidity. A normal component of wine but undesirable in excess, the danger signs being a vinegary smell and bitter/acid end taste. Excess volatile acidity cannot be remedied.

Weight. A measure of the body, *see* Alcohol.

Well balanced. All the components of the wine – fruit, acid, tannin, alcohol, etc. – in equilibrium. A highly desirable state and certainly expected of fine vintage wine, particularly when mature.

Well developed. Component parts blended together, a desirable state of full maturity.

Wishy-washy. Feeble, weak, loose, unknit components. Lack of character and quality.

Woody. In relation to a wine nose or taste, a pejorative term, as opposed to oak (q.v.), which is desirable. The result of wine kept too long in cask, particularly old casks with rotten staves.

Yeasty. Undesirable smell, usually accompanied by an unclean, beery end taste.

Zest, zing. Terms used to describe a wine with an abundance of life and, metaphorically, sparkle, racy acidity. An attractive quality.

Bibliography

Adams, L.D., *The Wines of America,* McGraw-Hill, 2nd edition, 1978

Allen, H.W., *A History of Wine*, Faber, 1961

Arlott, J., and Fielden, C., *Burgundy: Vines and Wines,* Quartet Books, 1978

Anderson, B., *Vino, The Wines and Winemakers of Italy*, Little Brown, 1980

Anderson, B., *The Mitchell Beazley Pocket Guide to Italian Wines*, Mitchell Beazley, 1982

Broadbent, J.M., *The Great Vintage Wine Book*, Mitchell Beazley, 1981

Broadbent, J.M., *Michael Broadbent's Pocket Guide to Wine Tasting*, Mitchell Beazley in association with Christie's Wine Publications, 1982

Chroman, Nathan, *The Treasury of American Wines*, Crown Publishers, 1973

Dallas, P., *Italian Wines*, Faber, 1974

Evans, Len, *Australia and New Zealand: Complete Book of Wine*, Hamlyn, 1973

Faith, N., *The Winemasters*, Hamish Hamilton, 1978

Forbes, P., *Champagne*, Gollancz, 1972

Hallgarten, S.F., *Alsace and its Wine Gardens*, Wine and Spirit Publications, 2nd edition, 1969

Hallgarten, S.F., *German Wines*, Faber, 1976

Hallgarten, S.F., *Rhineland Wineland*, Arlington Books, 1965

Hanson, A., *Burgundy*, Faber, 1982

Hogg, Anthony, *Guide to Visiting Vineyards*, Michael Joseph, revised edition, 1981

Jeffs, J., *Sherry*, Faber, 3rd edition, 1982

Johnson, Hugh, *The World Atlas of Wine*, Mitchell Beazley, 2nd edition, 1977

Langenbach, A., *German Wines and Vines*, Vista Books, 1962

Lichine, A., *Alexis Lichine's Encyclopaedia of Wines and Spirits*, Cassell, 1967

Lichine, A., *Wines of France*, Cassell, 5th edition, 1961

Livingstone-Learmonth, J., and Master, Melvyn, C.H., *The Wines of the Rhône*, Faber, 1978

Loeb, O.W., and Prittie, T.C.W., *Moselle*, Faber, 1972

Meinhard, Heinrich, *The Wines of Germany*, David and Charles, 1976

Meinhard, Heinrich, *German wines*, Oriel Press,

Ordish, G., *Vineyards in England and Wales*, Faber, 1978

Penning-Rowsell, E., *The Wines of Bordeaux*, Allen Lane, 4th edition, 1979

Peppercorn, D., *Bordeaux*, Faber, 1982

Ray, Cyril, *The Wines of Germany*, Allen Lane, 1977

Ray, Cyril, *The New Book of Italian Wines*, Sidgwick and Jackson, 1982

Read, Jan, *The Wines of Spain and Portugal*, Faber, 1973

Robertson, G., *Port*, Faber, 1978

Saintsbury, George, *Notes on a Cellar Book*, Macmillan, 1978

Siegel, Hans, *Guide to the Wines of Germany*, Pitman, 1978

Simon, André, *The Commonsense of Wine*, Michael Joseph, 1966

Simon, André, and Hallgarten, S.F., *The Great Wines of Germany*, McGraw-Hill, 1963

Stabilisierungsfond für Wein, *Deutscher Weinatlas mit Weinlagenverzeichnis*, Ceres-Verlag, 1976, translated into English by Nadia Fowler and published as *German Wine Atlas and Vineyard Register* by Davis-Poynter, 1977

Sutcliffe, Serena, *André Simon's Wines of the World*, 2nd edition, Macdonald Futura, 1981

Thorpy, Frank, *New Zealand Wine Guide*, Books for Pleasure, 1976

Thorpy, Frank, *Wine in New Zealand*, Collins, 1972

Which? Wine Guide 1983, Consumer's Association, 1982

Younger, William, *Gods, Men and Wine*, International Wine and Food Society and Michael Joseph, 1966

Yoxall, Harry W., *The International Wine and Food Society's Guide to the Wines of Burgundy*, International Wine and Food Society and Michael Joseph, 1968

Index

Acknowledgments

Special Photography: Michael Boys 2-3, 8, 15 above, 22, 48-9, 98-9, 101, 104 below, 105 left, 106-7, 108, 109, 113, 136 left, 137, 138, 139, 141, 142 right, 143, 145, 147; Chris Linton 28-9, 31, 32, 33, 34-5, 38-9 below, 44-5, 46-7; Colin Maher 14 below, 17 above, 19 below, 20 above, 21 above, 27 below, 50 left, 57, 59, 62, 63 left, 64, 65 below, 67 below left, 68-9, 70, 72-3; Charlie Stebbings 36-7, 38, 40-1; Jon Wyand 24, 120, 121, 126, 126-7, 128, 130-1, 132 above and below.

The publishers would like to thank the following individuals and organizations for their kind permission to reproduce photographs in this book: Hans Albers 16, 27 above, 40, 198, 198-9, 200 above, 204 above right, 208; Australian Picture Library 187 below right; Michael Boys 6, 6-7, 13, 25, 50-1, 86, 87, 103 below, 136, 142 left; British Tourist Authority (Eric Rowell) 183 below; Christian Bros. Wines 206-7; Cognac Information Centre 114, 114-5, 117 above; Cooks Wine 193; Decanter Magazine 160-1, 166 above and below left, 197; DWI 129, 130 left, 131 below; Patrick Eagar 175, 183 above, 187 above right, 189, 190-1, 191; Robert Estall 14 above, 94; Werner Forman Archive 12; Fotobank 200 below left, 201 right, 203 above right, 204 centre right; German Wine Growers Association 132-3, 134-5; Sonia Halliday Photographs 174, 176 above, 177 below, (FHC Birch) 171; Hargrave Vineyards 100 centre left; Hedges & Butler 160, 166 right; Percy Hennell 1, 18, 21 below, 43, 56 below, 74-5, 76 above left, 77, 82, 83, 85, 88-9, 110-11, 116, 158-9, 165, (by permission of Virtue & Co Ltd) 81; John Hillelson Agency (Bruno Barbey) 96 right; Hungarian Wine Association 23; Hungary (Counsel Ltd) 172 above; Luxembourg National Tourist & Trade Office 168; Fred Lyon Pictures 9, 19 above, 23 top, 42, 54-5, 60, 61, 63 right, 67 above left, right and below right, 78 above, 80 right and below left, 90, 91, 92-3, 98 below, 103 above, 112, 170 below; Madeira Wine Co (S & B Modules) 167; Colin Maher 10-11, 15 centre and below, 17 below, 56 above, 71, 72 left, 76 below left and above right, 78 below, 80 above left, 96 above and centre left, 100 right and above left, 102, 104 above, 117 below, 118-9, (QED) 20 below, 26, 30, 56 above, 65 above, 72 left; Novosti 173; Chuck O' Rear 203 left; The Photographic Library of Australia 185, 186, 187 left, 188, 190 above and below left, 192; Jan Read 148, 150 below, 151, 153 centre right and left, 155, 156, 157, 158, 161, 164; Rioja Wine Information Centre 153 above right; Sherry Institute of Spain 150 above, (Graham Harrison) 149; Top Agence (J Ducange) 94-5; Topham 172 below, 182, 195, 196, (Hambledon Vineyard) 180-1, (Osborne) 178 above, (Parkhouse) 177 above; Bill Wetmore 203 centre right; Charles Wetmore 204 left; Jon Wyand 122 above, 123, 124-5; Zefa (UK) Picture Library (Abril) 213, (E G Carlé) 163 above, (D Grathwohl) 212 below, (W Hasenberg) 210-11, (K Helbig) 176 below, (H Luetticke) 170 above, (C Maher) 84, (B Nash) 162 and 163 below, (E Rekos) 212 above, (W Schaefer) 169, (K Scholz) 178 below, (L Schranner) 179, (Starfoto) 4-5.

Author's Acknowledgments
Part of the text is based on a previous book by George Rainbird entitled *The Subtle Alchemist* (Michael Joseph, 1973). The text has been extensively revised, up-dated and expanded, and during his researches the author has had recourse to the expertise of a number of Masters of Wine, wine writers and importers. He is extremely grateful to them all for their help and advice. He would especially like to thank his friend Robert Misch for his chapter on the wines of North America; Penelope Mansell-Jones MW (Introduction and France); Helen Thomson of O. W. Loeb (Germany); Gordon Brown (Italy); Jan Read and Alejandro Cassinello (Spain); James Halliday (Australia); Ron Small (New Zealand); Nicholas Clarke MW (South Africa); David Stevens MW (South America); Bill Gunn MW (Central Europe and Eastern and Southern Mediterranean) and, of course, the many friendly growers, shippers and merchants he has known over the years. Among the latter he would like to mention the Avery's. Father and Son, of Bristol; Tom Abell of Edward Sheldon of Shipston and innumerable others who, in his opinion, can be trusted in their vinous selections.